MW01601697

READ CHINESE

WITHOUT KNOWING CHINESE

A complete guide to
Computer-aided Chinese Reading

George Kung

www.georgekung.com

Publisher: George Kung

Copyright © 2008 by George Kung

Notice of rights
All rights reserved. No part of this book shall be reproduced, stored in a retrieval system, or transmitted, in any form or by any means, electronic, mechanical, photocopying, desktop publishing, recording, or otherwise, without prior written permission from the publisher. For more information on getting permission for any form of reproduction, visit www.georgekung.com.

Notice of liability
The information in this book is distributed on an "AS IS" basis, without warranty. While every precaution has been taken in the preparation of this book, the publisher and author assume no responsibility for errors or omissions. Neither is any liability assumed for damages resulting from the use or unable to use of the information contained herein.

Trademarks
All brand names and product names mentioned in this book are trademarks or registered trademarks of their respective copyright owners.

Printed in the United States of America
10 9 8 7 6 5 4 3 2 1

First Printing: June 2008

ISBN-10: 0-9816933-0-X
ISBN-13: 978-0-9816933-0-9

In memory of my father, C.Y. Kung (龔乾一), a distinguished and modest Chinese engineer who worked diligently, achieved enormously, and contributed generously to his country and society.

Acknowledgments

I would like to give very special thanks to Dr. Bob Rich for his excellent editing work and so much valuable advice. My appreciation also goes to my brothers, C. L. and Charles, and my elder son William, for reading and editing my draft, and for their critiques, suggestions and comments. Much credit is due to my younger son, Albert, who has helped out with many housekeeping chores. I wish to thank my classmates, C. C. Feng (馮竹健) and Delin Din (丁燿仁), for recommending and help in looking up product information, and Ms. Shelly Rosenberg, for her help in proofreading. Last but not least, I would also like to thank my wife and my mother, for their love and support.

Contents

Preface

Chinese is a major language of the world, with over one billion native speakers. The opening up and reform in China's economy and its growing influence in the international community has further expanded the global nature of the language. In the foreseeable future, the ability to speak Chinese will become a very important skill in many professions. According to an article in USA Today on December 27, 2007, Chinese learning programs in US schools have doubled since the beginning of 2006.

Although the interest in Chinese learning has increased rapidly, in reality few foreigners have been able to successfully learn to read or write the language. Actually, the spoken part of Chinese is relatively easy, but learning to read or write is quite challenging. Unlike Latin-based languages that use alphabets, Chinese text consists of characters, which are created from strokes written in virtual boxes. To read newspapers or common text documents, one would need to know about 1,500 to 3,000 characters. This takes native Chinese speaking children three to six years to learn in a regular curriculum. For foreigners who do not use the language on a daily basis, the time needed may be longer. This simple fact may help explain why so many people feel that Chinese is difficult to learn.

Technologies are constantly changing. They offer new ways for us to do things that were not possible before. Just a few years ago, we needed dictionaries to help with unfamiliar Chinese characters encountered while reading. Looking up Chinese characters in a dictionary without knowing the pronunciation is not a simple matter; it requires not only knowledge about the shape of the characters and experiences, but also some luck and lots of patience. Recent advances in technology have made this task much easier. Nowadays, all we need to do is swipe a handheld scanner over a character, and the explanation of the character shows up immediately. To make things even more convenient, much of the information today is already in electronic format, ready to be viewed through a web browser or other software program. When we encounter trouble with a character or word, all we need to do is move the mouse cursor over the word and the definitions automatically pop up. We can even hear the character pronounced to us through the computer speaker.

With the help of new technologies, not only has language learning become easier than ever, but there are now practical ways for people who don't know a language to be able to read text written in that language. Scanners and digital cameras can be used to capture text into images. OCR (Optical Character Recognition) software can be used to transform text images into computer-readable codes. There are dictionary and translator software programs capable of translating words or sentences from Chinese to English. In recent years especially, these tools have become more powerful, reliable and very affordable. All people need now is some basic knowledge and practical guidance for putting these pieces together, which is where this book comes into play.

This book is intended to be a step-by-step guide for people unfamiliar with the language, who have the use of the Internet and the PC, and optionally with additional tools and devices, to read text written in Chinese. It starts with a basic introduction to Chinese reading: characters, words, sentence structures, reading directions, punctuations, writing styles, etc. After that, it explains some computer-related topics: traditional vs. simplified character sets, encoding methods, text fonts and so on.

Chapter 3 describes the overall process and tools used in computer-aided Chinese reading. A flow diagram is first used to give an overview. Following that, the book gives a general description of all the devices and tools that will be used in the process, including the scanner, digital camera, the OCR program, the dictionary software and the translation software. Some of the tools and devices are discussed in further detail throughout this chapter. This includes the setting up of Chinese language support in the Windows operating system, the display software, the image editing software, and the handheld scanner with built-in OCR/translator. Upon the completion of this chapter, readers will have a basic understanding of all the tools and how they fit in the process.

Chapter 4 is dedicated to the discussion of Chinese OCR. It gives step-by-step instructions for using three OCR products. It also describes approaches we can take to improve the recognized results. OCR is used for transforming printed text into computer-readable codes. This chapter can be skipped by readers wishing only to read text that is already in electronic format.

Chapter 5 gives thorough descriptions and detailed instructions for the core tools for converting Chinese to English: the translation and dictionary programs. Chapter 6 focuses on how to view machine-translated output. It describes techniques we can use to better understand and improve the translated results, as well as to resolve or avoid problems. Chapter 7 describes some advanced topics in translating Chinese into English. It also includes a brief discussion about seeking additional help on the Internet. Chapter 8 shows some real-life examples of using OCR and translator/dictionary programs to read Chinese from a magazine and a newspaper, as well as text on poster and signs captured by a camera. In there, you will see the practical use of many techniques described in earlier chapters. Chapter 9, the last chapter, has a few final words to wrap up.

This book covers both traditional and simplified Chinese. A lot of the discussion is related to properly setting things up in the software programs for supporting the two different character sets. There is also a dedicated section describing how to distinguish text from the two sets.

The descriptions about the language and computer-aided reading process are platform independent. However, the software programs covered in the book are mainly for Windows-based systems. Other than some web-based tools, which work in any platform, most applications and utilities described are for PCs using Windows 2000, XP, and Vista systems only.

This will be the first book to advocate Chinese reading without the actual learning of the language. Even though the book is intended for people who don't read Chinese but need to acquire information in Chinese-based text, it can certainly be used by people who already know some Chinese, or people who do intend to learn the language. Business-persons, tourists, students, scholars, public servants in foreign affairs, defense, trade and immigration departments, etc. can all benefit from this book.

Much of the content relates directly to software products, which, by their nature, are constantly changing. To keep them continuously up to date, I have created a supporting website for this book at www.georgekung.com. In addition to product information update, the website also contains test and benchmark data, product comparisons, links to tools, and other useful resources.

George Kung
Lexington, Massachusetts, USA
June 2008

1. Introduction

After a quarter of a century of reform and modernization, China has developed at a faster clip than any other major nation in recent years. With one fifth of the world's population and a continuous and massive boom in the country, it rocketed past the US in 2006 to become the second largest global exporter. It is also the world's fourth largest economy by GDP and second largest economy by purchasing power.

Ever since China's Open Door policy was initiated, virtually every outsider has been interested in doing business with this country. Importers are constantly looking to China for magnificent supplies of goods. Manufacturers go to China for cheap and reliable labor. Chinese-based factories produce 50% of the world's shoes and over 70% of the world's toys. On the other hand, exporters and trade industries wish to sell into its enormous market. China has 450 million mobile phone subscribers. It is the world's biggest consumer of basic agriculture and industrial commodities: grain, meat, coal, and steel.

Even though the most noticeable growth of China is in its economy, that is certainly not the only facet relevant to the world. There is much evidence that displays China's global power in other ways. Politically, China is certainly a key player in international affairs, having taken a major role in the matters concerning Korea, Iran, and Afghanistan. Military-wise, China's US$45 billion expenditures in 2007 rank at number seven in the world. Technology-wise, China launched its lunar probe satellite in October 2007, marking the beginning of an ambitious 10-year space program. In sports, China's gold medal count in the 2004 Athens Olympics was second only to the US. It is expected to win more when the 2008 Summer Olympics are held in Beijing. Of course, rapid economic growth has its negative impacts. China now consumes more coal than the US, Japan, and the EU nations combined, and sulfur dioxide pollution caused by coal combustion poses a major threat to the global environment.

As its world-wide influence becomes increasingly prominent, more foreigners interact with people from China for business, tourism, education, and other purposes. Over two million foreigners travel to China for business or pleasure every month. According to the data published in July 2007, China has 160 million Internet users and over 1.3 million websites, with more than 80% of the content written in Chinese. The huge population of China is certainly a big factor in its global dominance. Most importantly, even though people living in different areas of China speak unique dialects, they all share the same common written language. The language is used not only in mainland China, but also in the Republic of China (Taiwan), Hong Kong, Macao, Singapore and Malaysia. Each of these regions accounts for significant aspects of the world's economy and its population.

Even though English is now learned and used by many people in big cities, the vast majority of the population in Chinese speaking areas uses Chinese as the only form of communication. Foreigners who know the Chinese language are quickly able to get first-hand information, establish their networks, and get around just about anywhere more easily. In recent years, more and more foreigners believe that learning Chinese is increasingly necessary in all fields due to China's growing political and economic importance in the international arena. According to statistics from China's Ministry of Education in 2006, 40 million foreigners are learning Chinese in some 12,400 schools and universities around the world. That number is expected to reach 100 million by the year 2010. A separate article from USA Today on December 27, 2007 indicated that Chinese learning programs in US schools have doubled since the beginning of 2006.

By looking at the statistics, we can assume that many people have realized that knowing the language will give them a major boost for success in their endeavors. Nevertheless, in reality, not too many foreigners have learned to read Chinese, and even fewer can write Chinese text. The main reason for this is that Chinese is very different from the languages with which they are familiar, and it is just too hard to learn. The truth is, the spoken part of Chinese can be relatively easy, but learning to read or write is quite challenging. Unlike Latin-based texts using alphabets, Chinese texts consist of characters. To read newspapers or common text documents, one would need to memorize about 1,500 to 3,000 characters and know about 5,000 to 10,000 commonly used words made from these characters. It is estimated that Chinese children need to spend more than twice the amount of time in learning to read and write their native language than children in English-speaking countries. Since learning to read or write is not easy even for native speakers, it can be substantially more demanding for foreigners, especially people from western countries. The curriculum information from the United States Foreign Service Institute shows that Chinese takes three to five times the effort for English speakers to reach the same level of competence learning, compared to French or Spanish.

Fortunately, with recent advances in technology, Chinese learning has become easier. People previously spent a lot of time looking up unrecognized characters or words in dictionaries. Nowadays, there are many on-line materials we can read from our computers. By just moving our mouse cursor over a character or a word, we instantly get its meanings from electronic dictionaries. By clicking a button, we are able to hear the sound of the character or word pronounced to us. If the materials we need to read are in a book or magazines, we can capture the text image with a scanner and use OCR (Optical Character Recognition) software to get the text into our computer. There is even a handheld device that can scan, recognize and then translate the text for us.

In recent years, there also have been large improvements in MT (Machine Translation) technology. MT software is able to analyze and translate an entire block of text from one language to another. However, even with these continuous improvements, MT technology is still far from perfect. It is not expected to produce results that are comparable to human writing. Still, with some proper planning and tuning, MT software is able to render reasonable results for the purpose of understanding the text written in Chinese. The translated output may not read very English-like, but if all the key words of the text have been grasped, the readers usually do not have too much trouble understanding the meaning. With the help of MT software and other tools, people can now read Chinese text without actually having to learn the language.

This book describes the whole computer-aided Chinese reading process, with tools and methods to be used. It is intended to be a very thorough guide, showing readers how to use their PCs, the Internet, and other readily available tools to read, and optionally, learn Chinese. For each product, there is a detailed description of its usages, features, limitations, and comparative performance. Throughout the book, readers will also find tips, tricks, and supplemental resources that will be helpful for reading and learning Chinese. The methods described in the book can be used by anyone, regardless of their level of familiarity with Chinese. Readers can follow the process and apply these methods to read Chinese with no intention of actually learning the language. For readers who do wish to learn Chinese, the information provided will be very useful also in helping them to study.

China is a very old nation with a rich culture and heritage, and a long history that dates back thousands of years. There are many books, publications, documents, artifacts, and other traces of human civilization recorded in this old language. Large amounts of information also reside in Chinese-based websites, newsgroups, forums, chats, blogs, and other on-line resources. With the popularity of the Internet, you get lots of up-to-date, direct, first hand, unabridged, biased or unbiased, official or insider information quicker than ever. When something happens, you not only know the details of it but also understand the ways people react. You hear opinions from one side and the other, from both the experts and the public. There are opportunities to be discovered, ideas to be explored, and concepts from which to be inspired. All the useful information can be put to your use because you are now able to understand the text. It is my intention that, with the writing of this book, more outsiders will have the opportunity to access a whole new dimension of the world that was unfamiliar and unreachable previously. By lowering the language barrier for foreigners, hopefully they can now have a greater understanding of this old country, people, culture, and civilization that seems to have been mysterious in the past.

2. Chinese Language Basics

This chapter covers some basics of the Chinese language. Most of the information is closely related to Chinese text reading about which you should become familiar. A few topics may not be very relevant for our purposes. They are briefly mentioned because the terminologies and concepts may appear in the documentation of the tools we use.

2.1 Characters (字), Words (词) and Sentences (句)

Chinese is very different from western (Latin) style languages. First of all, the text in Chinese does not consist of alphabet letters; instead it is made up of characters (字). The character is the most basic element in the Chinese language. It is built from strokes written in a virtual rectangle box. Commonly used characters contain from one to twenty, sometimes thirty, strokes. Figure 2.1 shows some examples of strokes and characters containing these strokes.

Stroke	丶	一	丨	丿	乀	刁	乛	乙	乚	乀	乀	乚	乚	乚
Example Characters	小	素	上	分	人	羽	又	冠	能	代	化	去	女	以
	心	味	山	秒	定	扇	多	軍	見	我	水	公	災	切
	下	平	伐	必	勝	綸	子	完	尾	成	求	云	巢	比
	雨	生	木	爭	天	巾	孫	蛋	巴	戈	北	叁	好	鼠

Figure 2.1 Strokes and characters

Each character has its meanings, which can represent a thing or a concept. The sound of a character contains one syllable, and the pronunciation can be very different when spoken by people from different geographic regions. The Mandarin (国语), also known as Putunghua (普通话), is the pronunciation used by people from Beijing. It is the official standard pronunciation recognized by the governments from both the People's Republic of China (PRC) and Taiwan, the

Republic of China (ROC). Mandarin is estimated to be spoken by about 55% of the whole Chinese language population, and over two thirds of the population in the cities. Most Chinese whose primary language is not Mandarin can nevertheless understand it.

The Chinese character set is known as Han character or Hanzi (汉字) by Japanese and Koreans. Many Chinese characters have been adopted by the Japanese and Korean languages and given the same meanings with different pronunciations. In Japanese and Korean, a person's name is usually written in Hanzi.

It is hard to say how many Chinese characters there are in total. Generally, there are between 5,000 to 15,000 characters in standard dictionaries that people use regularly. The famous 康熙字典 (*Kangxi dictionary*) contains 47,035 characters. The most comprehensive Chinese dictionary that I know of, 中华字海 (*A sea of Chinese Characters*), even lists in excess of 85,000! Fortunately, most of these characters are rarely used; otherwise, people would have to spend all their lives learning the language. The most frequently used 1,000 characters cover about 90% of the usage. If you know 3,500 characters, the estimated number of characters an educated Chinese adult knows, the coverage rate reaches 99.5%.

The next level of elements in the language hierarchy above the 字 is the 词 (*word*). A general definition of the Chinese word is a combination of mostly two or more characters representing a specific thing or concept. Most characters have meanings but they may represent only a vague thing or concept, which is sometimes too ambiguous when used alone. When two characters are put together to form words, their meanings become more specific. Take the following character and words for example: the character 近 means near, close, or recent. When it is used together with another character, they become words with a more specific meaning.

近来 (*recently*), 近代 (*modern era*), 靠近 (*come close*), 近邻 (*neighbor*), 近视 (*near sighted*)

It is even harder to estimate how many total words there are in the Chinese language. A daily use dictionary may contain from 20,000 to 150,000 entries; the most comprehensive one that I know of, 汉语大词典 (*Comprehensive Dictionary of Chinese Words*), has a collection of 370,000! The word should be considered a critical if not the most important part of the Chinese language. It also plays an absolutely crucial role in reading. Even though functionally the Chinese word is very similar to the English word, there is one major difference. Unlike English or any other Latin language, there are no spaces in Chinese text to break different words apart. Each sentence only consists of characters that concatenate together, with no indication of which characters form a word. It is the sole responsibility of the reader to identify all the words inside the sentence to interpret the meaning of the text. For an MT (Machine Translation) program to get good translation results, it is critical to have a dictionary that contains all the words people commonly use. If an MT program lacks a word in its dictionary, it would have to interpret that word as two or more separate characters. This may work well sometimes, but usually it doesn't. The same situation may even occur for human readers. Sometimes a writer uses a word that is not commonly seen, or is only known to people from a specific geographic area. Readers from other places will have a hard time comprehending the word, even if they know all its constituent characters.

Let us use the sentence "美国东接大西洋。" for example. It is to be interpreted as: 美国 (*USA*) 东 (*east*) 接 (*connect to*) 大西洋 (*Atlantic*). The readers need to know that 美国 means "thc USA," and not the character-by-character interpretation of 美 (*beautiful*) and 国 (*country*). They also need to know that 大西洋 means "the Atlantic ocean," instead of 大 (*big*) 西洋 (*occident*), or 大 (*big*) 西 (*west*) 洋 (*ocean*).

Some words can have multiple meanings; sometimes the meanings are completely unrelated. It is up to the reader to determine what the word means under each circumstance. For example, 大班 means the top class in a kindergarten, and it also means the manager in a dance hall. 小時 stands for an hour, or it can mean in one's young age. 出口 can mean export or an exit. In circumstances like these, readers need to look at the context to determine what the words mean.

Another element in the language is the 成语 (*idiom*), which usually consists of four characters. The English equivalent of 成语 is an idiom or a phrase. It is similar to a word but it is longer and in most cases is used to describe a specific situation. One unique thing about 成语 is that most 成语 have stories behind them. For the purpose of Chinese reading, you can treat them the same as regular words.

One other element that is in the same hierarchy with word is what I call "pattern." I do not have a linguistic name for it. These are characters that are used together, based on certain rules to form words, but actually they are not "words." For example, consider the modification of the following words when the character 们 is added:

我	I
你	you (singular)
老鼠	mouse

我**们**	we
你**们**	you (plural)
老鼠**们**	mice

Each word refers to a living being. The extra character has made it into a plural.

Similarly, the following examples show that adding the character 的 converts a noun into its possessive form (this rule applies to inanimate as well as living objects):

我	I
你	you
我们	we
老鼠们	mice
北京园	Beijing Garden (a restaurant)

我**的** ~	my ~
你**的** ~	your ~
我们**的** ~	our ~
老鼠们**的** ~	~ of a group of mice
北京园**的** ~	~ from Beijing Garden

In order to identify these patterns in sentences, the readers (or the MT programs) have to have some kind of intelligence to follow the rules. We can't simply use a dictionary to list all the words in such a situation, because there will be an infinite number of words of this form.

The next level of element above "word" in the hierarchy is the 句 (*sentence*). It is equivalent to the sentence in English with a very loose grammatical rule. Basically, a Chinese sentence consists of words and characters concatenated together. The subject can usually be implied and omitted in a sentence. In many cases, a sentence does not contain a verb. For example, people always say: "晚上 很冷。" (*Night very cold*).

Unlike English, there is no capitalization to help us identify proper nouns in a Chinese text. To make things worse, it allows just about any character for the names of people, places, business, etc. Because of this, sometimes it can be a challenge to distinguish a person's name from other part of the sentence.

Remember I said that each character is always pronounced as one syllable. A sentence is made by putting multiple characters together, and the way to speak the sentence is just to concatenate all the single syllable sounds. From what I can see, this is about the only place where the Chinese language is easier to learn than Latin-based languages.

Chinese is an old language and over time people have used it in different ways. Writers like to be free, creative and do not want to obey rules or follow conventions. They also tend to be lazy and dislike the idea of doing extra work to make their writings more understandable. Perhaps writers consider writing to be the work of geniuses. If readers cannot follow the great concepts behind their masterpieces, then the readers must not be smart enough. Some writers like to use obscure words to deliberately make their writings not understandable to the general public; otherwise their works would be considered 俗 (*vulgar*). This way of thinking leaves a large burden on the readers.

2.2 Writing Directions

Chinese text consists of characters in virtual rectangle boxes of the same size concatenate together. Text can go either vertically or horizontally. In the old days when I was still young, people had all the freedom in the writing directions. Horizontal writing could go from left to right or right to left. Vertical writing always goes from top to bottom, but as they form multiple columns, the column could cither go from right to left or from left to right (Figure 2.2). This makes the usage of spaces in tighter areas such as newspapers and street signs more effective. However, sometimes this can cause confusion even for native readers.

When text appears in large paragraphs, you can easily tell how they go by just taking a glimpse of the contents. People unfamiliar with the language can still identify it by looking at the spaces at the beginning and end of the paragraphs. You can also tell by the spacing between characters, because that is usually smaller than the spacing between rows or columns. The real challenge is reading text from banners, signboards, classified ads, etc. where there may be only a single row of text. In some interesting cases, text can even be read both ways.

Take the phrase 人人愛我 for example. When reading from left to right it means "Everyone loves me," but it means "I love everyone" when read from right to left.

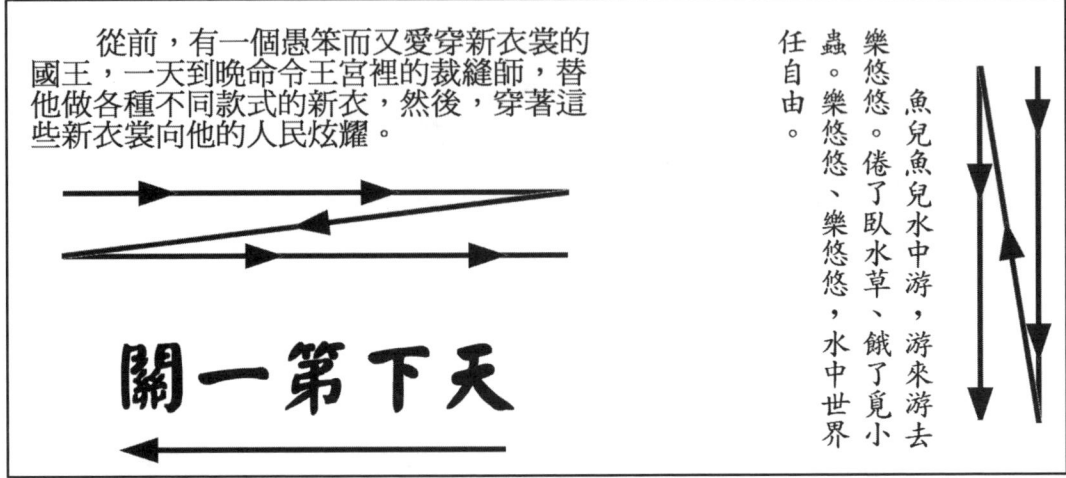

Figure 2.2 Chinese text writing directions

To avoid confusion, both Taiwan and China now have standardized the writing direction of Chinese text. For horizontal writing, they go from left to right for the convenience of mixing with Latin letters and numbers. For vertical writing, the sequence of columns goes from right to left because that is the traditional way used in all the books and other printings that have been in existence for thousands of years. This writing standard certainly makes everyone's life easier and reduces guessing. However, bear in mind that there are many writings that existed way before the introduction of the standard. Horizontal text written before the modern era are most likely to go the other way—from right to left. The other thing to remember is that a standard is just something for people to follow. Even though you can expect it to be obeyed in the printing for books, magazines, etc., there is no guarantee that people will always do the "right" thing when it comes to private or informal usage.

I have trouble understanding the rationale behind the traditional way of writing from right to left. The strokes within each character actually go from left to right; to me it would make more sense for the characters to go from left to right as well. Another inconvenience that I recall from this is doing paint-brush homework when I was little. Because of going from right to left, my hand always smudged the fresh writing I just made on the previous column, and that often resulted in a big mess.

In Taiwan, vertical writing is still the most common method used in books, magazines and other printed literary works. For text in electronics format, such as in websites or e-mail, writing goes horizontally. In mainland China, writing almost always goes horizontally from left to right. Occasionally, you may see vertical text printed by the side of pictures in newspapers, or on spring couplets pasted by the door. In such cases, the vertical columns progress from right to left. For the purpose of reading Chinese, you don't really need to worry about the writing direction if the materials are already in electronic format. When reading text from books, posters, or other non-electronic sources, you have to use a scanner (or camera) and OCR to capture the text. In such situations you may need to know which way the text goes in case the OCR program cannot recognize the blocks correctly. We will discuss this in more detail in the future sections that cover OCR software and handheld scanner devices.

2.3 Pinyin and Zhuyin

All Chinese characters have exactly one syllable in sound when pronounced. The pronunciation varies from region to region, and the differences can be quite significant. Mandarin Chinese is the pronunciation used by people in Beijing, and it is the official standard in both China and Taiwan. Mandarin Chinese has fewer sounds than English. One unique aspect of spoken Chinese is its use of tones. Pitches of voice are used to help differentiate among characters. There are five tones used in Mandarin. Considering that different tones sound differently, there are only about 1,300 unique sounds in Mandarin. Since these will be used for more than 47,000 characters (based on the *Kangxi dictionary*), many characters have the exact same pronunciation. There is no standard method that will tell us how to pronounce characters. Basically, all you can do is memorize the sound of each of the characters as you learn them. A simple rule of thumb is to see if the character contains other simpler characters in it, and then pronounce it using the sound of the simpler character. While this rule does not work well, it is better than a random guess.

Pinyin (拼音), also known as Hanyu Pinyin, is an effort by PRC for Romanization of the Chinese language. The idea is to represent Chinese characters using their sound (based on the Mandarin standard), which can then be represented by Latin alphabets using some simple rules. This standard was first introduced in 1958, but the idea of Romanization is certainly not a new concept. A similar system called Wade (aka Wade-Giles), developed by Thomas Wade and Herbert Giles, has been widely used to Romanize Chinese since the 19th century.

Pinyin was adopted by the ISO in 1979, and is now the most commonly used Romanization standard for Mandarin Chinese. Pinyin is used for its close resemblance to the phonetic system with which people are already familiar. The phonetic system is called Zhuyin (注音), aka Bopomofo, and was invented in 1913.

The Zhuyin system consists of 37 Chinese phonetic symbols and four notations to represent the five different tones in Mandarin. The system contains consonant and vowel symbols. It represents the pronunciation of each character using one consonant and one or two vowels put together, along with a tone notation. The sole purpose of Zhuyin is to provide phonetic annotation of the Mandarin sounds of Chinese characters. We can find the use of Zhuyin in many of the dictionaries published after 1913.

Other than in dictionaries, one major use of Zhuyin is for annotating text so it can be read by children, or people who are starting to learn the language. As of today, Zhuyin is still used in Taiwan, Hong Kong, and some overseas Chinese communities.

The way to use Zhuyin is to place these symbols on the right-hand side of each character. Figure 2.3 shows an example of text printed with the Zhuyin symbols. One other use of the Zhuyin system is to input Chinese characters into the computer.

Figure 2.3 Text with Zhuyin annotations

One major drawback with the Zhuyin system is that it uses a special set of symbols that is unfamiliar to foreigners. From what I can see, the symbols are not strongly correlated to Chinese characters either. It has always been a mystery to me why people choose to use them. Pinyin closely resembles Zhuyin, but it uses the Roman alphabet to replace the phonetic symbols. As such, it can be used for both Romanization and phonetic annotations. When used for annotation, it is usually put on top of the characters, as shown in Figure 2.4.

Figure 2.4 Text with Pinyin annotations

Figure 2.5 shows a list of phonetic symbols used in Zhuyin and a mapping of Pinyin.

Consonants

ㄅ	ㄆ	ㄇ	ㄈ	ㄉ	ㄊ	ㄋ	ㄌ	ㄍ	ㄎ	ㄏ	ㄐ	ㄑ	ㄒ
b	p	m	f	d	t	n	l	g	k	h	j	q	x

ㄓ	ㄔ	ㄕ	ㄖ	ㄗ	ㄘ	ㄙ
zh	ch	sh	r	z	c	s

Vowels

ㄧ	ㄨ	ㄩ
i	u	u
y	w	y
yi	wu	yu

ㄚ	ㄛ	ㄜ	ㄝ	ㄞ	ㄟ	ㄠ	ㄡ	ㄢ	ㄣ	ㄤ	ㄥ	ㄦ
a	o	e	e ie	ai	i ei	ao	u ou	an	n en	ang	ong eng ing	er

Figure 2.5 Zhuyin phonetic symbols and their mappings in Pinyin

The main purpose of Romanized Chinese is to represent names of people and places in alphabetic form, so they can be used by foreigners. From this, some people arrived at the concept of replacing the entire Chinese system of writing. I suppose when people compared Chinese with Latin-based languages, they realized that learning it is far more difficult. A conclusion was then drawn that there must be something very wrong with the language, so they decided to have it reformed.

The full Romanization of Chinese was advocated many years ago. I believe there was a time when people were seriously considering it. It was when computers made their way to rule the world, but before Chinese input and output methods were invented. People began to panic and thought they would be extinct if they did not abandon the language. I imagine what happened next was that there must have been some strong objection coming from vendors who made ink and brush pens. Now come to think of it—there were many old comrades in the Communist Party who took charge of the government at that time. These poor old fellows spent the first half of their life adapting from their dialects to Mandarin. After that they spent another 10 years struggling with simplified Chinese characters. Now they were in their 70s, and they were really not too keen on the idea of learning a new language all over again with their grand-children. Even though they realized they would be labeled as counter-revolutionists by history, guilty for thirty thousand years after they die and responsible for the vanishing of the Chinese civilization, they decided to procrastinate…to do nothing…to wait until the last minute of their lives. Fortunately, the waiting paid off. Before long, smart people had invented new ways for this old language to get along with this monster from the New Imperialism. They were acceptable, although far from perfect. People are happy once again and very quickly everyone has forgotten about this full Romanization nonsense. As of today, there are still die-hard advocates, but they are no longer taken seriously.

Anyway, one technical difficulty I can see for full Romanization is that multiple characters can have the exact same sound. When we write the Pinyin of a single character, people will not be able to tell which character it is. The situation is improved when it comes to words. Usually you can identify commonly used words by their sounds, but in some cases even different words may have the same Pinyin. For example, the word 榆树 (*elm*) and 馀数 (*remainder*) have two characters with the same pronunciations, but both characters are different and they mean completely different things. Another example is the word 捣蛋 (*mischief*) and 导弹 (*missile*).

Despite the great ambition of reforming the Chinese language system, there are actually practical situations where you have to use Pinyin instead of the Chinese characters. One example is to display Chinese text on a (very old) computer system that does not support the display of Chinese characters.

2.4 Radical

部首 (*radical*) is the semantic root of a character and it usually appears as a part of a character. Characters of the same radical usually have related meanings. Sometimes people say that a character is derived from a radical. Learning radicals helps understand the origin of characters, just like the prefix or postfix helps learning words in Latin-based languages.

For example, the following characters have the same radical 木 (*wood*). They all contain 木 either on the left side or on the top. The meanings of all these characters are also related to wood.

本 (*root*), 札 (*tablet*), 朽 (*rotten*), 杏 (*apricot*), 材 (*material*), 李 (*plum*), 杖 (*stick*)

It is easy to identify the radicals of certain characters. For instance, when you see the character 木 (*wood*) or 女 (*female*) at the left-hand side of a character, you can almost know for sure that it is the radical. On the other hand, there are peculiar characters with radicals that are hard to guess, for example, 粤 or 艱.

The most common use of radicals is for indexing characters in dictionaries. In Chinese dictionaries, characters of the same radical are grouped together and listed in the order of the number of strokes. Here is the scenario: when you see an unfamiliar character, you look at its shape and make a guess at what the radical is. Based on that radical, you count the number of strokes (excluding the radical) and look that up in the dictionary. If you don't see it listed under that radical, you come back to make another guess. You may have to repeat these steps two or three times until you either find it or give up and convince yourself that it is not in the dictionary. There are times you may need to revisit the same radical because it is not unusual to miss the character or miscount the strokes. The whole process is tedious and may not be very much fun, especially for the impatient. Sometimes I hear people shout out joyfully as they locate a character from the dictionary; you might actually think they have hit the lottery or something.

I am not going to spend too much time describing radicals because most likely you will not be concerned with them. There may be one occasion in which you can use them—to tell if a text is written in simplified or traditional Chinese. I will explain this in more detail when I cover that topic.

2.5 Writing Styles—Vernacular vs. Literary

Chinese is a very old language and it has evolved over time. The modern Chinese writing style that we commonly see these days has only been used since the twentieth century. Before 1900, with the exception of some novels, most Chinese literature used the "Literary" writing style. This is a traditional writing style whose text reads quite differently from the regular spoken language. It is more concise and uses many single characters instead of words. Since a character in Chinese is vaguer than a word, literary writings tend to be ambiguous. At times when it actually uses words, the words being used are usually not commonly heard in the spoken language. By their nature, literary writings are more difficult to understand. When people read literature from older generations, they may need to refer to study guides with annotations to understand the text in the original writings. In the old days, reading and writing were only meant for intellectuals and not the general public.

Because of the inconvenience and the awareness of the need for a wider population to become literate, in 1919 there was a motion led by scholar Hu Shih (胡適) to advocate "Vernacular Chinese" writing. It promoted the use of spoken words in writings and considered the literary writing style to be an obstacle to Chinese civilization. This idea gained popularity and was gradually accepted by people all over the country. After that, the vernacular style became the main stream in Chinese writing.

Nowadays, writing in the real literary style is rare. The ability to write in this style requires formal training that is usually provided only to college students who study Chinese literature. Nevertheless, you can see a lot of mixed use of writing styles everywhere. People sometimes like to use more "formal" words in their writing, especially when it comes to things like essays or regulations, etc.

Since literary writing style uses more single characters in places where words would be used in spoken language, it is more difficult for the software to handle. Often the software would have to do a character-by-character translation of the text. By doing so, it often misses the closest interpretation of the English word, or even worse, picks an irrelevant word. Also, I have not seen any translation software that makes a distinction between the different writing styles. Fortunately, most of the writing you see today is very vernacular-like. In case there is a need to study literary-style texts, my suggestion is to use dictionary software to supplement the translation software. Dictionary software gives you a thorough list of the meanings of each character. By checking all the meanings of characters and words, you can do your translations manually in case the output from the translation program makes no sense.

2.6 Chinese Punctuation

Like vernacular writing, punctuation was only introduced to Chinese writing in the modern era. There is no punctuation in ancient Chinese printings. When people read, they took out the brush pen and put pause marks and periods in the book. They also put down explanatory notes and comments because the literary style of writing was not easy to understand. What I am talking about here is the "real" ancient printings. You are unlikely to see any of these sorts of printings these days. The famous books from ancient times that you will likely see today will be the modern editions, which are edited with punctuation and have been reprinted many times.

With the influence of foreign languages as well as the vernacular writing style, the use of punctuation has become popular in modern Chinese writing. It makes reading much easier. It also eliminates confusions, as sometimes a text can be interpreted in a completely opposite way when paused at different places.

Most punctuation symbols used in modern Chinese are similar to those used in English, so you should already be familiar with them. Here is a list of commonly seen punctuation signs in the Chinese language:

Comma (逗号)   ，
The shape and use of a comma is the same as in English. It is used to reflect pauses in speech.

Period (句号)   。
The use of a period is the same as in English. It is used to terminate a sentence. The period symbol in Chinese looks like a small circle.

Exclamation mark (惊叹号)   ！
The shape and use of an exclamation mark is the same as in English. It is used to terminate a sentence with an exclamation.

Question mark (问号)   ？
The shape and use of question mark is the same as in English. It is used to terminate a sentence with question.

Semicolon (分号)   ；
The shape and use of semicolon is the same as in English. It separates parts of a sentence that have independent clauses.

Colon (冒号)   ：
The shape and use of colon is the same as in English. It indicates that what follows is an elaboration of what precedes. In Chinese, a colon is also used between a quotation and the person who says or writes the material being quoted.

Pause mark (顿号)   、
A pause mark is a special type of comma used to separate words constituting a list.

Ellipsis mark (略号)   ……
An ellipsis mark indicates that some parts in the text have been eliminated for reasons of being concise. An ellipsis mark in Chinese consists of six dots that occupy the space of two characters.

Quotation mark (引号)   " and "   ' and '   (simplified Chinese)
                                           「 and 」 『 and 』 (traditional Chinese)
Quotation marks are used in pairs to set off speech, a quotation, or to express a "special" meaning. In simplified Chinese, double quotation marks are used first to denote a quotation. If there is another quotation inside of the first quotation then the single quotation marks are used for the embedded quotes. If more levels are needed then the double and single quotation marks will be used alternatively inside of each other. In traditional Chinese, the idea is similar but another set of symbols is used. Also, the single quotation marks will be used first and if there is another quotation inside of the first one, then the double quotation marks are used next. The other thing about traditional Chinese is that the symbols drawn above are for horizontally written text. For text written vertically, the symbols are turned 90 degrees.

Bracket (括号)   （ and ）〔 and 〕〔 and 〕
Brackets (Parentheses) are used in pairs to set apart or interject text within other text, for annotations, etc. The symbols drawn above are for horizontally written text. For text written vertically, the symbols are turned 90 degrees.

Book name mark (书名号)   《 and 》〈 and 〉
Book name marks are used in pairs to enclose the name of a book, an essay or other literary works. Double book name marks are used first, and if there is a need to describe a special variation or addendum of a book, the single book name marks will be used inside of the double book name marks. For example:

Have you finished reading 《 The study guide of Homer's 〈 Odyssey〉 》 ?

The symbols drawn above are for horizontally written text. For text written vertically, the symbols are turned 90 degrees.

Book name mark (书名号)   ⸑ or ﹏
An alternative way of marking book names is to put wavy lines beside or under the name of a book. When the text is vertical, the vertical book name marks are used, and they may appear either on the left (new style) or right (old style) side of characters. When the text is horizontal, the horizontal book name marks are placed underneath the characters.

Proper name mark (专名号)   ｜ or __
Proper name marks are placed beside or under characters to denote personal or geographic names. When text is vertical, the vertical proper name marks are used, and they may appear either on the left (new style) or right (old style) side of the characters. When text is horizontal, the horizontal proper name marks are placed underneath the characters.

Long hyphen (破折号)   ——
This mark occupies the space of two characters. It is used to represent a sudden change of topic in a speech, or to denote an annotation. The symbols drawn above are for horizontally written text. For text written vertically, the symbols are turned 90 degrees.

Hyphen (连接号)   — or ~
The hyphen mark is used between two items to represent "from one to the other." The regular hyphen is used between numbers, places, etc. The tilde hyphen is used between numbers that represent eras. The symbols drawn above are for

horizontally written text. For text written vertically, the symbols are turned 90 degrees.

Dot (间隔号)   •
This symbol is a dot in the middle of the character space. When a foreigner's name is translated into Chinese characters, the dot mark is used to separate the first name from the last name. It is also used to separate things into a hierarchy. For example, it can be used between the name of a country (where the city is located) and the city name to present the full name of a city. In Chinese, the country name is placed before the city name.

Emphasis mark (着重号)   .
Emphasis marks are dots placed underneath characters to denote the emphasis of word(s) when the text is horizontal. For vertical text, the symbols are placed on the right side of the characters.

2.7 Traditional and Simplified Chinese

There are currently two different sets of characters used in Chinese writing: simplified Chinese and traditional Chinese. Simplified Chinese was introduced between 1950 and 1960 by the People's Republic of China in an attempt to promote literacy. It is currently used in Mainland China, Singapore and Malaysia. Traditional Chinese is used in Taiwan, Hong Kong, Macau, and in overseas Chinese communities. The existing of two different character sets in Chinese means you may see two different ways of writing when it comes to reading the same text. Simplified and traditional Chinese are taken by some people to be different languages. This is not true: they merely use different ideographic symbols to represent (some of the) characters. It's true that people from different places may use different words for certain things; for example; "air conditioner" is called 冷气 in Taiwan and 空调 in most of China. However, that is a different aspect in the language, and has nothing to do with the two systems. It is like in English someone may refer to dinner as supper and to lunch as dinner.

Simplified characters, as their name implies, are derived by simplifying them from the traditional character set. Simplification is performed by either decreasing the number of stokes from the original characters to form new characters, substituting complex characters with simple ones, or by some other means that yield similar results. There are also many common characters between the two systems. From a usage point of view, you really don't need to be too concerned about how the simplification is performed. All you need to know is there may be these three scenarios:

Scenario1: Simplification
A simpler ideographic symbol replaces a complex one. Sometimes the character still looks similar to the original but just has fewer strokes, i.e., 变 for 變, or 话 for 話. Other times the characters may look very different, i.e., 仅 for 僅, or 华 for 華.

Scenario 2: Merging
Use a simpler character to substitute for another. In such a situation, one character is eliminated from the simplified system and the simpler character now needs to be used in two different places. This kind of substitution does not happen very often and usually applies to situations when two characters have some kind of similarity. An example is the substitution of 醜 (*ugly*) by 丑 (*a clown; a buffoon*). In the simplified Chinese system, the character 醜 is eliminated, and 丑 now is used in all the places that contain either 醜 or 丑 in the original usage. Another variation of merging is to create one simplified character to replace two traditional characters. For example, use 发 to replace both 髮 and 發.

Scenario 3: No change
The same character is used in both systems.

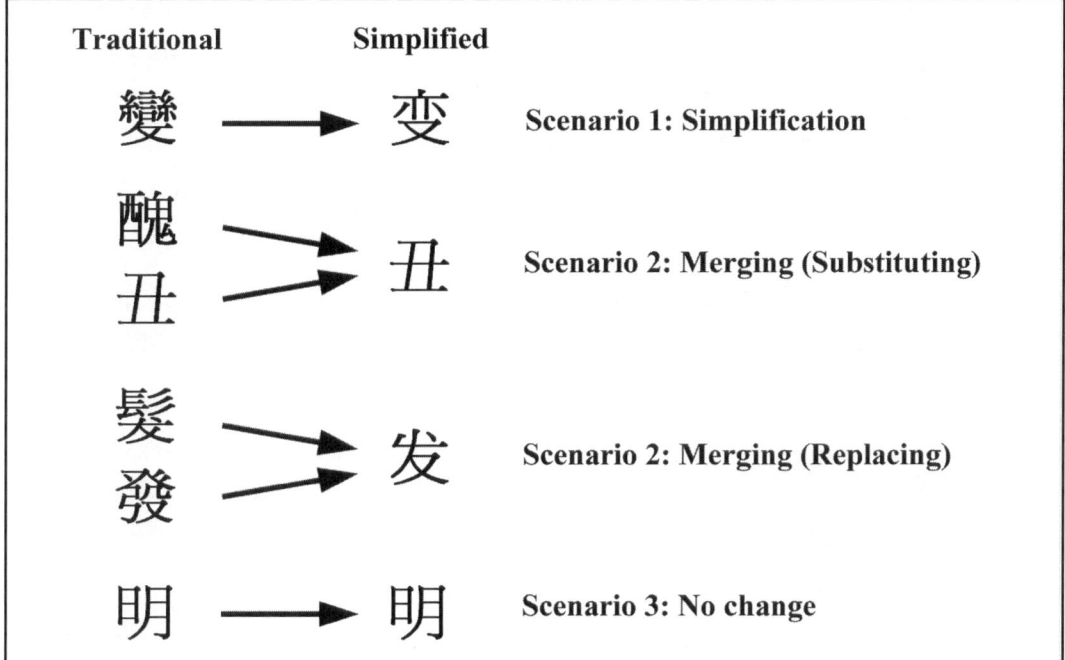

Figure 2.6 Mapping between traditional and simplified characters

Figure 2.6 shows some examples of the mapping between traditional and simplified characters. Note that because of the merging (using one character in places where multiple characters were used originally), mapping from traditional Chinese to simplified Chinese will have a multiple-to-one relationship. Conversion from traditional to simplified Chinese can be easily done by looking up a mapping table. Converting the other way is difficult, because you may need to examine the context to know which characters to map to.

When displaying or entering text on the computer, the existence of two different systems is not a problem per se, but there are pitfalls to watch for. One basic thing you need to know is that there are different encoding standards associated with the two systems. I will cover the encoding standards in more detail in the next section. In Chapter 2.12, I will discuss a related topic: determining which system a passage is written in. This is necessary because you may need to tell a program the system of writing being used before it can correctly recognize the characters or translate the text.

2.8 Encoding Standards of Chinese Characters

Encoding is to represent a set of characters in codes (numbers) so they can be used by computer programs. The need for encoding is not specific to Chinese, but to English and all other languages as well. It has been less of a problem for Latin-based languages because they contain only a small number of alphabetic symbols, while Chinese contains over ten thousand characters to encode.

An encoding standard defines two things: the character set and the encoding method. The character set is the collection of characters covered by the standard. The encoding method defines how the actual codes are mapped to represent the characters. For Chinese characters, there are three major encoding systems in use currently: GB, Big5, and Unicode. Within each system, there is more than one standard for various reasons. All systems contain different versions as they grow over time, with new versions superseding the old versions. Some systems may have different "extensions," which are custom character sets implemented by different software vendors. Even within a system, there are different encoding methods to represent the same set of characters differently.

The Guobiao (国标), aka GB, which means "National Standard" in Chinese, is the official standard used in mainland China. It is usually associated with simplified Chinese characters. There are two major GB versions currently in use. The original GB, aka GB2312, was introduced in 1980. The standard contains about 7,000 simplified Chinese characters (including characters common to both simplified and traditional), but does not include any traditional-only characters. As time went by, I suppose the government authority realized that it would be inappropriate for GB to be a "National Standard" if it did not include characters used by people from other areas that it considered to be part of its "Nation." The superseding standard GB18030, published in 2000, contains more than 27,000 Chinese characters to include the support for traditional Chinese characters as well. There are also other GB versions, but GB2312 and GB18030 are the two major ones. There is a variation of GB2312 that is commonly known as "HZ." It encodes GB2312 character sets using a different encoding method to facilitate the special requirement for transferring text through e-mail.

Another system is known as the Big5 (or Big-5), with its name representing a standard agreed upon by five big software vendors in Taiwan. Big5 was the de facto standard in ROC (Taiwan) and Hong Kong for use with traditional Chinese. The original standard introduced in 1984 defined about 13,000 traditional Chinese characters. It is widely used by companies that make Chinese-related software products. Since many characters are missing from the original standard, over time, vendors started to add new characters for their own needs. This resulted in the many different extensions of the standard published by various vendors and organizations. For example, the Hong Kong government created its own extension HKSCS (Hong Kong Supplementary Character Set) to accommodate Cantonese colloquial characters. The biggest problem with these extensions is that they are incompatible with one another. One code in one extension may conflict with a different character in another extension. As such, each extension can only be used by specific software products that support it. In 2003, the ROC government officially adopted Big5 as its "national standard," and published a revised version of the standard known as Big5-2003.

The third major standard for Chinese character encoding is Unicode. This is a worldwide standard intended to cover not only Chinese, but all the popular written characters that have been invented. It includes the ideographic symbols used in all languages, punctuation marks, mathematic symbols, etc. It defines uniform methods of encoding multilingual text so data can be exchanged internationally, laying the foundation for global software. Just like the other two systems, Unicode has been through different revisions since its first release in 1991. The latest major release is version 5 introduced in July of 2006. It covers about 70,000 CJK (Chinese-Japanese-Korean) unified ideographs, including traditional and simplified characters. Within Unicode, there are different encoding methods defined for its covered character set. The most commonly used encoding method these days is a variable-length encoding method called UTF-8. Unless otherwise specified, I always assume UTF-8 encoding whenever I mention Unicode encoding in this book. Unicode is maintained by the Unicode Consortium, a non-profit organization founded specifically to develop and promote the use of Unicode. Since Unicode is a universal standard and is politically neutral, even though it is relatively new, it is quickly getting popularity in all communities. As of today, Unicode is widely supported by all the major software and hardware vendors, and is expected to replace the other two standards in the future.

The majority of websites originating in China and Singapore were created in simplified Chinese, using GB encoding. Most existing websites from Taiwan, Hong Kong, and overseas Chinese communities were created in traditional Chinese, using Big5 encoding. Many new websites, regardless of whether they are in simplified or traditional Chinese, use Unicode encoding. A web page usually consists of an HTML file, which contains the text encoding information within the file. The web browser only needs to look at this encoding information and it knows how to display the contents.

There are other types of files that do not contain encoding method information. To view such files you may need to explicitly specify the encoding method used in them for some programs to work properly. There are also situations when the software blindly assumes that the system always displays texts in GB or Big5. To accommodate this, you may need to make a special adjustment to your Windows system. I will cover these in more detail in future sections as we come to use the specific programs.

I have covered a lot of technical details in this section. It is perfectly fine if you are still not very clear about most of these things. All you need to remember now is that there are three basic encoding systems: GB, Big5, and Unicode. GB is associated with simplified Chinese, and is used in mainland China. Big5 is associated with traditional Chinese, and is used in Taiwan and Hong Kong. Unicode covers both character sets, and is used everywhere.

2.9 Calligraphic Styles and Fonts

Chinese characters consist of strokes drawn in virtual rectangle boxes of equal size, regardless of the number of strokes. Commonly used characters contain from one to about twenty-five stokes. Occasionally you may see characters with over thirty strokes.

Many different calligraphic styles (体 or 书) are used in writing Chinese characters. I use the phrase "calligraphic style" loosely here as a general term for describing different ways of writing or printing characters. As I understand, some ancient calligraphic styles have characters with very different appearance from their common, modern equivalents. Even though the literature on calligraphic styles usually describes them together with other common styles, I really think they should be categorized differently. These styles were used in ancient times, and few people know how to write or read them any more. I will just call these ancient styles, and won't cover them in our discussion.

The Chinese characters we commonly see in printing or writing use one of a few calligraphic styles or their variations. Even though some of them may have already existed for more than a thousand years, they are considered modern calligraphic styles because they are still in use.

宋体 (Song)   Song is also known as 明体 (Ming). This is the font commonly used in printing. The strokes consist of straight, thin lines going across and thicker lines going down, for easy carving on wood. It has been used in printing for almost a thousand years. This font takes the least space compared to other fonts. The fine, square-looking characters commonly seen in the newspaper are printed using Song.

仿宋体 (FongSong)   FongSong is similar to Song but it looks more like hand writing. The character 仿 means "imitate" in Chinese, which suggests that it is a variation of Song. The strokes of FongSong are still straight lines, but they look less mechanical and monotonous. The other difference is that all strokes are of the same thickness. Characters written in FongSong usually appear in longer rectangles instead of squares. FongSong is usually used in engineering drawings, maps, diagrams, etc.

楷体 (Kai)   Kai is the font used in regular hand-writing. Characters in Kai look like writing made with traditional brush pens. Nowadays people write with ballpoint pens or fountain pens, but the writing is still made in Kai. The shapes of the characters look similar even though the strokes do not appear as fat. The characters that appear on people's tattoos are made in Kai.

黑体 (Hei)   The characters of the Hei font look like writing made using a thick Sharpie pen. All strokes have a constant thickness from beginning to end. Each stroke turns with no hesitation, and terminates abruptly at the end. It is usually used in titles or on posters where you want to give a crisp, strong impression.

圆体 **(Yuan)**   Yuan is a variation of Hei. It looks similar to Hei but has replaced the sharp turns with curves, so the characters have a smoother look. Yuan is commonly used on street signs, banners, etc.

隶书 **(Li)**   Li is a font that originated from ancient times with artistic-looking strokes. Nowadays, it is mainly usually used in large titles, signage, or places where people demonstrate the art of calligraphy.

Figure 2.7 gives an illustration of sample characters written in these fonts. Be aware that what I have described here is only a general categorization. What you actually see in the real world may be some variation of these fonts. Also, the implementation from various vendors may make them look different.

國這來個說　国这来个说	**Song**
國這來個說	**FongSong**
國這來個說　国这来个说	**Kai**
國這來個說　国这来个说	**Hei**
國這來個說	**Yuan**
國這來個說　国这来个说	**Li**

Figure 2.7 Common Chinese fonts

When a computer displays Chinese text, it relies on the installed text font files to render the characters on the screen. Just like having different fonts such as Times Roman or Arial when displaying English alphabets, you can choose different Chinese fonts to make Chinese text look different on the screen.

The question of which font is used become important when we use OCR software to recognize text on printed materials. If the text is printed using a font that is too special, the OCR software may not recognize it correctly. Most OCR software should be able to recognize characters printed in the commonly used fonts that I have described above.

There are times when you need to proofread and correct misrecognized characters from the OCR software. The proofreading process involves comparing the original text image with the text output from the software. To make comparisons easier, it is better to install the same font as what is used in the source.

2.10 Chinese Input Methods

To input Chinese text into a computer is not an easy task. Not too long ago, the only method you could use was to type it using the (English) keyboard. This is still the most common way of entering Chinese into the PC because there is no additional hardware required. You do need a special type of software to perform such tasks, and this is commonly known as IME, the Input Method Editor. A few years ago you might have had to pay for this kind of software, but nowadays it comes with the Windows system. There are also many web-based IMEs that can be used free of charge. Over time, people have invented many different Input Method Editors based on the sound, shape, or other categorization of characters. New input methods are still being invented these days because the prevailing methods still have problems. The Windows built-in tool supports only the most common methods.

Using a regular keyboard for inputting Chinese characters involves categorizing Chinese characters so each one can be represented by a sequence of English letters. This task sounds simple, but is almost impossible to do well. There is no simple method to categorize Chinese characters based on their appearance. There are many input methods invented to do this, some based on the shape, others based on the strokes. Unfortunately, they all have some drawbacks and most of them require non-trivial learning by users. A different approach is to categorize using the Mandarin sound of the characters. This method requires the least effort in learning, because many people already know either Pinyin or Zhuyin when they learn the language. The English keyboard can be used directly for the Pinyin method. The Zhuyin method requires one more mapping from the phonetic symbols to the English alphabet on the keyboard. Currently, these two are the most widely used methods for inputting Chinese characters into computers. The biggest problem with the Mandarin sound input is that each pronunciation has multiple characters associated with it. Usually you need to select from a list of characters presented by the software to finalize your steps. This makes the input process slow. The other problem is that you cannot input a character if you don't know the sound of it, but this should not usually happen while writing. One last issue is that some people may not have learned Zhuyin or Pinyin, and some may not know the correct pronunciation in Mandarin.

Other than using IME software with a keyboard, you can use a speech recognition program or a hand-writing pad for Chinese input. With continuous developments and improvements in recent years, these two technologies have now become quite reliable for practical use.

None of the methods I have discussed are practical to use for people who do not know the language. Fortunately, there is only one instance in our process that requires you to enter Chinese characters into the system. On that one occasion, you would not use any of the input methods that I have just described. The software will provide you with a list, and all you need is to select a character from that list.

2.11 Hand-Writing Chinese

Since it is not very easy to type Chinese characters, hand-writing with a pen and paper is still very common for writing Chinese. As of today, no OCR software program is able to recognize hand written Chinese characters well enough by itself. When they are used for recognizing hand-writing characters, significant human effort is required to correct the misrecognized results.

Until a better technology is invented, I will have to say the process described in this book cannot be used for reading hand-written text.

2.12 Distinguishing Chinese Character Sets

This might sound odd, but there are actually times when you need to tell a computer program what character set (traditional vs. simplified) you have in the text for it to tell you what characters they are. Most Chinese OCR software programs are able to recognize both traditional and simplified characters, but they are all designed in a way that they can only recognize characters from one system at a time. Most translation programs have the exact same problem—they support both systems, but don't allow the mixed use of characters in a text. What makes things worse is that the user has to specify the proper character set for the program to operate properly.

It is not easy for someone unfamiliar with Chinese to tell in which system a document is written from the text. One way to guess is to go by the geographical origin of the document. If it is something printed before 1960, you can safely assume that it is in traditional Chinese. For materials printed after that time or for electronic documents, see if you can find out where they come from. If they are from China, Singapore, or Malaysia then most likely they use simplified Chinese. If they are from Taiwan, Hong Kong, or other places in the world then you can assume they are in traditional Chinese.

When the materials are from a book or magazine, there is one other way to tell. If it is printed vertically and opens in the reverse direction to English books, then it is almost certainly traditional Chinese. If the book or magazine is printed horizontally and is opened in the same way as English books, then it is hard to determine. Even though most simplified Chinese texts are printed this way, more and more traditional Chinese texts have begun to use the horizontal printing style as well.

If the methods mentioned above do not give you an answer, you can probably use one of the following tips:

Figure 2.8 is a list of frequently-used Chinese characters that are different in the traditional and simplified systems. If you see any one of them then you know immediately what system it is.

Traditional:
國這來個說們爲時會過學對麼還發當無開見經頭從動長

Simplified:
国这来个说们为时会过学对么还发当无开见经头从动长

Figure 2.8 Frequently-used characters that look different in the two systems

If you don't see any of the characters in the list, try the following method. In Figure 2.9, I have listed some radicals that are written differently in the two systems. If you can spot any character in the text to contain any characters that use these radicals, then you have solved your mystery.

Group	Character Set	Radical	Characters					
1	Traditional	言	計	訂	話	記	討	訊
	Simplified	讠	计	订	话	记	讨	讯
2	Traditional	門	閂	問	悶	閃	間	閣
	Simplified	门	闩	问	闷	闪	间	阁
3	Traditional	糸	糾	紀	紅	約	細	紙
	Simplified	纟	纠	纪	红	约	细	纸
4	Traditional	貝	財	貞	販	貨	貼	賀
	Simplified	贝	财	贞	贩	货	贴	贺
5	Traditional	食	飢	飲	飯	飼	飽	餅
	Simplified	饣	饥	饮	饭	饲	饱	饼
6	Traditional	金	針	釘	釣	鈔	鈴	錦
	Simplified	钅	针	钉	钓	钞	铃	锦

Figure 2.9 Radicals and example characters that look different in the two systems

If you are still not able to find any character in your text that uses one of these radicals described above, then I am running out of tricks to use. Your last resort will be just to make a wild guess. If you need to specify this in the software then just choose the simplified Chinese and see what happens. When you do this to the OCR software with a wrong setting, most of the output characters will be incorrect. It is usually very easy to spot this kind of error once you are familiar with the operation of the program. I will cover this in detail when I describe using the software.

2.13 Distinguishing Chinese Text from Japanese and Korean

CJK stands for the three East Asian languages: Chinese, Japanese, and Korean. When it comes to describing computer software, the three languages are sometimes mentioned together. The reason is that all contain ideographic symbols, and there are common characters used among them. Ancient Japanese and Korean languages use a lot of Chinese characters which are called Hanzi (汉字). These Chinese characters have their own pronunciations in Japanese and Korean, but the meanings are still the same. This is much like the situations where Chinese characters are used in different parts of China. Chinese characters have been greatly reduced in modern Japanese, and are rarely seen in modern Korean. The most common place you see Chinese characters is in the names of people or places.

There may be times when you need to know whether the text you are reading is Chinese and not the other two languages. This is relatively easy compared with telling simplified Chinese from traditional Chinese. Here are a few methods that you can use:

Japanese text contains a random, mixed use of Japanese syllabaries and Chinese characters in a sentence. My estimation is that roughly 50% of each is used in an average document. Japanese syllabary symbols are simpler in shape and some look like worms or hooks. Listed below are some symbols from the Japanese syllabaries:

の て か つ し カ ノ タ ミ

As you can see, these are very simple symbols that contain fewer than five strokes each. Chinese characters are usually more complex and contain ten or even more strokes on average. When you see a lot of mixing of these two kinds of characters, it is safe to assume that the writing is Japanese.

The other thing you may notice is the frequent appearance of the symbol の in Japanese texts. When you see that symbol in the text you are almost certain that the text is written in Japanese.

Characters in Korean texts contain a lot of circles and bars. They look like some sort of stick figure drawing. For example,

으 이 의 여 인 유 모 일 임

I do not know if other languages also contain symbols like these, but when you see characters that contain circles, they are almost certainly not Chinese. Chinese characters are made of strokes, and in ancient times they needed to carve them in wood. It would not be very convenient to make many hollow circles like those.

3. Process and Tools

This chapter is an introduction to the tools and overall process that we will use for Chinese reading. It starts with a diagram displaying an overview of the entire computer-aided reading process. From this diagram, you will have a basic idea of the flow of activities, as well as an understanding of which tool is used in each step. The subsequent sections give detailed descriptions of some of the devices and tools. I will cover the two main tools, the OCR (Optical Character Recognition) and MT (Machine Translation) software, in separate chapters.

3.1 The Process Flow Diagram

There is a famous saying "A picture is worth a thousand words." The Chinese equivalent of this is:

百闻不如一见 (*Hundred hearing not match one seeing*)

The English text after the Chinese is a direct, character-by-character interpretation of the original Chinese proverb. Similar texts may appear frequently when reading machine translated results. I figured it is better for you to get used to it first.

I'll describe many devices and software tools in this book. To help you more easily understand the role of each of the tools and how they fit together, I have created a process flow diagram of computer-aided Chinese reading (Figure 3.1).

On top of this diagram, we can see three sources where our documents may come from. Starting from the left, we have books, magazines, newspapers, etc. These documents are not in electronic format, but they are accessible through the use of a scanner. The second type of sources, shown in the middle of the diagram, is texts on banners, posters, street signs, etc. They are not in electronic format and can only be captured with a camera. The third type of source is materials already in electronic format, such as websites, e-mail, text files, etc.

Sources already in electronic format can be sent to translation or dictionary software directly to produce English text. For the other two types of sources, we need to capture the text image and convert it into text codes first.

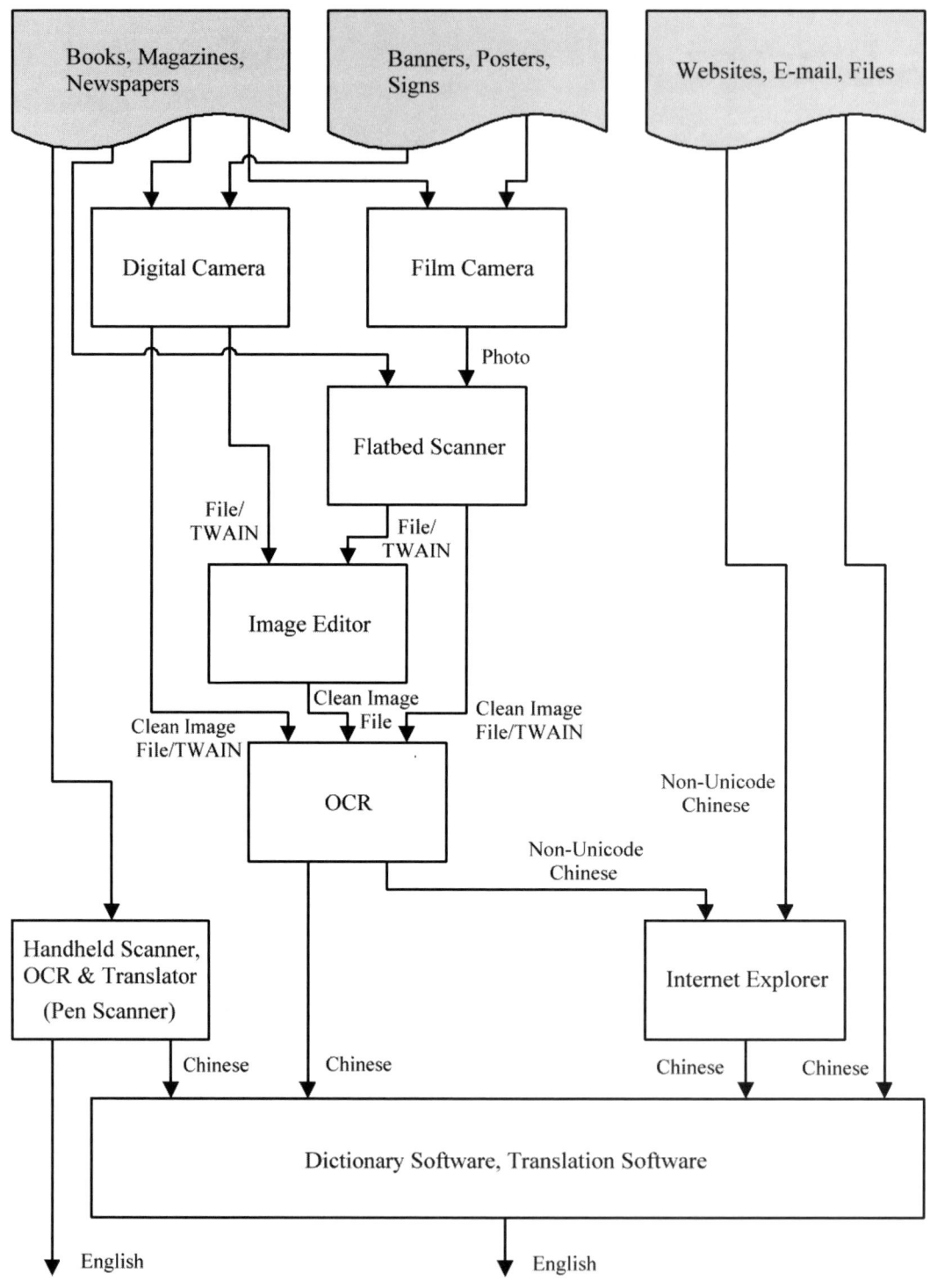

Figure 3.1 Process flow diagram of computer-aided Chinese reading

There are several devices available for image capture: flatbed scanners, film cameras or digital cameras, and handheld scanners. For capturing text on paper, a flatbed scanner is most commonly used. A camera is mainly for capturing text not accessible from a scanner. It works well with larger text, but requires some careful adjustments for getting smaller text, and the results are generally unsatisfactory. The pen-shaped handheld scanner is a relatively new device. It resembles a marker pen, and it scans one line of text at a time. It comes with built-in OCR and translation software to convert the scanned images into text codes and then translate the results to English. Since the quality of the built-in translator in the handheld scanner may be inferior to standard translation and dictionary software, we sometimes take the output from the handheld scanner and feed that to other translators and dictionaries to get better results. I will talk more about the flatbed scanner, the digital camera, and the handheld scanner in Chapters 3.5, 3.6, and 3.11 respectively.

Texts on banners, posters, signs, etc., are acquired through the use of a camera. Images captured from a camera may need some editing before they can be utilized by the OCR. When using a film camera, a flatbed scanner is needed to capture the developed photos. Texts captured through a digital camera can be sent directly to the image editor or the OCR. Thorough descriptions of an image editor are given in Chapter 3.7.

The outputs from a scanner or a digital camera are text images, which need to be sent to the OCR to produce text codes. In situations where the images produced are less than satisfactory, an image editor program is used to tidy things up. An image editor can be used to cut, paste, resize, transform, or perform other processing needs to the images, producing better recognition results when they are sent to the OCR software. Images can be passed between applications through the saving and opening of image files, or they can be transported directly using a software interface standard called TWAIN, a protocol for different image processing programs to communicate with one another.

The OCR software takes text images and converts them into text codes. Some OCR programs produce output texts that are Unicode encoded, which can be used by the translation or dictionary software. Some older OCR programs only produce non-Unicode (GB or Big5) texts. In such cases we may need to convert them into Unicode texts before feeding them to the translation or dictionary software. This conversion can be done using the Internet Explorer program, which I will cover in Chapter 3.3. The OCR software will be mentioned briefly in Chapter 3.8 and thoroughly in Chapter 4.

Chinese texts already in electronic format, such as texts on websites, e-mail, files, etc can be used directly by the translator or dictionary software if they are Unicode encoded. If the texts are encoded in other methods then we may also need to use the Internet Explorer to convert them.

The bottom of the diagram shows the core tools for the process: dictionary software and translation software. Dictionary software gives definitions to individual Chinese words in English. Translation software translates whole sentences or paragraphs. They will be mentioned briefly in Chapter 3.9 and 3.10 respectively and covered in full in Chapter 5.

One essential piece of software not showing in this picture is the Windows system itself. Certain installations and configurations may be needed for the US or the other English version Windows systems to fully support the display of Chinese characters. I will cover these details in the next section. The other tool that we may need is the Windows Notepad or WordPad, for viewing or editing files. The topics related to these two programs will be covered in Chapter 3.4.

3.2 Chinese Language Support in Windows

The very first thing I would like to describe is an essential piece of software that allows us to display Chinese texts in all the applications that we will use. This piece of software does not appear in the diagram because it is actually part of the Windows system and gets used by most blocks in there.

Certain language-specific files need to be installed in order to display Chinese texts on a Windows-based computer. The US version of the Windows 2000 and XP systems comes with support for reading and writing Chinese, but mostly likely you need to install them separately because they are not selected by default when you set up your Windows system. For Windows Vista, the Chinese language supports are installed by default, so these extra steps are not needed.

To install the Chinese language related files on a Windows XP system, follow the steps described below. Depending on how the Windows system was installed previously, you may need to have the original Windows installation CD handy.

1. Go to Windows **Start** menu, select **Control Panel**.

2. Double click the **Regional and Language Options** icon if the Control Panel is displayed in **Classic View**. If the Control Panel is displayed in the **Category View**, you can do this by clicking the **Date, Time, Language, and Regional Options** category link, followed by the **Regional and Language Options** link. This opens the **Regional and Language Options** dialog window (see Figure 3.2).

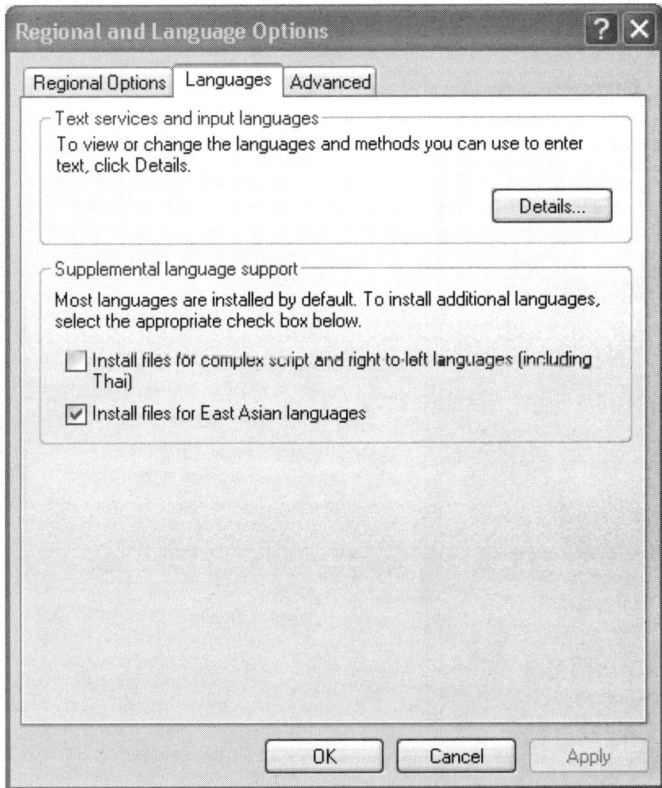

Figure 3.2 Install Chinese language support on Windows XP

3. Select the **Languages** tab on the **Regional and Language Options** dialog.

4. In the **Supplemental language support** section, verify the status of the **Install files for East Asian languages** checkbox. If this checkbox is checked, it means the system has already had the language files installed and you don't have to do the following steps. Just click the **Cancel** button to exit out of this. If the checkbox is not checked, proceed with clicking the checkbox. A message box displaying information will appear. Click the **OK** button to continue, and then click the **Apply** button to begin installing the language files. During the installation process, you may be asked to insert the Windows CD-ROM. Follow the instructions on screen to complete the installation. After these steps are completed successfully, your Windows system is ready to display Chinese.

For Windows 2000 users, follow the steps described below. Depending on how the Windows system was installed previously, you may need to have the original Windows installation CD handy for use.

1. Go to Windows **Start** menu, select **Settings**, and then select **Control Panel**. Double click the **Regional Settings** icon to open the **Regional Options** dialog window (see Figure 3.3).

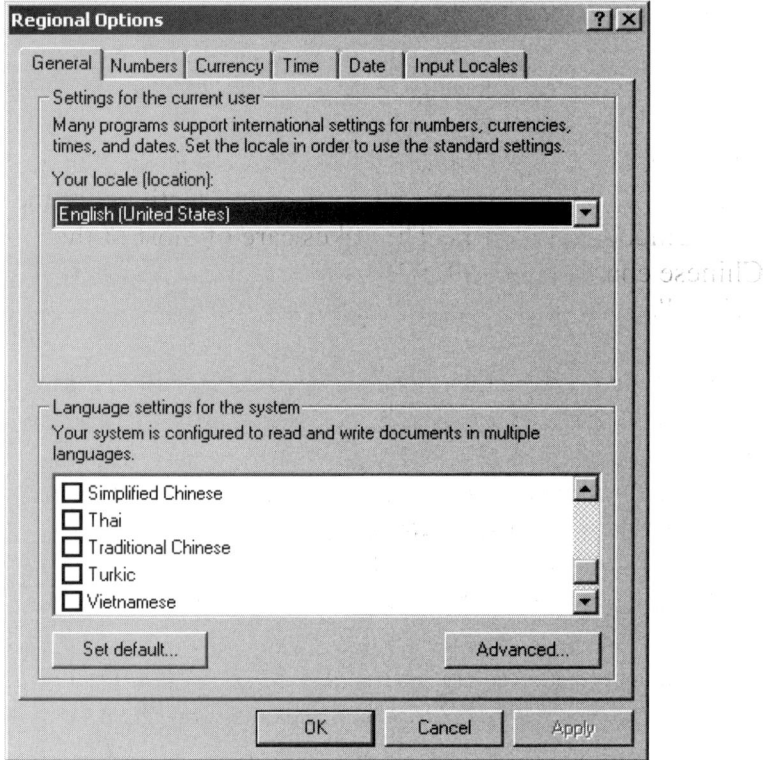

Figure 3.3 Install Chinese language support on Windows 2000

2. Select the **General** tab.

3. In the **Language settings for the system** section, check both the **Simplified Chinese** and the **Traditional Chinese** checkboxes.

4. Click the **Apply** button to start installing the language files. During the installation process, you may be asked to insert the Windows CD-ROM. Follow the instructions on screen to complete the installation, and also to reboot the system when asked to. After these steps are completed successfully, your Windows system is now ready to display Chinese.

After the installation, you can perform a quick verification by visiting some Chinese-based websites. If the language files are properly installed, you will see all the Chinese characters on these web pages; otherwise, you may see boxes, question marks or other strange symbols. Please refer to Appendix C for a list of some websites with Chinese content. Be aware that some of the materials on a website may contain graphics with text (not the real text). In these places, the text image will show up correctly even though the character display function is not working, so, needless to say, they are irrelevant. Make sure that the places displaying real text show up correctly. Also remember to perform tests on both simplified and traditional Chinese-based websites to verify that both are working properly.

The language file installation added several Chinese text fonts, so that the Chinese characters can be displayed. It also updated some text displaying functions for the system to support the use of Unicode characters. This takes care of most of the problems in displaying Chinese characters in a US Windows system. The only remaining issue now is to handle the non-Unicode Chinese text displays.

As mentioned in the previous chapter, two other major systems exist for encoding Chinese Characters besides Unicode: the Big5 and the GB. As of today, these two encoding methods are still widely used in Chinese-based websites, and they are not likely to go away soon. Luckily, for reading materials from websites, the web browser programs are able to take care of displaying the Big5 or GB encoded characters automatically. There are a few things we should pay attention to concerning the usage of web browsers, which I will cover in the next section.

For many applications developed before the popularity of Unicode, the texts on menus, dialogs, buttons, etc are encoded in Big5 or GB code. Such applications are designed for Chinese versions of Windows, or they require the installation of a special Chinese-language framework on top of the Windows system. These software programs always assume that the encoding system is in either Big5 or GB. When these applications run under a US version of Windows, even with the installation of the East Asian Language files, the Chinese characters will still not show up correctly. This being said, we will not be too concerned about the Chinese UI of an application. For our purposes, we always need to use the English UI. For practical considerations, the biggest concern with these old programs is that the Big5 or GB encoded text they produced can not be used by other programs that only take Unicode encoded text.

To resolve this issue, Windows has included a setting that allows the system to handle characters encoded in non-Unicode codes. This solves the problem of using non-Unicode texts within an application as well as in the UI. The caveat is that you can choose only one of the encoding methods to deal with. There is no way to display Big5 text and GB text together, because their code spaces overlap. When the setting is selected to one system while viewing text encoded in another system, most characters may still be in Chinese, but they will be totally wrong.

Follow these steps to set up the Windows XP system to display non-Unicode encoded texts:

1. Go to the Windows **Start** menu, select **Control Panel**.

2. Double click the **Regional and Language Options** icon if the Control Panel is displayed in **Classic View**. If the Control Panel is displayed in **Category View**, click the **Date, Time, Language, and Regional Options** category link, and then click the **Regional and Language Options** link. This will open the **Regional and Language Options** dialog window (Figure 3.4).

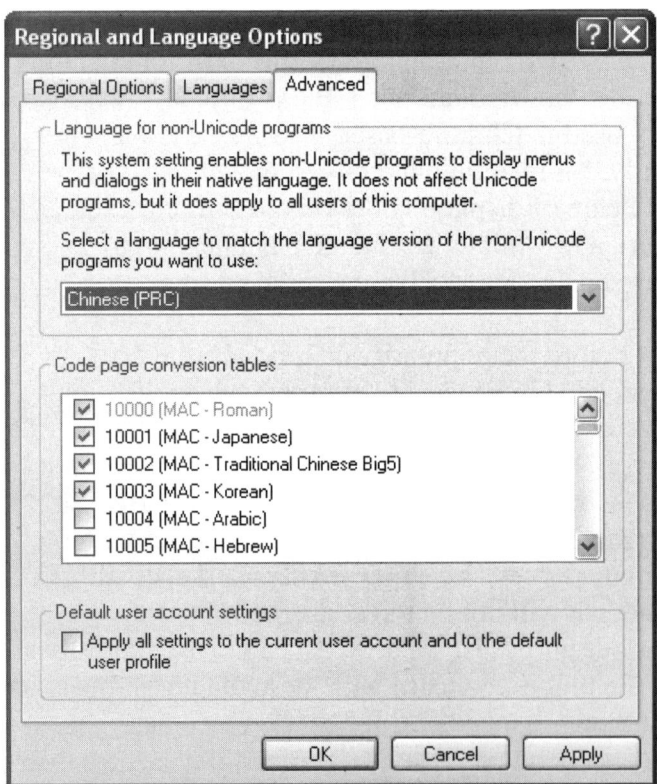

Figure 3.4 Set up Windows XP for showing non-Unicode texts

3. Select the **Advanced** tab on the **Regional and Language Options** dialog.

4. Under the **Language for non-Unicode programs** dropdown box, select the appropriate language by region, such as Chinese (Taiwan) or Chinese (PRC). Do not change the selections in the **Code page conversion tables**. Leave the **Default user account settings** checkbox unchecked if you only wish to use this setting for the current user. Check the checkbox to apply this setting to all users of the computer.

5. Click the **OK** button and follow the instructions on the screen to finish the setup.

Follow these steps to set up the Windows 2000 system to display non-Unicode encoded texts:

1. Go to the Windows **Start** menu, select **Settings**, and then select **Control Panel**. Double click the **Regional Settings** icon to open the **Regional Options** dialog window (Figure 3.5).

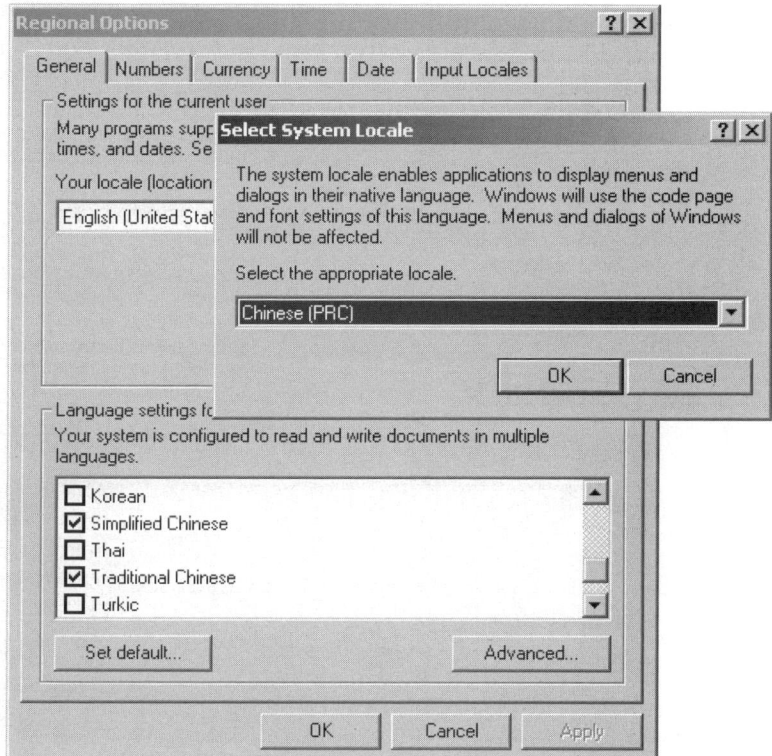

Figure 3.5 Set up Windows 2000 for showing non-Unicode texts

2. Select the **General** tab.

3. Click the **Set default** button in the **Language settings for the system** section.

4. In the **Select System Locale** dialog window, select the appropriate language by region, such as Chinese (Taiwan) or Chinese (PRC). Click **OK** to accept the selection.

5. Click the **Apply** button and then follow the instructions on the screen to finish the setup.

Follow these steps to set up the Windows Vista system to display non-Unicode encoded texts:

1. Go to the Windows **Start** menu, select **Control Panel**.

2. Double click the **Regional and Language Options** icon if the Control Panel is displayed in **Classic View**. If the Control Panel is displayed with categorized selections, click the **Clock, Language, and Region** category link, and then click the **Regional and Language Options** link. This will open the **Regional and Language Options** dialog window (Figure 3.6).

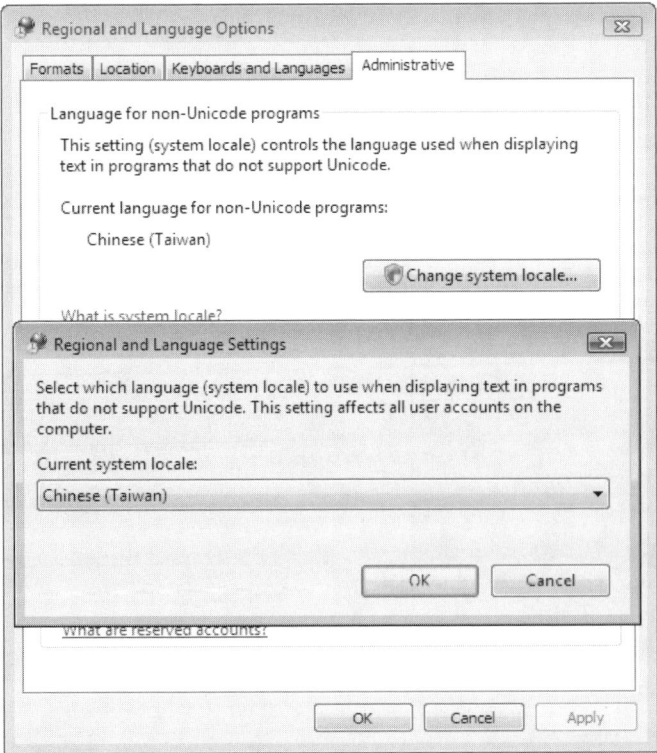

Figure 3.6 Set up Windows Vista for showing non-Unicode texts

3. Select the **Administrative** tab on the **Regional and Language Options** dialog.

4. Under the **Language for non-Unicode programs** section, click the **Change System Locale** button. From the **Current System Local** dropdown box in the **Regional and Language Settings** dialog window, select the appropriate language by region, such as Chinese (Taiwan) or Chinese (PRC). Follow the instructions on the screen to finish the setup.

Instead of relying on the functions of the Windows system, some applications handle their own character display. For example, Adobe Acrobat uses it own set of font files for displaying Chinese. If Acrobat cannot find the fonts to display in a PDF file, it will automatically download and install the font files from its website. We will not use Acrobat in our process and the detailed discussion of this topic is beyond the scope of this book.

3.3 Web Browser

In this section, I will describe the use of web browser software. It is assumed that readers are already familiar with regular web browser tasks, so I will focus only on specific topics related to Chinese reading. At the end of this section, I will cover a unique but important task the web browser can do, so please don't skip this section just yet. The East Asian Language files installation should already have been completed on your Windows system. If not, please refer to the previous section to complete that installation before reading any further.

As I have mentioned previously, there are three commonly used encoding systems for Chinese text: GB, Big5, and Unicode. Websites from mainland China and Singapore are usually encoded using GB. Websites from Taiwan, Hong Kong, and overseas Chinese communities are usually encoded using Big5. Nowadays, more and more sites are starting to use the Unicode encoding as well. While browsing web pages, the web browser can usually determine the encoding method automatically, based on the information provided from the web pages. Try the following simple experiment to see how this works. (**These steps are used only to help you understand how the web browser works. You don't need to actually follow them.**)

1. Navigate to a Chinese language website, for example, the Yahoo! Taiwan home page (http://tw.yahoo.com/)

2. Right click the mouse button while the mouse cursor is on the page (but not on any texts or pictures). A pop-up menu should appear with a menu item **View Source** or **View Page Source** (Figure 3.7). Select that to view the source of the web page, i.e., the HTML file. HTML stands for "Hyper Text Markup Language," which is used for describing web pages. This opens a new window (either Windows Notepad or a text viewer utility used by the web browser), as shown in Figure 3.8.

Figure 3.7 Use **View Source** to view the code in a web page

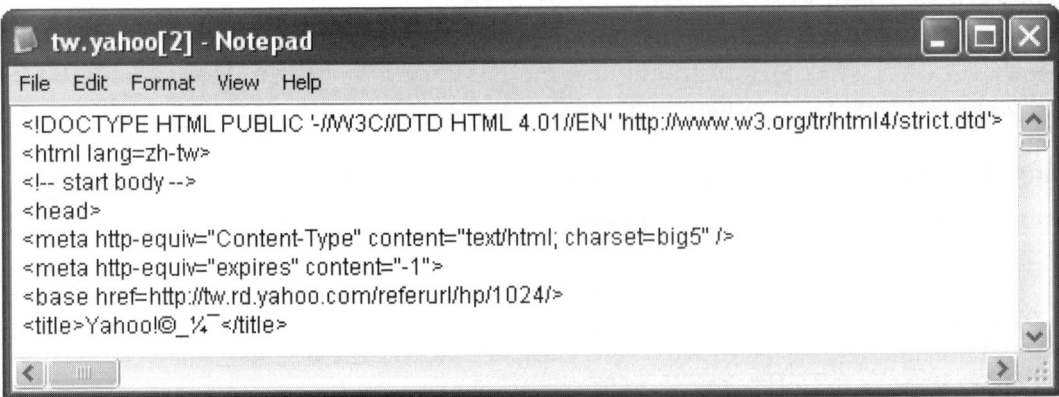

Figure 3.8 Character encoding information (Meta tag) embedded in a web page

3. Look at the fifth line in the Notepad window (Figure 3.8), it says:

```
<meta http-equiv="Content-Type" content="text/html; charset=big5" />
```

This is where the character encoding method is specified in the web page.

4. Click Internet Explorer's **View** menu and then choose **Encoding**. If the **Auto-Select** option is checked, the program will automatically choose the **Chinese Traditional (Big5)** (Figure 3.9). For readers using Firefox, the operation is similar: Choose **View** and then click **Character Encoding**. If the **Auto-Detect** option is on (i.e., the **Auto-Detect** submenu is set to select **Chinese** or **East Asian**), the program will automatically choose the **Chinese Traditional (Big5)**.

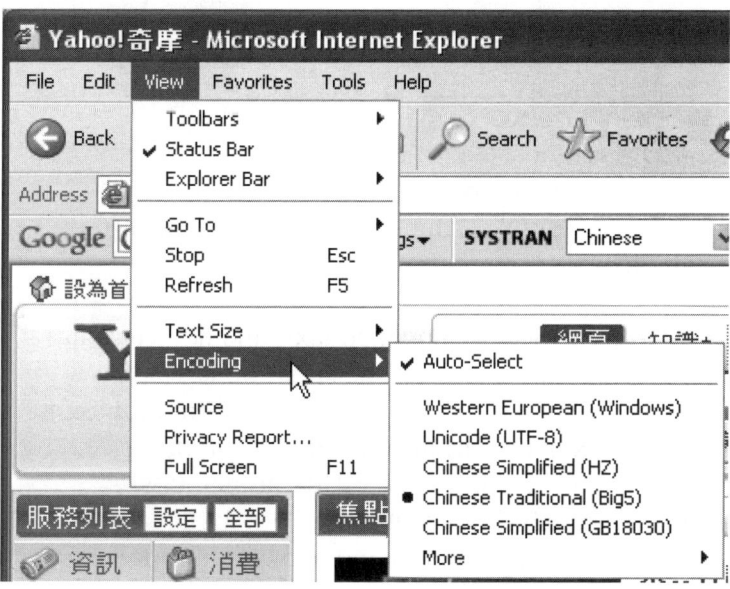

Figure 3.9 Internet Explorer selects the encoding automatically

Once again, you don't actually need to perform these tasks. I have only used them to demonstrate the location of the encoding information on a web page, so you can see how the web browser identifies it. I also want to emphasize that, in order for a web browser to recognize the encoding methods of web pages automatically, the encoding selection must be left on **Auto-Select**.

5. If an incorrect encoding method is used to view a web page or a text file, the contents will not be displayed properly. In this situation, you will most likely see a mix of Chinese characters with boxes and some special symbols. To experience this, uncheck the **Auto-Select** checkmark, and then choose a different encoding

method that we know is incorrect, for instance, **Chinese Simplified (GB18030)**. Now, the same page will show some boxes, question marks, strange symbols and unusual spaces. In some instances the browser may even stop displaying the entire page. Figure 3.10 gives some examples of Chinese texts displayed with incorrect encoding methods.

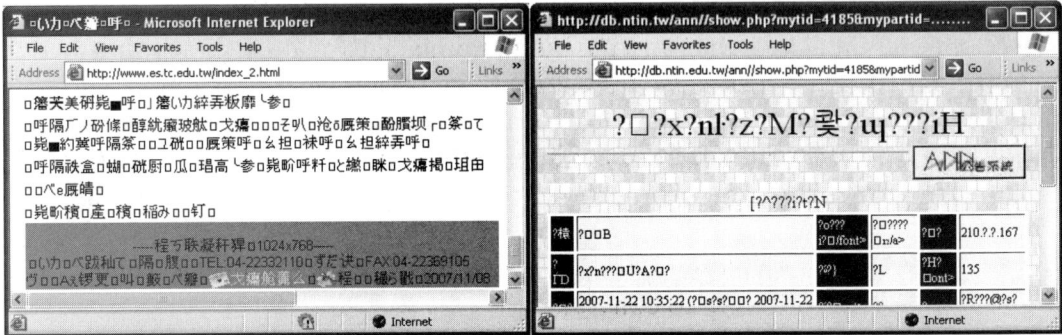

Figure 3.10 Viewing Chinese texts with incorrect encoding methods

6. This is the end of our experiment. If you have followed along with step 5, please do not forget to change the encoding setting (click **View**, **Encoding**) on your browser back to **Auto-select**.

Occasionally, you may come across incorrectly encoded text, and need to adjust the encoding methods for text to show up properly. One situation is when a web page either does not contain the encoding tag, or has incorrect information on it. Situations such as these, while not frequent, certainly do exist. A similar scenario is when a web page contains text encoded from many different methods. A practical example of this is when we accessing a web-based e-mail account using the web browser. On the "Inbox" page of the web e-mail account, normally shown is a list of entries with the date, senders and subjects. Since the subject contents come from different senders, they may well contain texts encoded through different methods.

Another practical situation is when the web browser is used to view files that are not created in HTML. As we have seen in our first experiment, an HTML web page uses Meta tags to describe the appearance of a document. This tag exists only in HTML files, and not other types of file, such as a plain text file. Even though web pages are usually written in HTML, sometimes you may find places that have plain text files on their websites. To view plain text files containing Chinese or other non-Roman characters using the web browser, you need to manually set the encoding method for the text to show up correctly.

There is an "Internet Explorer" step in the process flow diagram (Figure 3.1). This represents a special task that we want the Internet Explorer program to do besides browsing web pages—to convert Big5 or GB encoded files into Unicode.

When the non-Unicode support is set up on the Windows system, most Windows applications should work properly even with the Big5 or GB encoded texts. However, one limitation of using the non-Unicode support in Windows is that you need to choose either the Big5 or GB, but not both. To avoid confusion, it is better to convert them into Unicode encoded files.

Follow these steps to convert the encoding method of a text file or an HTML file using the Internet Explorer:

1. Start the Windows Explorer application (not the "Internet Explorer") and navigate to the file you wish to convert.

2. Click the right mouse button while the cursor is on the filename. This will bring up a pop-up menu. Select the **Open With** menu item and then choose **Internet Explorer** (see Figure 3.11).

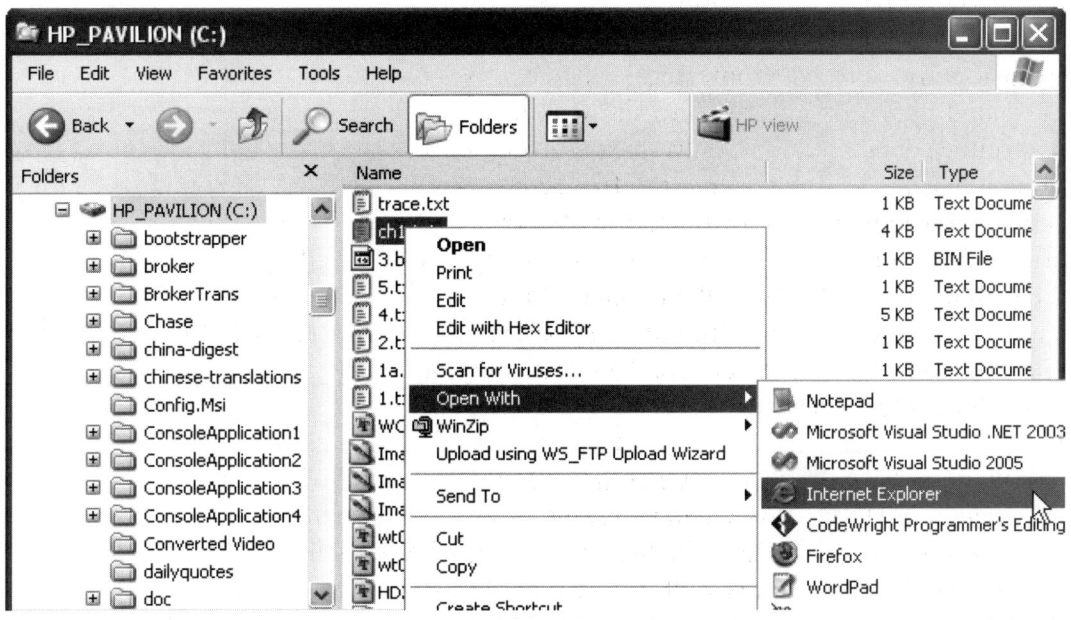

Figure 3.11 Open a file with Internet Explorer

3. The file will now open from the Internet Explorer window. If the text fails to show up with proper encoding, you need to change it manually. To do this, Click

View, select **Encoding** and then select the proper encoding method. The text should appear properly in the Internet Explorer window.

4. From the Internet Explorer main menu, select **File**, then select **Save As**. The **Save Web Page** dialog comes up as in Figure 3.12. Click the **Encoding** selection box and select the **Unicode (UTF-8)** to choose the Unicode encoding. Enter a new file name in the **File name** area to prevent it from overwriting the existing file. Click **Save** to save the new file.

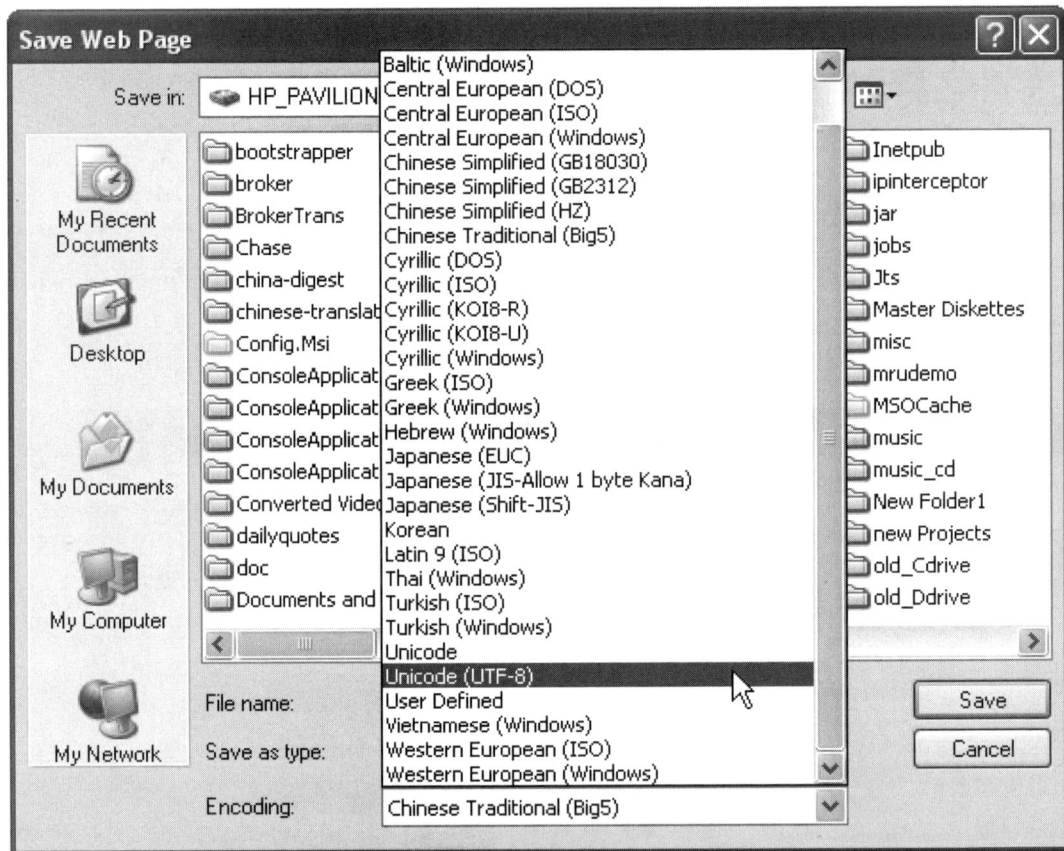

Figure 3.12 Save a file and choose the encoding method using Internet Explorer

For readers using Firefox, the steps for opening the file (step 1 to 3) are similar. I have not found a similar option for the last step (my version is 2.0.0.7). Firefox always saves the file using the original encoding method. To work around this, select **Edit**, click **Select All**, click **Edit** again, and then click **Copy.** This will copy the contents into the Windows Clipboard. After that, start Windows Notepad or WordPad program, paste the contents from the Windows Clipboard, and then save the file using the Unicode (UTF-8) format.

3.4 Notepad and WordPad

Notepad and WordPad are two utilities included with Windows. After the installation of Chinese language support files in the Windows system, both utilities can be used to view and save files containing Chinese characters.

Notepad can only be used to open and save plain text files, and it only handles texts with Unicode encoding. After setting up the non-Unicode texts function (see Chapter 3.2) in Windows system, it can also open and save either Big5 or GB encoded texts, depending on the setup in the Windows system.

WordPad is able to handle plain text files in the same way as Notepad. In addition, it reads RTF (Rich Text Format, .rtf) files, Windows Write (.wri) files, and Microsoft Word document (.doc) files. However, it only saves RTF files, not Windows Write or Microsoft Word files.

3.5 Flatbed Scanner

A flatbed scanner looks like a small copy machine. It usually connects to a PC through a USB port. You place materials such as papers, photos, magazines, and books face down on top of its glass pane. When the scanner operates, a light and an array of optical sensors move underneath the glass pane. This mechanism captures the image of the document and sends it to the computer.

For good scanning quality, make sure the material is positioned well on the glass pane and properly aligned with the edge. Make sure the material stays close to the surface, so the images aren't distorted or blurred. Keep the scanner cover on and make sure it is pressed down firmly against the documents so they won't move during scanning. Keep the glass pane clean and be careful not to scratch it so the outputs won't contain dirty spots or unwanted marks. If the document is wrinkled, press it using a heavy book before scanning. If the scanning result is not satisfactory, then by all means scan it again. Do not count on the downstream steps to fix the problems caused by sloppiness in scanning. That would end up wasting more time and could even jeopardize the entire process. Having a good scan is essential for having the text properly recognized by the OCR, which is again essential for getting the document properly translated by the translator software. Do everything possible to ensure that the early steps are performed properly. It is very much like building a house; you need to make sure the foundation is solid before continuing the rest of the structure.

The output from the scanner either goes directly to the OCR software or to an image editor first, and then to the OCR. There are two ways to transport the output from the scanner to its downstream applications. One is to save the scanning output to a graphic file, and then open it with the OCR or the image editor. The other way is to go through a common interface that is widely used among image devices and software, called TWAIN.

Almost all scanners nowadays support the use of TWAIN. Even though it has not been officially documented, TWAIN is widely known to stand for "**T**echnology **W**ithout **A**n **I**nteresting **N**ame." For our purposes, all you need to know is that it defines an interface standard for the low level software of image capture devices (scanner, digital camera, etc.) to communicate with the high level (application) software. The low level software is usually provided by the hardware vendor to give a uniform user interface for controlling the device. The application software can be any program that needs to use images in it, such as an OCR, an image editor, or a word processor. Just think of it this way: Any application that uses images can either open them from graphic files or get them directly from a device (the scanner). When you open a graphic file, you see the Windows **Open File** dialog to navigate through a directory tree to the file. When you get them from a device using TWAIN, you see a dialog window provided by the image device vendor for specifying parameters such as the resolutions, formats (color vs. B&W), color intensity, etc. The good thing about this is that you are presented with the same TWAIN dialog window with the same UI no matter what applications are used. Using TWAIN saves you the trouble of having to save the scanned images into files, then opening them from other applications.

The flatbed scanner I purchased years ago for my daily use is an old outdated model from the Windows 95 era: the Astra 600P from UMAX. I am using it with Windows 98 SE because it does not have the driver for Windows 2000 or later systems, and the company has stopped supporting it. However, since the setup works flawlessly for my scanning needs, I plan to use it until the hardware finally breaks down, but I doubt very much that this will happen. From my experience, this kind of old hardware lasts and lasts, just likes an old TV. It never breaks at the time you wish them to, giving you an excuse for buying that new big-screen TV. This seems to be in strong contrast to all those iPods that my son got, which always die right after their warranty expires. One other problem with keeping my old PC with Windows 98 is that it adds to the ammunition for my wife to support her claims that I keep all the junks in the house.

In order to continue writing this book, I had no choice but to get myself a new scanner. With the old UMAX, I was unable to run tests on Windows 2000, XP or Vista. In addition, installing the latest OCR software to the old PC with Windows 98 SE would be a real stretch. This is really not a big deal, because the price of this equipment is now quite low. For $100, I was able to get a Canon CanoScan 4400F from my local computer store. It has an optical resolution of 4800 DPI and it is even able to scan 35mm film. This is much more than I needed. The UMAX Astra 600P connects to the PC using the 25 pin parallel port, which is almost obsolete now. The Canon CanoScan 4400F, like most other flatbed scanners these days, connects to the PC through a USB port. In the section below, I am going to describe some general basics with using the flatbed scanner. This does not cover the detailed operations for any specific scanner model or its software, which is beyond the scope of this book.

A scanner normally comes with various pieces of software. Usually, the installation software will install the device drivers and the TWAIN software automatically. There are also other application programs bundled with scanners, which you can choose to install. This varies for different vendors. Both the UMAX and Canon come with Presto! PageManager as the default application. This is a File management application similar to Windows Explorer, with some additional functions for viewing and organizing image files and controlling image input devices. As I have described before, the real work of showing the scanning dialog window and controlling the device are actually performed by the low level TWAIN software. This low level program is provided by scanner manufacturers, and it varies with the model. Basically, the program lets you preview the document, set the scanning area, and adjust detailed settings before the scanning. These settings include the document type (color vs. B/W), resolution, intensity or other color related parameters, and so on. After scanning, you can view the image, open the image from another application or store the scanned image to a file.

The scanning software usually gives you at least three different document types to select from: "B/W Document," "B/W Photo" and "Color Photo." For OCR, you can usually use the basic "B/W Document." This setting gives you the simplest black and white output with no grayscale. It works fine on most black and white texts, or texts that appear on a simple colored background with strong contrast. If the colors in the text areas are too complex or not distinct enough for the texts to stand out, you may need to scan it using "Color Photo" and then manually process it. Even though many OCR products are able to take color images and process them directly, sometimes it is better to manually convert them to B/W documents with the image editor before handing them to the OCR.

In many cases, the most critical adjustment is the intensity setting for the B/W Document scanning. The scanner software usually has an option to automatically adjust the intensity. However, the automatic adjustment usually tries to make the picture look best as a whole, which is not necessarily the optimal setting for the purpose of identifying text. It is often better to manually adjust the intensity for each page, to optimize the quality of the scanning. The other setting that we usually need to adjust is the DPI, which is the resolution of the scanning. For small Chinese characters commonly seen in books and magazines, assuming the printing quality is good, the resolution should be set at 300 DPI. For newspapers, you can start with 300 DPI and then increase to 400 DPI if the 300DPI setting does not work. Appendix A gives a detailed reference of text size and recommended DPI usage. Sometimes, when the paper is too thin, you may see through to the contents of the page beneath it. Depending on the thickness of the document and the scanner, you may also need to adjust the illumination intensity of the scanner.

After scanning, check the results to make sure the intensity and DPI are set properly. Watch for the thinnest strokes of all the characters, to make sure they are intact. If any line is broken, it is an indication that the scanning is too light, i.e., the intensity is too high (Figure 3.13b). Also make sure the hollow areas within all the characters remain hollow. If there is any nearby stroke smudged inside of them, the scanning is too dark, i.e., the intensity is too low (Figure 3.13a). If you can't find an intensity setting to make both happen, it usually means the DPI setting is too low, and you should increase it (Figure 3.13c).

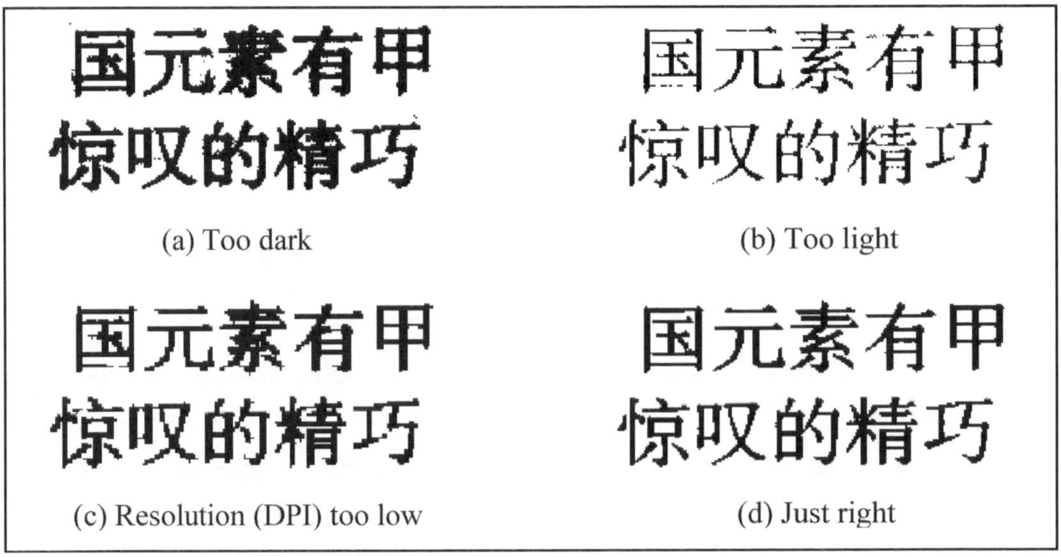

国元素有甲
惊叹的精巧

(a) Too dark

国元素有甲
惊叹的精巧

(b) Too light

国元素有甲
惊叹的精巧

(c) Resolution (DPI) too low

国元素有甲
惊叹的精巧

(d) Just right

Figure 3.13 Example of scanning results

Usually, I start with the "B/W Document" document type, using the automatic intensity settings given by the software, and use the 300 DPI. After scanning, I check the results against the breaking/smudging rule and adjust the intensity if necessary. Unless there are special reasons, the intensity setting usually has a good amount of margin without the need to go back and forth to adjust it. When I find the intensity is hard to adjust, I increase the resolution value to 400 DPI, which usually gives satisfactory results. For color printings, a suitable intensity setting may not exist, simply because the contrast between the text and background is insufficient, or there are different colors in different areas. In this case, I need to scan to the "Color photo" document type and manually process the image. I will cover the details of color image processing in Chapter 3.7.2, when I describe the image editor software.

Figure 3.13 shows some examples of scanning results. The intensity in (a) is adjusted too high. You can see some extra black spots around characters, and also some characters have their strokes smudged together and show lumps of black areas. Chinese characters should consist of clearly distinctive strokes, without smudges. In (b), the intensity is adjusted too low. You can see that some horizontal going strokes are broken in the middle. Figure 3.13(c) has some areas with broken strokes and other areas with smudges. This gives you a hint that there is no way to fix both the breaking and the smudging by merely adjusting the intensity. You need to increase the DPI to the next higher level to see if that can fix the problem. Figure 3.13(d) shows a good quality scanning result.

3.6 Digital Camera

Digital cameras are most useful in places where text is inaccessible to flatbed or handheld scanners. They can be useful for capturing text from banners, posters, signage, inscriptions on steles, etc. I have included a few real-life examples of using a camera to capture images from signs and posters in Chapter 8.

The quality of digital cameras has been improved substantially with continuously lowering prices during the last decade. It is now possible to use a regular digital camera to take pictures of books and magazines, and get the text recognized by OCR software. However, I would not recommend using one in place of a scanner, because it requires careful adjustments, and the results are often unsatisfactory. A flatbed scanner should always be the primary choice unless the materials are located in a place only accessible with a camera.

I did some tests with an older digital camera, a Nikon Cool PIX 4300 with 4.0 M pixels, introduced in 2002. I have tested it with characters the same small size one finds in a Chinese newspaper. I mounted the camera on a tripod, and placed it approximately 9 inches away from the newspaper, using close-up mode, with the zoom setting adjusted to its widest position. This setting allows me to take a picture in an area of about 7 inches by 5 inches while yielding a reasonably clean text image.

Keep in mind that when using a camera, position it at the center of the shooting area and keep the shooting direction perpendicular to the surface of the document. This keeps the four corners of the document evenly distorted. The other thing to remember is to use the close-up mode. Also ensure that you have good illumination on the document, and to keep the document neat, flat, and straight (not tilted). The camera lens should be kept clean as well. The output from cameras may require editing before they can be used by the OCR. I'll discuss the image editor in great detail in the next section.

3.7 Image Editor Software

Image editor software can help to tidy captured images before they are sent to the OCR for recognition. It can also be used to transform one image file type to another, or to change the color encoding formats or compression methods. Sometimes an OCR program may not be able to read certain image file types or images saved using a special color encoding or compression scheme. An image editor can be used to open these files and then save them to another type. Here is a list of features I look for in an image editor program:

1. It should support the opening and saving of a wide range of image file types and formats. At the very least, it should support the most commonly used file types, including Windows bitmap (.bmp), TIFF (.tif), JPEG (.jpg), and GIF (.gif). Note that within each file type there may be different variation of formats. These various formats may include different versions, different encoding/compression methods or different color formats (e.g., 24 or 32 bits color, or 8 bits palette color). Even though a program may state that it supports a certain file type, in reality it may or may not support every format defined by the file type, or it may have problem when working with certain formats. Finding image editors that support a rich variety of file types may help minimize the issue. This is important because OCR software may only be able to open specific types of file, and we need the image editor to convert them for us.

2. The image editor should be able to easily cut and paste areas by selecting a rectangle or a hand drawn region. This is a very basic function of most image editors. We use this feature very often, for tasks such like cutting away unwanted areas, rearranging characters or text blocks, and so on.

3. The image editor should have basic painting tools such as paint, erase, flood (bucket) fill, etc., for touching up or erasing images. The image editor should be able to resize, rotate, and deform (horizontal or vertical perspective) images. We need these functions to adjust the text size and compensate for any misaligned or distorted areas. The rotation should support custom angles as well as 90 degrees or 180 degrees. It should also allow us to adjust the canvas size.

4. The image editor should be able to perform many color processing functions. It should easily make adjustments for colors, brightness, contrast, and the intensity of B/W (black and white) images. It should allow for the decrease or increase of color depth, and be able to invert between the black and white. It should be able to convert images from color to B/W with simple steps for specifying the converting criteria. These color processing features are critical in order to extract the text from background pictures or noise.

5. The image editor should be intuitive and easy to use. It should allow us to undo or redo many steps. It should let us preview results before a lengthy processing, e.g., color adjustment, or custom rotation, etc.

In the rest of this section, I will introduce a software program that fits this bill. The reason I listed the criteria for an image editor is that you may already have a program that satisfies them. In that case, by all means use the good old program that you are familiar with. This will save you all the trouble of having to get and install new software on your computer, learn the new program, and deal with any issues that might occur.

My all-time favorite image editor software is Paint Shop Pro, made by the company JASC. It was at version 5 when I got it in 1998, and that already had all the features listed above. It is a general raster graphics editing software that can perform many more tasks than these requirements. I have been using it on a regular basis for most of the common graphic editing tasks. Even without any patch or update since 1998, so far I have not experienced any major issue with it. This product was acquired by the Corel Corporation a few years ago, and it is currently at version 11. There is no doubt that the program has much more enhancements and new features than version 5. However, this product is not what I am going to describe below, because currently it is going to cost us $80. At the time I am writing this book, my feeling is that with the advancement in software products and our moderate requirements, we should be able to find something to use free of charge.

After researching on the Internet through testing and comparison, I have found my current favorite free image editor: GNU Image Manipulation Program (GIMP). The software I installed and tested is version 2.2.17 and it has all the features that I was looking for. I have also put it to use for quite some time on a regular basis. While not as defect-free as my good old Paint Shop Pro 5, it has proven to be reasonably reliable.

3.7.1 GIMP—Installation

The full GIMP program is not only free to use, it is also an open source software product. Open source is a set of principles and practices to make the source codes of the software available to the general public, so many developers can contribute to product enhancement and support in a collaborative manner.

For end users, one problem with open source software is that there is much more information out there than needed. There are usually various versions of binary and source codes available for many different platforms. There are also patches, frameworks, development kits, release notes, readme files, documents, help files, etc. Some of these can have different versions for different languages, which gives us a whole new dimension of stuff. For software developers, the availability of such rich resources is paradise. However, users looking only for a tool to accomplish a special task may feel overwhelmed.

To download a stable, installable version of the GIMP software for the Windows platform, please visit the following website:

http://gimp-win.sourceforge.net/stable.html

There are two separate files that you need to download. The first file contains the GIMP for Windows software and the GTK+ runtime environment that the program needs to run on. The other file is the Help document. For the Help document file, there may be different language versions to choose from, and you can download the English language only version. Download and save these two files to a temporary location on your computer. These are self-executable EXE files and they will run and install the software program when started. The version that I have tested is 2.2.17. You will find a newer stable version at the time you read this book, because the program gets updated frequently. The reason they call it a "stable" version is that there are even newer versions available out there for pioneer users. These newer versions have been released only recently, and have not been widely tested yet. To avoid unfamiliar issues or unpleasant surprises, it is better to stick with the stable version.

You may feel intimidated by the defect reports as you read them, either from this site or other places that discuss the GIMP software. Please do not conclude that it is an inferior or unstable product simply because there are many discussions about the defects in each release. In fact, this particular software is reasonably stable, and may be more defect-free than many other software programs released by some big and well known vendors. The discussions about defects, patches, known issues, etc. are just the nature of a software product of this magnitude.

Actually we can consider bugs (defects) in software similar to germs in our body; they are things that we live with. The managers from my previous employer love this concept, and often apply it to the extreme. They start out by setting up very aggressive schedules, and then do whatever they can to stick to it. To them, missing a release date is as disastrous as missing the estimation in an earning report. They will basically release just about anything regardless of how un-releasable a version can be, as long as it sticks to the release date. The argument is that an issue is not really an issue as long as it gets documented in the release notes. Once that's been done, an issue becomes a "known issue" that can be fixed later, and will not jeopardize or hold back the release.

Anyway, let us go back to our discussion of the GIMP. After using the software for some time, I have actually found a few issues. Only one of these can cause us real problems, and I will describe it later in this section. Hopefully, by the time you read this book, it will already have been fixed, otherwise you will need to work your way around it.

3.7.2 GIMP—Basic Operations

When you start the GIMP program from Windows, the first thing you see is the GIMP **Main Toolbox** (Figure 3.14). This is the command center of GIMP, and it contains menus and controls for you to perform different tasks. The **Main Toolbox** of GIMP does not take up large amounts of space because it is not the place that you do most of your work from. As you open an image file, GIMP creates a separate window to hold the graphics, and that is the working area where you view and edit your image from. You can open as many images as needed, and each image will be placed in a separate **Image Window**. Each **Image Window** has its own main menu. The main menu on the **Image Window** mostly contains functions related to the specific image file, but there are also functions that are overlapped with those in the **Main Toolbox**.

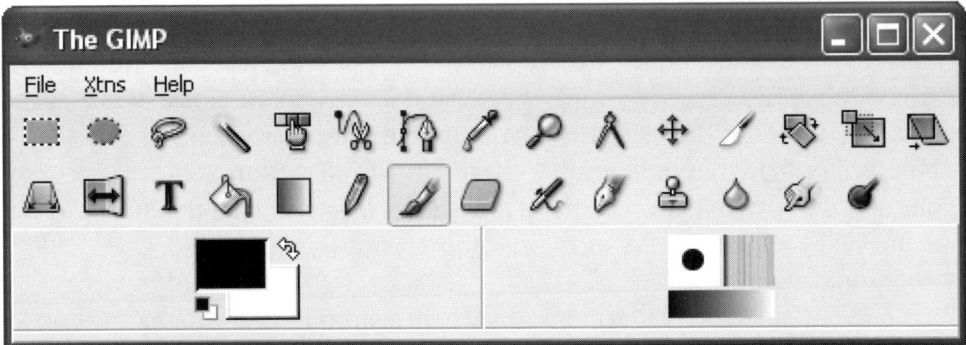

Figure 3.14 GIMP—**Main Toolbox**

Select **File** and then **Open** from the **Main Toolbox** to open an image file for editing. The image will be opened in an **Image Window** (Figure 3.15).

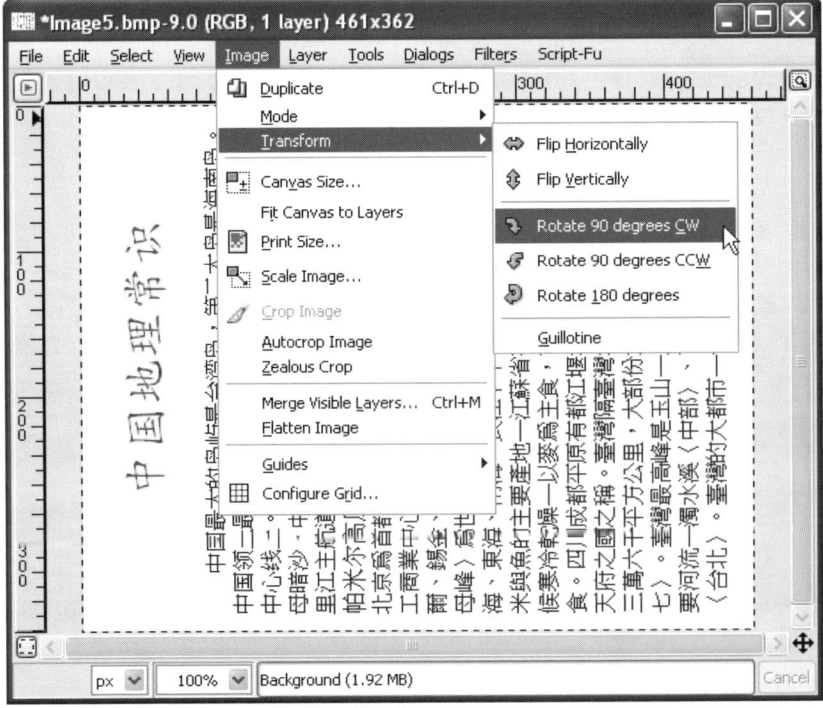

Figure 3.15 GIMP—**Image Window**

Click **View** and then select **Zoom** from the main menu in the **Image Window** to adjust the magnification of the document in the **Image Window**. This only affects the viewing size and does not change the real size of the image.

One common task often required right after opening an image is rotating it 90 degrees. From the main menu on the **Image Window**, select **Image, Transform,** and then select the command to rotate the image 90 degrees clockwise, counter clockwise, or 180 degrees.

Sometimes you may need to rotate an image a certain degree angle other than 90 and 180 degrees. This is necessary when an image is tilted, which can occur if the document was not properly aligned when you scanned it. Even though they may feel similar, custom angle rotation needs to be treated differently from the 90 or 180 degree rotation.

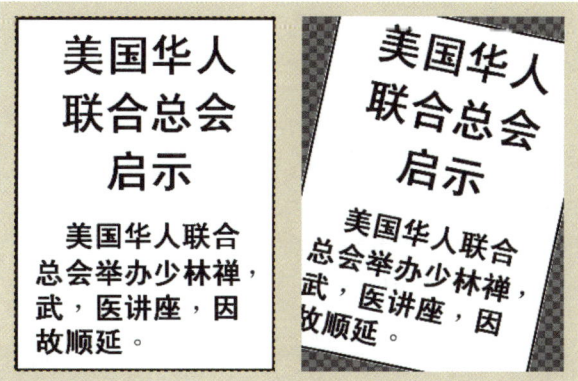

Figure 3.16 Rotate an image for a custom angle

Essentially, every graphic needs to be fitted on a rectangle-shaped canvas. With 90 or 180 degree rotation, you can rotate the whole canvas without any issue. However, with custom angle rotation, after the rotation the shape of image will no longer be a rectangle. When you rotate a custom angle, what you are actually doing is rotating the image layer while leaving the canvas intact. Imagine that there is a background layer associated with the image. The rotation keeps the background of the image intact and rotates the image around the center of the background. Figure 3.16 shows the effect of such a rotation. The image on the left of this figure is the original, and the one on the right is after the rotation. Note that some part of the original image has been cut out because of the rotation. In other places, you see some checkerboard-like regions. They represent areas with only background layer with no graphics (i.e., it becomes transparent) after the rotation. By doing a layer rotation, technically you have created a new Alpha channel to the image. An Alpha channel specifies which areas contain graphics and which areas are hollow (transparent). For the purpose for making an image file for use by an OCR program, you shouldn't care about any Alpha channel or multiple layers. To make things simpler, you can merge the layers together after the rotation.

"Layer" and "Channel" are special concepts related to image editing. If you are unfamiliar with this terminology, think of the image as multiple layers that stack up together. One layer may contain pictures while the other contains text, etc. Each layer can be edited separately without interfering with others. Within each layer, the image can be further broken down to different channels, for example, Red, Green, Blue, and Alpha component. Not all image file formats support the concept of layer or transparency, so you may need to merge multiple layers into one layer or to flatten the Alpha channel when you convert between file formats. For our purposes, everything should be just on one layer and you don't need to work on multiple layers or an Alpha channel.

Now let us look at the step-by-step instructions for these tasks. First, make sure the image margins are large enough all around. This prevents useful information from being cut away when you rotate the image. If these margins are too small, you should increase the canvas size of the image by selecting **Image** and then **Canvas Size**. From the **Set Image Canvas Size** dialog window (Figure 3.17), you can increase the canvas size. Remember to click the **Center** button before hitting the **Resize** button. This keeps the original image in the center and adds the extra spaces to the outsides.

To perform a custom angle rotation, click **Layer**, select **Transform**, and then click **Arbitrary Rotation** from the main menu on the **Image Window**. This will bring up the **Rotate** dialog window. From the **Rotate** dialog window, set the rotating angle by either typing the value into the **Angle** text box or dragging the scrollbar. The **Image Window** displays a preview of the image after the rotation. Once you are satisfied, click the **Rotate** button to perform the actual rotation.

As I have described earlier, the rotation of the image layer automatically creates multiple layers within the graphics. Merge the layers in order to keep things simple and to prevent seeing those unpleasant hollow areas. This process simply fills the hollow regions with the background color. Before doing this, first make sure the background color is set properly. The current foreground and background colors are shown on the **Color area** in the **Main Toolbox** (see Figure 3.14). Normally, the colors of the foreground and background are set to black and white, respectively. Click the background color display area twice (select it first and then click it again) to open the **Change Background Color** dialog window to change the background color if needed. You can also click the small curved line with two arrowheads to swap the foreground and background colors. After the background color is properly selected, you can then choose **Image** from the main menu of the **Image Window**, and then click **Flatten Image** to merge the layers.

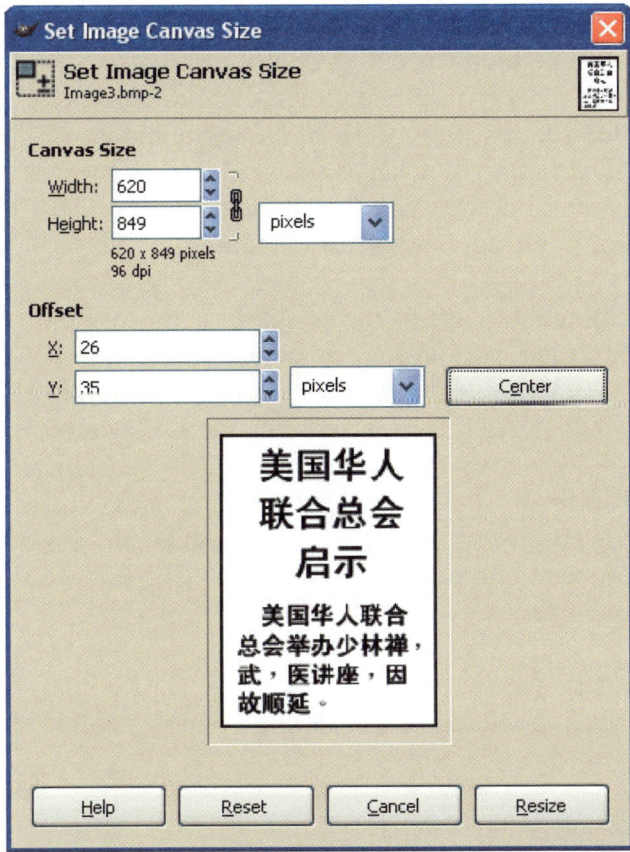

Figure 3.17 Use the **Set Image Canvas Size** dialog to increase canvas size

Cut and paste are commonly used image editing functions. A scanned document usually contains things that we don't need and wish to cut away. Sometimes it is easier to cut around the portion we wish to keep and discard the rest. There are also times when we need to combine small pieces into a large document, or to rearrange different portions within a document.

To cut out an area, use the **Select rectangular regions** or **Select hand drawn regions** control on the **Main Toolbox** to select the desired area first. Click the **Select rectangular regions** control on the **Main Toolbox** to enter the rectangle area selection mode. In response, the mouse cursor changes its shape into an arrow with a small rectangle by its side. Click the left top corner where you want to select and then drag the cursor to the right bottom corner to complete the selection. To cut the selected rectangle into a new image, click **Edit**, click **Copy**, click **Edit** again, and click **Paste as New** to create a new image. To cut away the selected rectangle, click **Edit**, and then click **Clear**. This will fill the rectangle area with the background color.

You can also select by drawing around an area with the **Select hand drawn regions** control on the **Main Toolbox**. In response, the mouse cursor changes its shape into an arrow with a small rope-shaped symbol. Hold down the mouse button and drag the cursor around the region you wish to select. After a region is selected, it can be treated in exactly the same way as with the rectangle selections—either paste the selection into a new image, or clear out the selected region. When pasting a hand-drawn selection into a new image, the size of the new image is chosen to be the bounding rectangle of the selected region. Within this rectangle where no image is presented, you will see a checkerboard pattern, indicating that there is nothing there (a hollow area). Since you won't need the outline of the selection any more, you can click **Image** and then click **Flatten Image** to remove the Alpha channel. I have briefly mentioned the Alpha channel earlier in this section. For more information about the Alpha channel, please refer to the help manual of GIMP. For our purposes, all you need to know is that some functions make the Alpha channel appear automatically. When that happens, you can do a **Flatten Image** to merge the layers.

There are times when you need to make the image larger or smaller. To do this, click **Image**, then **Scale Image** to open the **Scale Image** dialog window (Figure 3.18).

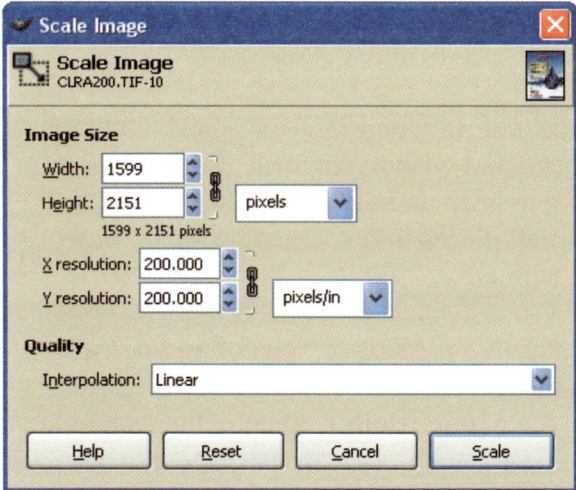

Figure 3.18 Adjust image size using the **Scale Image** dialog window

From the **Scale Image** dialog window, you can change the values in the **Image Size** selection boxes and then hit the **Scale** button to scale the image. The chain icon next to the **Width** and **Height** selection boxes is for preserving the aspect ratio (the ratio between the width and height) when doing the scaling. When this chain is on, as you adjust either the width or height of the image, the other value will be changed automatically to maintain the aspect ratio. If you don't want the aspect ratio of the image to be preserved, just click the chain icon to break that chain. Once the chain is broken, you can change those two values independently.

Sometimes, you may need to scale just one portion of the image instead of the entire canvas. To do this, click the **Select rectangular regions** control on the **Main Toolbox** to select the desired rectangle area to be scaled first. Click the **Scale the layer or selection** control on the **Main Toolbox** to enter the scaling mode. After that, drag one of the four corners of the image in the **Image Window** to scale the rectangular region to the desired size. As you do this, a **Scale** dialog will pop up automatically, and you can click the **Scale** button in there once you are satisfied with the preview. Note that the scaling done this way only scales the image layer while leaving the canvas size and the unselected portion of the image intact. When you scale an image down, empty spaces will appear in areas where the scaled image no longer resides. When you scale an image up, the selected region will go over and overlap with other parts of the image, or even go outside of the canvas. If these results are not desired, you should adjust the canvas size of the image and rearrange the image so that useful information will not be affected.

At times, the scanned image may be distorted at the corners or on the sides. This usually occurs when an image is taken using a camera, or scanned from a book that was unable to be laid completely flat on the scanner. Such problems can be fixed to a certain degree by using the **Perspective Transform** tool. This tool can be selected by clicking the **Change perspective of the layer or selection** icon located in the **Main Toolbox**. It can also be started from the **Image Window** by clicking **Tools**, **Transform Tools**, and then **Perspective**. Just like using the **Scale the layer or selection** tool, you can use the **Select rectangular regions** control to select a region first, and do the transformation on the selected region only. To do the transformation, drag one of the four corners and watch the preview of the transformation from the **Image Window**. When satisfied, click the **Transform** button on the dialog window to proceed with the changes. Similar to scaling an image, you also need to leave some margin space when doing the transformation, so the image will not be stretched off the canvas. If the margins are not large enough, you need to first increase the canvas size of the image.

3.7.3 GIMP—Color Processing

Most OCR products are able to use color images directly, but sometimes you need to either adjust the color, or convert into a B/W image before sending it to the OCR. One reason is that some OCR programs may have trouble reading certain color formats. Another important reason is that OCR may not produce good recognition results when the image color is too complex. The color processing algorithms used by the OCR software are usually not sophisticated enough to tell important from unimportant regions, which may not contain any text at all. When images contain simple colors with good contrast between the text and the background, the software can handle them properly; otherwise, you need to manually process them first.

Figure 3.19 shows an example of a color image that contains text buried in color backgrounds. When this image is fed to an OCR program directly, the program processes it into the image shown in Figure 3.20. As you can see, a big chunk of the text area appears totally black.

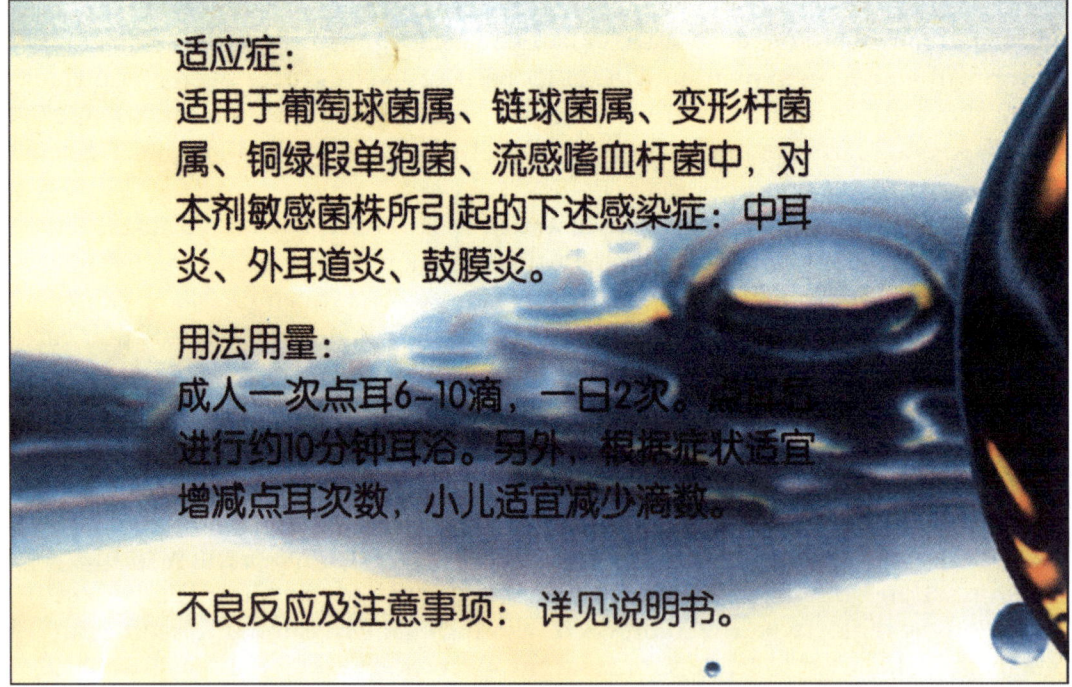

Figure 3.19 Complex color image

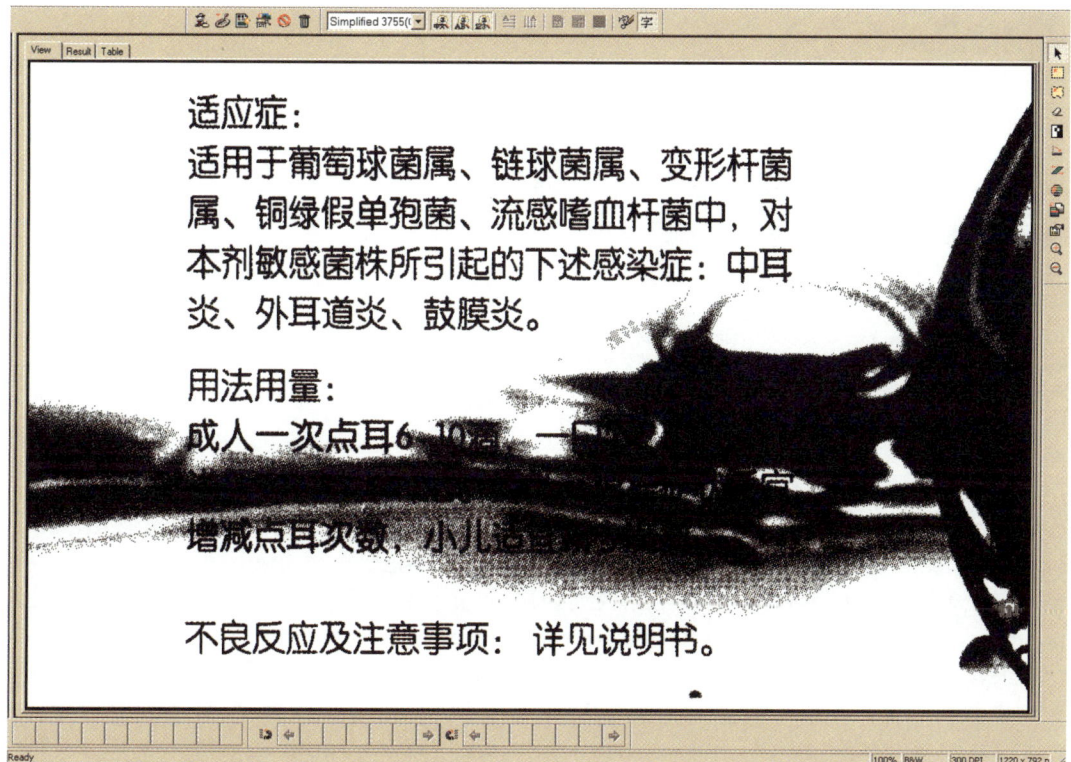

Figure 3.20 OCR color processing result

The color processing tools in GIMP are accessible from the **Layer – Colors** menu. From there, select **Threshold** to open up the **Threshold** dialog window. This tool allows you to convert a color image into B/W based on a comparison of the intensity of each pixel with a threshold value. When the intensity of a pixel is higher than the threshold, it is converted into White, otherwise it becomes black. This is a very simple tool to use, but a lot of the time it is all you need for color processing.

Figure 3.21 show the **Threshold** dialog window. Check the **Preview** checkbox to allow for a preview of the converted image. Drag the scrollbar to adjust the threshold value and preview the results in the **Image Window** as you scroll. When you are satisfied with the result, click the **OK** button to make the change.

You may notice a problem: there is only one threshold value to be used for the entire image. When an image contains different colors in different areas, it may be impossible to find a suitable threshold for all locations. In our example, the region on the bottom right is buried in dark blue background. In order to extract text from there, you will need to adjust the threshold to a very low value, jeopardizing text in some other places by making them too light.

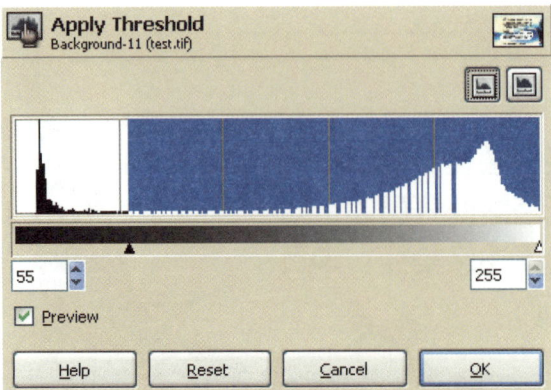

Figure 3.21 **Threshold** dialog window

In a situation like this, you can still use the **Threshold** tool, by separating out the treatment of different areas. First, use the **Select hand drawn regions** tool that you have seen previously to enclose the area with the dark blue background. After that, use the **Threshold** tool to convert the color into B/W within the selected area (see Figure 3.22). After the change in that region is completed, do a **Select – All** to select the whole image. After that, use the **Threshold** tool again to change the whole image use a different threshold value. Since the area that was changed in the first round is already in black and white, the two extreme values, it will not be affected again. By making changes in two steps, you can set different thresholds to different areas separately. This technique can be easily applied to more regions as needed.

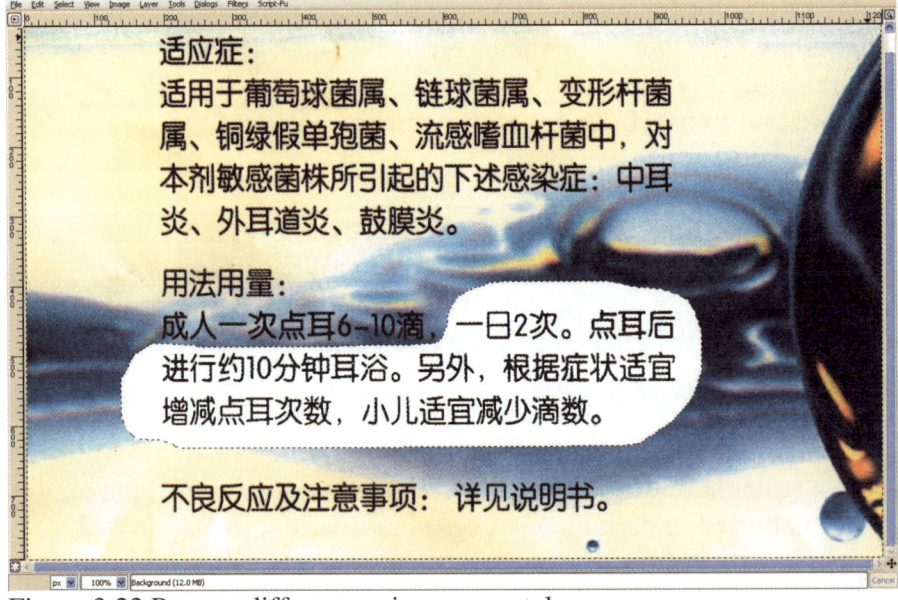

Figure 3.22 Process different regions separately

Some OCR programs do not work when fed with "inverted" color texts—white (light) text on black (dark) background. To fix inverted text, select **Layer** from the menu on the **Image window**, choose **Colors** and select **Invert**. This will invert the color of both B/W and color images. Some images may contain both white text on black ground and black text on white ground. To invert only a portion of the image, use either the rectangular region or hand-drawn region selection tool to select the area first, and then apply the inversion.

Sometimes you may need to use the **Eraser** or the **Pencil** tool to touch up your images for erasing unwanted specks, or fixing spots that are erased accidentally. To use them, select the tool from the **Main Toolbar**, hold down the mouse button and drag around the places where you want to erase or touch. The **Pencil** and **Eraser** tools work homogeneously; the **Pencil** paints in foreground color and the **Eraser** paints in background color. You have already seen how to change the background color and also to swap the colors between the foreground and the background earlier in this section. The foreground color can be adjusted in a similar way. To change the size of the tip of the tools, select the **Active Brush** control from the **Main Toolbox** to open the **Brushes** dialog window (Figure 3.23). From there you can choose the different sizes and types for the tip for painting and erasing.

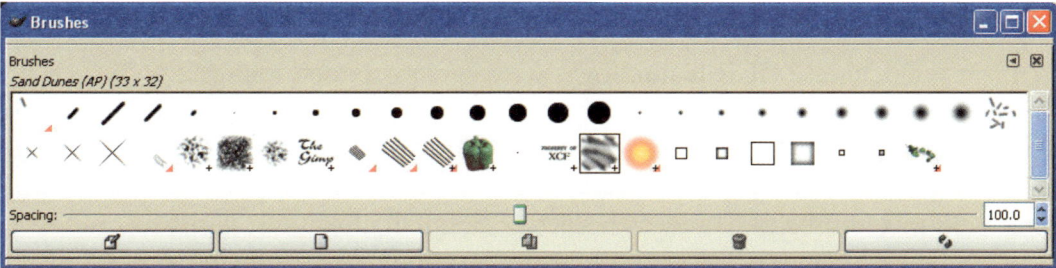

Figure 3.23 **Brushes** Dialog for adjusting the size and type of the painting tools

After finishing editing, select **File**, and then click **Save** from the main menu on the **Image Window** to save the change. I usually save files using the TIFF (tif, tiff) format, and choose the LZW compression algorithm. This should work with all the OCR programs I shall describe in this book. One other use of GIMP is to convert image file format. If for any reason an image file cannot be read correctly from the OCR software, you can open that file from the GIMP, and then save it using another format that is supported by the OCR software.

One of the issues I found with the GIMP is that it has trouble saving files in TIFF format using indexed (palette) color. Indexed color describes the color of an image using a color table instead of color values directly, for the purpose of reducing the file size. There are some older OCR programs I know that can only read indexed color images if the file is in TIFF format. To avoid such a problem, you can always save your files using the Windows BMP image (bmp) format. Windows BMP image format is the most basic image format used in Windows, so most software should be able to work with it. The Windows BMP file format is sufficient for all your needs as well. The only disadvantage is that the file size is likely to be bigger than the TIFF file.

3.8 OCR Software

Outputs from a scanner, a digital camera, or the image editor software are only graphics with images of Chinese characters on them. The information stored in these graphics consists of color or B/W pixels arranged in a two dimensional array. In order for a translation or dictionary software to understand the contents in the graphics, we need Optical Character Recognition (OCR) software with Chinese recognition ability to convert the images into the actual codes that represent characters. Once these codes have been generated, they can be used in the translator or other computer software, such as a word processor or a web browser.

With current Chinese OCR technology, we can expect good recognition rates (over 95%) for printed characters from high quality images. Most OCR software is able to recognize characters printed with commonly used fonts, including Song (宋), Kai (楷), FongSong (仿宋), Yuan (圓), and Hei (黑). They are able to handle texts with mixed uses of Chinese characters, English alphabets, numbers, and commonly used symbols. Most of them support both traditional and simplified Chinese characters, but only one of the two can be used at a time, and it must be specified. For hand-written characters, the recognition rate is low. Even with clean and neat hand writing, the OCR results are usually too poor to use. In addition, it is not easy to come up with statistics of the recognition rate because people's hand writing can vary a lot. I cannot find any data concerning the recognition rate for hand writing Chinese from OCR vendors or other sources. From my own experience, I would guess the recognition rate is less than 50%, even with very neat, stroke-by-stroke writings, which you don't usually see in real-life. Even though many OCR products include functions for comparing and fixing misrecognized characters, it is too much work for people who do not know Chinese characters to try to use. At this moment, I do not consider reading hand written characters with OCR to be a feasible task for people unfamiliar with the language.

I would like to mention one other thing about hand writing recognition technology. When searching the Internet, you may find products on Chinese hand writing recognition with very high recognition rates. What they are talking about is a totally different kind of product. This is an electronic writing pad for people to write on, and the device recognizes characters by the writing strokes. Such devices have been equipped in handheld electronic dictionaries and even some cell phones for text messaging. They are also used as general-purpose input devices for people to enter Chinese characters to their PCs. I do not know why knowing the strokes can make such drastic difference, but the writing pad actually has a very high recognition rate. I have a Besta CD-89 electronic dictionary which is at least seven years old, and it had this technology even back then. Recently, I have also tested a writing pad called Crystal Touch, introduced by PenPower Technology, just to see how well it functioned. I was impressed to find that many times it correctly recognized all the characters I wrote in a sentence. Hopefully in the future there will be a break through in OCR technology, so it can recognize scanned images with the same accuracy as recognizing strokes.

3.9 Dictionary Software

You may have seen a stand-alone, handheld electronic device with a small screen and keypad that resembles a PDA. You enter words on the keypad and it shows the translation on the screen. This device is commonly known as an electronic dictionary, but it is not what we will be discussing here. When the name "electronic dictionary" is used in this book, it refers to the dictionary software that we run on our PCs. It usually comes as a stand-alone program that gets installed locally to the PC, and can be used either on-line (connected to the Internet) or off-line. The Chinese to English version of the dictionary takes a Chinese character or word as input, and produces a list of explanations in English. It does not have the functionality to analyze the sentence structure, and also, it is not intended to translate a whole sentence. It gives a list of all the possible meanings of a character or word in English that it knows about, and you have to decide the meaning that suits the circumstance.

Dictionary software can be used together with translation software as supplements. It can be very helpful when results from translation software are ambiguous, nonsensical, or questionable. There are also dictionaries for words of specific categories, such as medical or legal terms, etc. If a sentence cannot be translated properly because a special word is missing from the translator's internal dictionaries, you may be able to find a meaning in these special dictionaries. The contents of different dictionaries vary as well. Some dictionaries include pronunciations, strokes, and other useful information about the character or word, so they can be very useful in learning the Chinese language. People born in this era are very lucky to have the help of computers for so many things. When I was young, we had to use the real dictionary to look up characters using radicals, and that is really painful. Some characters have irregular shapes and they need a lot of guesswork to locate in the dictionary. When you can't locate a character after several attempts, you won't be sure if it is listed under another radical, or if it is just not in the dictionary.

Dictionary software products vary in their user interface design. The most primitive ones require you to enter or paste characters into a text box and then hit a button to get results displayed. Such programs usually have an application window displayed for input, and to show results. Sophisticated dictionary programs allow you to use them directly from another Windows application. You can highlight or place the mouse cursor on a word while viewing a document, then hit a hot key to activate the dictionary look up. The results can show up in a pop-up window. The most convenient ones I found are those that provide the "mouse-over" lookup. All you need is to place your mouse over a character or word for a certain period of time, and the software will look up the character's definition and show the results in a pop-up window. Depending on the design of different programs, some mouse-over operations can only work with a certain application, such as with a web browser. More advanced mouse-over design works in many applications.

3.10 Translation Software

The process of using computer software to automatically translate text is sometimes known as Machine Translation (MT). MT software is the core tool for computer-aided Chinese reading. I will talk about this briefly here in this section, and then have the descriptions of many MT products in great detail in Chapter 5.

We can roughly break down MT software into two parts: the UI (user interface) and the translation engine. The UI part determines how the software interacts with users and the translation engine does the translation. There are different ways translation software can be used from a user's perspective. The most basic way is to copy the source text to Windows Clipboard, and then paste that to a text input area of the translator. As we hit a button, the program starts the translation and shows the results in a text display area. Another way is for the software to read a

Chinese text file and translate the whole contents into English. There are also MT programs that allow the translation of a whole Chinese web page. This can be done by specifying the URL (address) of the web page to the program and then waiting for the page to be translated. A more elegant way of doing this is for the software to integrate with the web browser program. As you navigate to a web page containing Chinese text, the click of a button on the web browser's toolbar will activate the translation. The translated web page can be shown in the original window, or a new one.

The translation engine is the part that performs the actual translation. It can be broken down further into two components: the core engine and the dictionary or dictionaries. The core engine identifies Chinese words in the source sentences, analyzes the words and the structure of the text, picks suitable English words based on the analysis, and constructs the English sentences for output. The dictionary part contains a list of Chinese characters and words, with their interpretations in English, and attributes that the core engine can use for mapping. Recall from the discussion in Chapter 2.1 that each Chinese word (词) is made of two or more characters put together, and it is a critical part of the language. All the translation software products contain a large collection of these words in their dictionaries. A large part of the translation engine's work is actually just to search for words in the text from these dictionaries. The accuracy of the translation depends more heavily on the dictionaries than on other factors, such as the ability of the engine to analyze the grammar or the structure of the sentences. From what I can see, a large part of incorrect translation by MT is caused by the failure to recognize some words. Even the best MT program I used has missed some common words from time to time. As such, it is my belief that at this time there is still room for significant improvement in Chinese to English MT technology.

3.11 Pen Scanner

A pen scanner is a pen-shaped, handheld scanner that combines the functions of a scanner, an OCR program, a dictionary program and a translation program. There are many pen-shaped scanner devices out there, but their functionalities vary greatly, so you must be careful. Some devices allow only scanning and recognition, with no translation. Others have the translation feature, but do not handle Chinese. There are also different types of devices depending on how they are connected. The regular type contains only the scanner, which must be connected and used with a PC. The OCR and translation functions are all performed in the PC. There is also a fancier type that can operate in stand-alone mode. It not only has its own processor that runs the OCR and translator program, but also displays the translated results on its own LCD screen. Some advanced models even speak out the results using TTS (text to speech) technology.

The only pen scanner I have evaluated is the MiniScanEYE II made by PenPower Technology Ltd. This is the latest handheld scanner and translator product from this company. It can recognize more than 13,000 traditional Chinese characters, 6,700 simplified Chinese characters, 4,000 Hong Kong Chinese characters, and 3,500 Japanese characters. This product connects to the PC through a USB port, and it needs the PC to operate. The PenPower Technology also has another pen scanner product called Super ScanEye that comes with a built-in LCD screen. The Super ScanEye can be used as a stand-alone scanner and translator without the use of a PC. One special note is that the traditional Chinese version and simplified Chinese version of Super ScanEye are actually two separate products. When operating in stand-alone mode, one product cannot read the characters from another system. I have not tried the Super ScanEye myself, but according to the salesperson, each can recognize text from the other system when operating with a PC. In this book, I will only cover the MiniScanEYE II.

3.11.1 MiniScanEYE II—Installation

There are a few things to note when installing the software for the MiniScanEYE II. The first thing is that you should install the software first, and remember not to plug in the pen scanner before the software installation is complete. The second is specific to Windows Vista. At the time this book is written, the software that comes on the installation CD is for use in Windows 2000 and XP only. Windows Vista users must download a newer version of the software. This can be found at the following URL:

http://penpowerinc.com/download/miniScanEYEIIv21.exe

If this link does not work any more, please refer to our supporting website at: http://www.georgekung.com/pen-scanners.html for the latest information.

You can save this file to a temporary location on your PC and run the self-extract EXE file. It will extract the installation package, containing a collection of files, into a folder. After that, run the setup program (setup.exe) from that folder to start the installation. Windows XP and 2000 users can run the setup.exe program from the installation CD and then select **miniScanEYE** to start the installation. During the installation, choose **English** as the installation language, and also select **miniScanEYE II** as the device to use. Check the **HK CharSet** checkbox to allow the installation of the Hong Kong regional specific characters. This feature can be disabled later if you are not going to use it, but there is no harm in installing it first. After the software installation is completed, plug in the pen scanner to an USB port. The system should detect the device automatically and display a hardware wizard to install the device driver. Follow the instructions from there to finish the installation. After that, you are ready to use the pen scanner.

Three pieces of software are installed: miniScanEYE II, TransEYE, and VoiceReader. MiniScanEYE II is the software for scanning and recognition. TransEYE is the software used for translating, and it is a separate application from the miniScanEYE II. The third program VoiceReader is for pronouncing the Chinese characters after each scanning, but it is not useful for our purposes.

3.11.2 MiniScanEYE II—Settings

Click the **PenPower miniScanEYE II** program link from the **PenPower miniScanEYE II** program group to start the scanner program. The miniScanEYE II program displays a splash screen and then minimizes to an icon on the Windows Taskbar (see Figure 3.24). The program does not have a main window because you don't need to interact with it normally. When you need to adjust some settings, click on its icon to bring up a menu and make selections from there. Since this is your first time starting the application, you should click the icon to bring up the menu.

Figure 3.24 MiniScanEYE II icon on the Windows Taskbar

Select **Settings** to open the **Setting** dialog window and then select the **Recognition setting** tab (Figure 3.25). On the left-hand side, there is a **Recognition** selection for **BIG5**, **GB**, **Japan**, and **English**. This is for selecting the character set for the source document, but the naming here is very misleading. The selection **BIG5** actually means traditional Chinese characters and **GB** means simplified Chinese characters. Depending on which character set you wish to recognize, choose either **BIG5** or **GB**. The **Recognise HK** checkbox is for recognizing Cantonese (Hong Kong regional specific) Chinese characters and can

only be used with the traditional character set. You can leave that unchecked
because we won't discuss the reading of Cantonese characters.

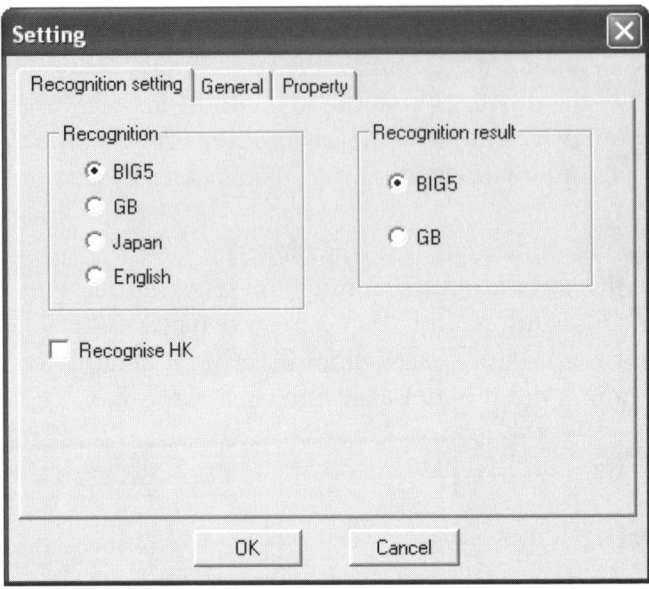

Figure 3.25 MiniScanEYE II settings (**Recognition setting** tab)

On the right-hand side is the **Recognition result** section, with two selections:
BIG5 and **GB**. The wording in here is once again incorrect. The output text from
this application is encoded in Unicode, and not in Big5 or GB code. The selection
in here is to decide whether to write the output in traditional or simplified
characters. The **BIG5** selection allows you to save the output in traditional
characters. The **GB** selection allows you to save the output in simplified
characters.

Click the **General** tab (Figure 3.26) to make adjustments of the scanning
directions. This screen contains selections that say **Left-handed** and **Right-
handed**, but the naming is useless and confusing. For horizontal text, the program
always assumes that the text runs from left to right. It doesn't matter if you choose
Left-handed or **Right-handed**, you can either hold the device with your right
hand and scan from left to right, or hold it with your left hand and scan from right
to left. As long as you don't hold the device up side down, the scanning will
always be correct (Figure 3.27).

For vertical text, the scanning is a little tricky. When selecting **Right-handed,**
you need to turn the document 90 degrees clockwise and scan from either left to
right or right to left. When selecting **Left-handed**, turn the document 90 degrees
counter-clockwise and scan either way.

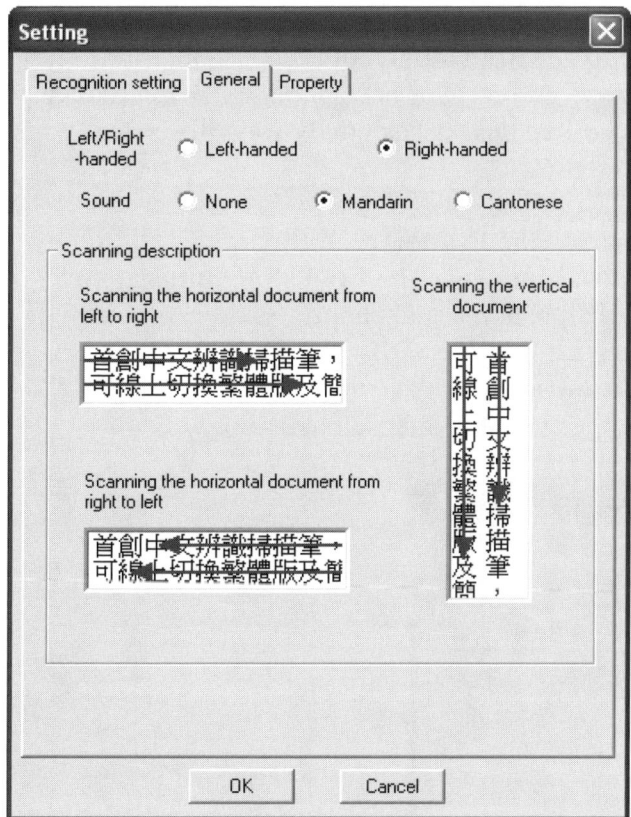

Figure 3.26 MiniScanEYE II settings (**General** tab)

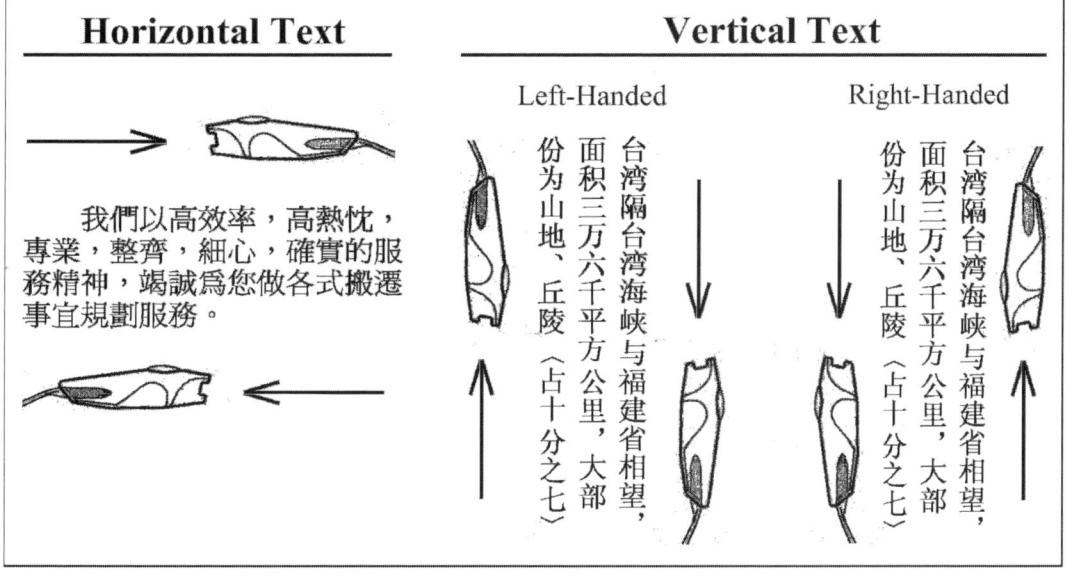

Figure 3.27 Scanning direction

One limitation with the miniScanEYE II is that it always assumes that the source text run from left to right horizontally, or from top to bottom vertically. For vertical text, this assumption is always correct. For horizontal text, even though for most modern printing is produced like that, occasionally we still see text going the other way.

There are three selections to be made on the **Property** tab (Figure 3.28). In the **Recognition** section, check both the **Chinese** and the **English&Numeral** boxes to recognize the mix of Chinese and alphanumerical characters. For the **Content** section, always choose **Printed** because we are not discussing work with hand-written characters. For the **Orientation** section, leave the selection on **Auto**. Click **OK** at the end to accept all the changes made and close the dialog window.

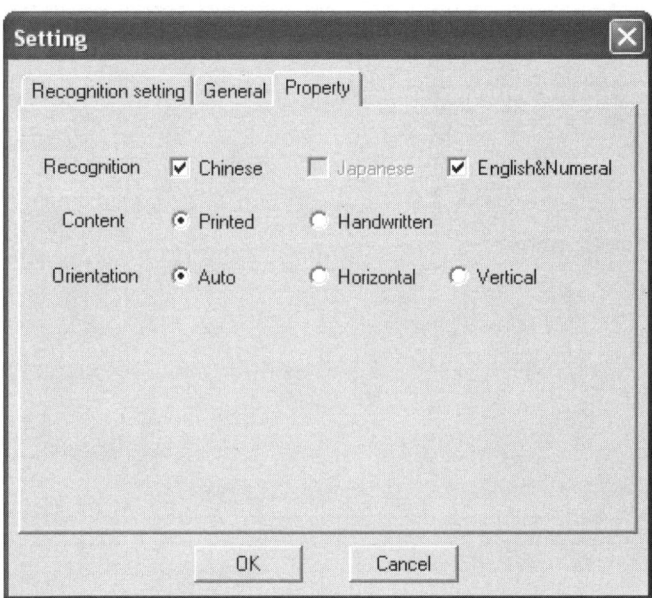

Figure 3.28 MiniScanEYE II settings (**Property** tab)

3.11.3 MiniScanEYE II—Operations

After all the settings are adjusted, the next step is to start the backend application, i.e., the program that uses the outputs from the pen scanner. Usually, you would like the scanned text to go to the translation software. The backend application can be either the PenPower TransEYE, or any other translation or dictionary program that you wish to use. Initially, I recommend using the Windows Notepad as the backend application, to learn how the pen scanner functions. After you are familiar with its operations, you can then use it with real translation programs. For now, let us run the Windows Notepad and start a new document. Make sure to leave the mouse focus on this new document.

One special note is that MiniScanEYE II only works with dark text on light background. If the document is in color, make sure the text is darker than the background.

To operate, hold the pen scanner as you would hold a marker pen (Figure 3.29). The device scans one line of characters at a time. Align the center of the pen scanner with the line of text being scanned. There is a function button on top of the pen scanner and a small scan button near the scan tip. The function button is used to insert new lines after each scan, and should not be pressed during scanning.

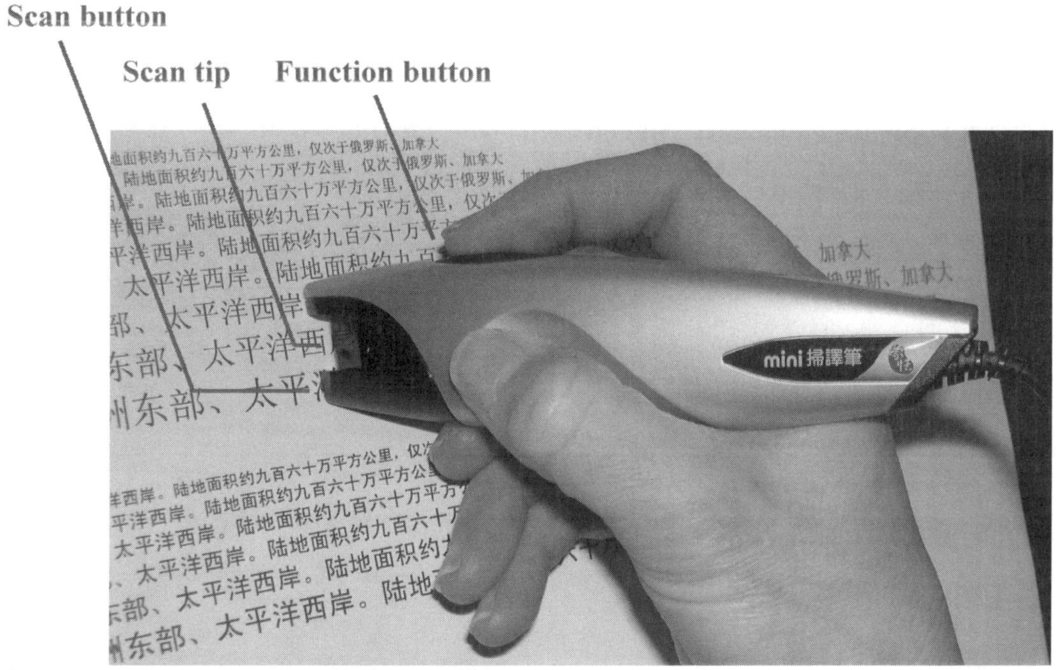

Figure 3.29 Operating the MiniScanEYE II

When scanning, press the pen scanner against the document so the scan button is pushed in, and keep it like that for the entire course of the scanning. As the scan button is pushed in, you will see a beam of light emitted from the scan tip area. Press the pen scanner against the document and swipe it along the line of text at a steady speed. The swiping can be relatively fast but the trick is to maintain a constant speed and also to keep the text at the center of the scan tip. The swiped path should be straight and not twirled. During the course of the swiping, the scan button should stay down and the light should stay on. The characters scanned must be smaller than the width of the scan tip and covered fully by the light beam during the scanning. After a line is scanned, you should see the scanned text on the Notepad window. You can press the function button once. This will insert a new line in the result text, so the next scan will be written to the next line.

Much practice is needed when first starting out, to get a feel of how the swiping works. You must learn to operate it comfortably in a consistent manner before it will yield satisfactory results. During practice, scan the same source line multiple times and press the function button after each scanning. This will place the scanned text in successive lines in the Notepad document for comparison. You can easily see if a character is missed or scanned incorrectly by comparing the two adjacent lines.

MiniScanEYE II comes with an editing tool for correcting misrecognized characters. To use the tool, just point the mouse cursor at a misrecognized character and leave it there for a while. As you do that, a pop-up window like the one showing in Figure 3.30 will come up. This **Editing Toolbar** contains a list of candidate characters, which look similar to the character in the image. Pick the desired character from the list to correct the error.

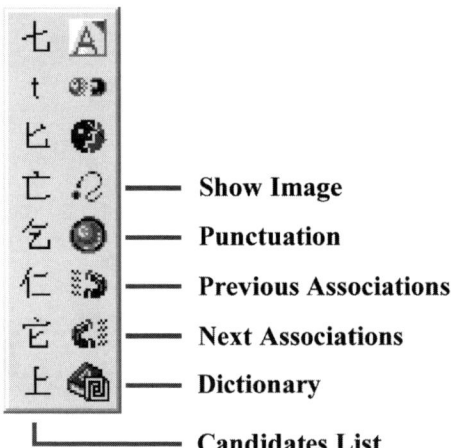

Figure 3.30 MiniScanEYE II—**Editing Toolbar**

In addition to the **Candidates List**, there are a few other helpful tools from the **Editing Toolbar**. The **Show Image** tool can be used to view the scanned image. When the mouse moves over the **Show Image** icon, you will see a section of the original scanned image displayed, with the character highlighted by a red rectangle enclosure (Figure 3.31). The **Punctuation** tool allows the addition of punctuation marks to the text. When you move the mouse over the **Punctuation** tool, another pop-up window containing punctuation symbols will appear, and you can click on a symbol to insert it into the text output.

Figure 3.31 MiniScanEYE II—**Editing Toolbar—Show Image**

The **Previous Associations** and **Next Associations** tools provide lists of candidate characters based on the forming of Chinese words, for replacing the currently edited character. Association means that one character forms a valid Chinese word with another character. As the mouse cursor hovers over a character and brings up the **Editing Toolbar**, the character that you are focusing on is the current character, and the character before the current one is the previous character and the character next to the current one is the next character. The **Associations** tools assume that the previous and next characters are correctly recognized. Base on this assumption, the **Previous Associations** tool gives you a list of all Chinese words (that it knows) with the previous character in the front position. By the same token, the **Next Associations** tool gives you a list of all the words that have the next character in the back position.

For example, let us take a look at Figure 3.32. Assume you leave the cursor at the third character 特. The current character is 特, the previous character is 部, and the next character is 近. When you move the mouse cursor over to the **Next Associations** button, the **Next Associations** tool gives you a list of all the Chinese words that end with the character 近, with the hope that the beginning character of one word will be the character that you are looking for. In this example, you found that the fourth word 將近 in the list is indeed what you are looking for, so you click on it for replacement.

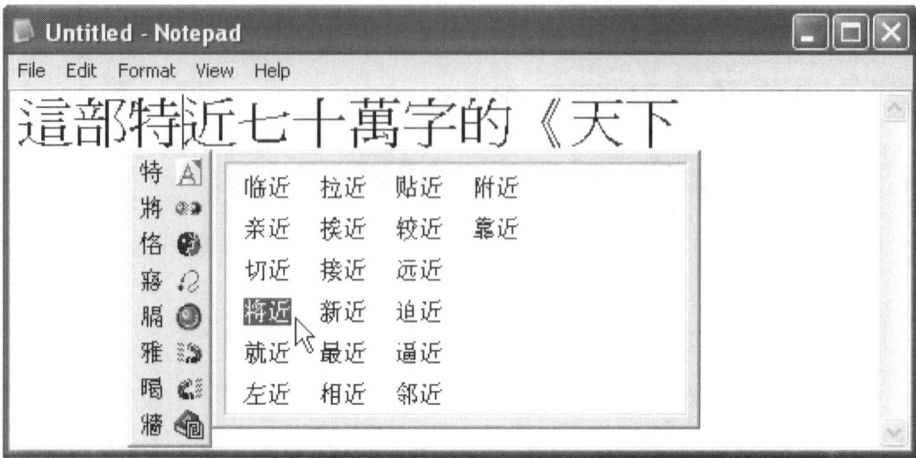

Figure 3.32 MiniScanEYE II—**Editing Toolbar—Next Association**

One problem with the **Editing Toolbar** is that the characters are very small, and there seems to be no way of adjusting the size of the display. Another thing is that these tools may not be very practical to use by people unfamiliar with Chinese. For our readers, I would think that the easiest way to correct misrecognized characters is to just rescan the line. The easiest way to identify misrecognized characters is to scan the same line twice and have the results in two adjacent lines for comparison.

One other tool from the **Editing Toolbar** is a pop-up dictionary (Figure 3.33). It finds all the words that begin with the current character, and shows the meaning of each word. You can click the up and down triangles to navigate between the previous and next word in the list.

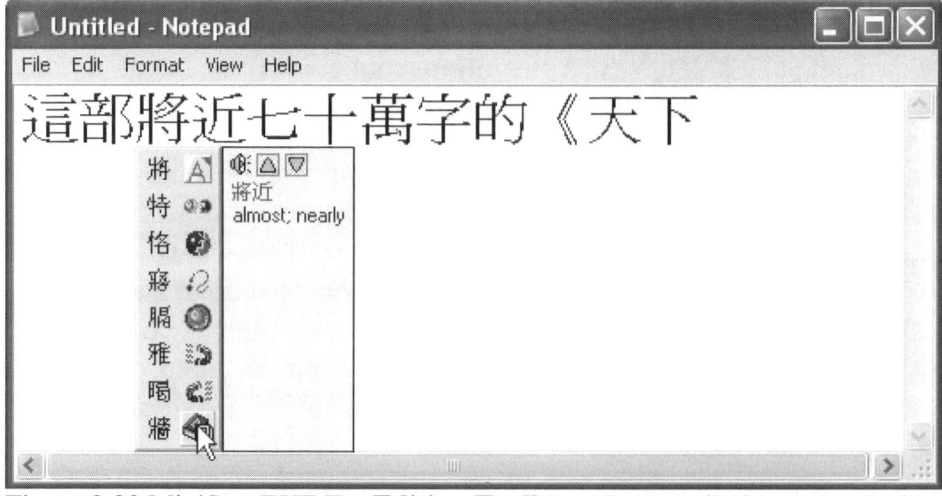

Figure 3.33 MiniScanEYE II—**Editing Toolbar**—Pop-up dictionary

3.11.4 TransEYE—Settings

Now that you are familiar with the operation of the pen scanner, the next step is to use TransEYE. TransEYE translator is a completely separate application from the miniScanEYE II program. This application not only runs independently from miniScanEYE II, but it actually contains all the functions of miniScanEYE II. Earlier in this section I discussed having TransEYE as the backend program for using the output from miniScanEYE II, but that statement is not completely true. TransEYE is actually both the front and the backend program. When you use TransEYE, it controls the pen scanner directly and you do not need the miniScanEYE II program. To be more exact, TransEYE translator maintains its own group of settings and will ignore the settings in miniScanEYE II. In reality, I have found that miniScanEYE II actually interferes with the operations of TransEYE, so please remember to close miniScanEYE II when you are working with TransEYE.

Figure 3.34 shows the main window of TransEYE. First, click the **Settings** icon to open the **Settings** dialog window to adjust the settings.

Figure 3.34 TransEYE Translator main window

Most selections in the first two tabs (**Recognition settings** and **Property**) are similar to what you have seen in the miniScanEYE II program, so I will not repeat them here. The **Property** tab in here contains most of the selections in the

General and the **Property** tabs in miniScanEYE II. TransEYE always recognizes the mix of Chinese characters and alphanumerical characters, so there are no separate selections like those in miniScanEYE II. The third tab, **Version**, in TransEYE is for adjusting the language used in the application's UI (user interface). Leave the selection on **English**.

3.11.5 TransEYE—Operations

After the settings are properly adjusted, choose one of the modes in which to operate. The program allows you to translate either from English to Chinese or vice versa. For each of these two types, you can have a word-by-word translation, or translate a whole sentence. For our purposes, you will use the two translation functions from Chinese to English only.

Let's start with the word translator. Do this by clicking the **Translate Words** (Chinese to English) button. After that, start using the pen scanner to scan Chinese text. In the word translator, you can only scan one line of text at a time. After each scanning, the scanned image will appear in the **Graphics Area**, and the recognized Chinese words and their English translations will appear one word at a time in the **Text Area**. You can use the **Previous** and the **Next** buttons to navigate to different words in the text. In the **Graphics Area**, a blue rectangle will highlight those characters that are currently displayed in the **Text Area**. The program identifies Chinese words (词) in multiple rounds, starting from words with the most number of characters. As it reaches the end of the text, it will restart from the beginning and look for words with fewer characters. It will repeat this process until all the single characters are translated.

Take the text 美國東接大西洋 for example. Ideally, the text should be translated to:

美國 (USA) 東 (east) 接 (connect to) 大西洋 (Atlantic)

The word translator does not perform any analysis of the sentence. It only looks for words from the text and lists them in the order of the number of characters each contains. In our example, the program finds 大西洋 (Atlantic) as the first word (the first line in Figure 3.35) because it contains the most number of characters (3). After that it restarts from the beginning and finds all the two-character words, 美國 (USA) and 西洋 (occident) (the second line in Figure 3.35). After all the two-character words are found, it restarts from the beginning and lists all the single characters, one at a time starting from 美 (beautiful), 國 (country) (the third line in Figure 3.35), and so on.

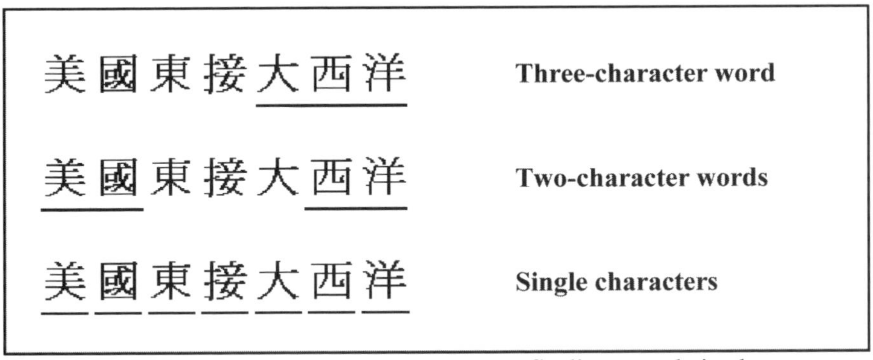

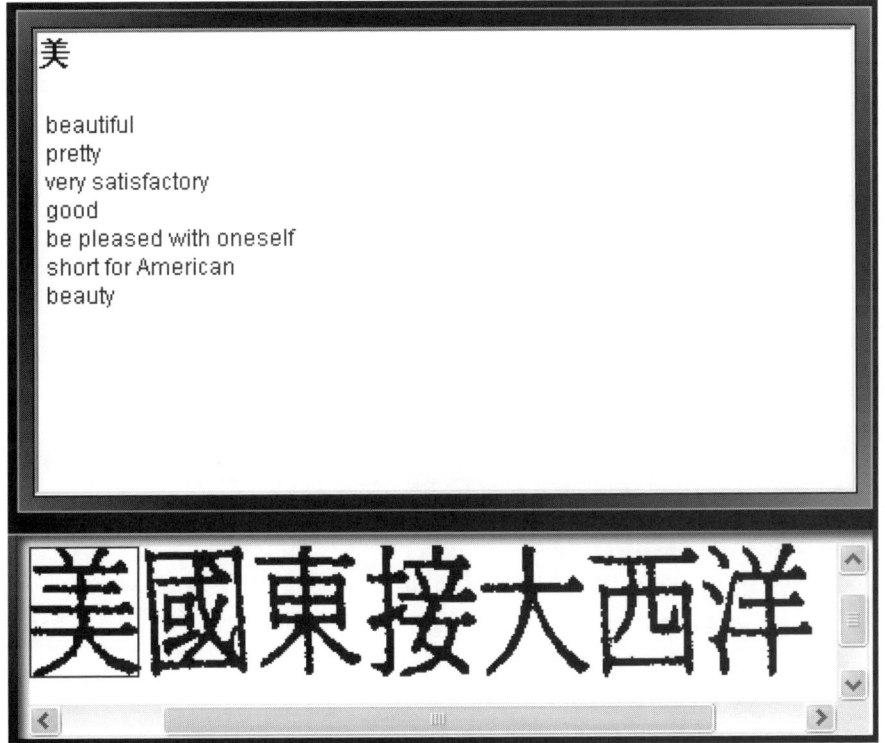

Figure 3.35 TransEYE—Word Translator—finding words in the text

When using the word translator, the **Text Area** displays the Chinese word on the top in black, followed by all the possible English translations in blue. The **Graphics Area** shows the scanned image, with the currently identified character(s) highlighted by a blue rectangle enclosure (see Figure 3.36).

Figure 3.36 TransEYE—Word Translator

Click the **Translate Sentences** (Chinese to English) button to do whole sentence translation. As you do that, the **Text Area** is split into the top and the bottom parts (Figure 3.37). After scanning each line, the recognized Chinese text appears on the top half of the **Text Area**, and the scanned image appears in the **Graphics Area**. The **Editing Toolbar** that we had seen in the miniScanEYE II is also implemented in the TransEYE, which can be used to correct misrecognized characters. Unlike the Word Translator, which accepts one line at a time, the Sentence Translator accepts multiple lines of scanning. As you scan more lines, the newly recognized results will be appended to the original text. After scanning, you can click the **Text Area** to edit and remove extra characters from the output.

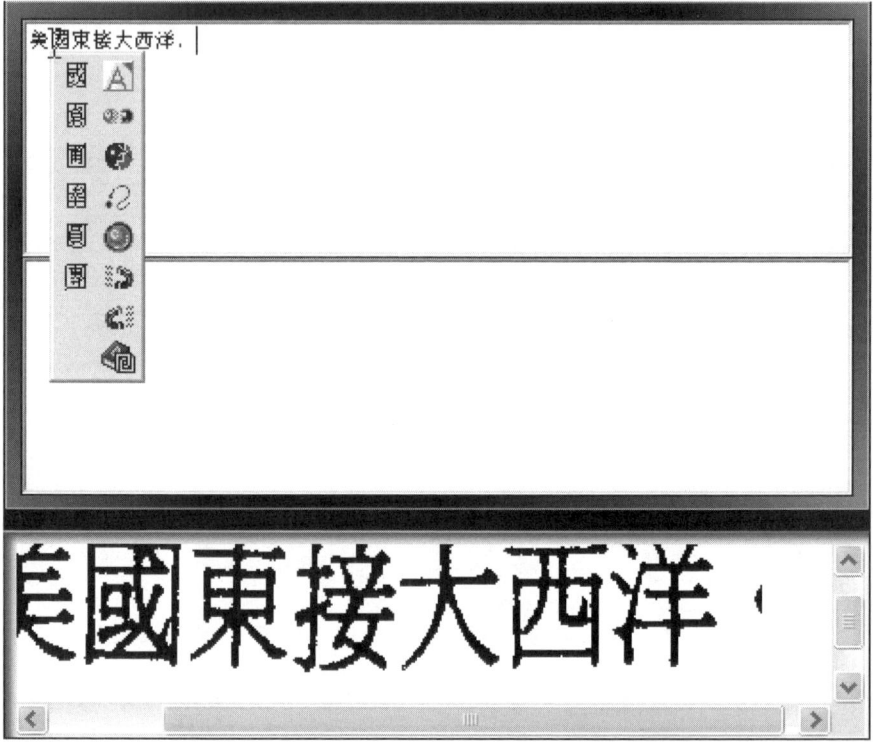

Figure 3.37 TransEYE—Edit misrecognized characters in the Sentence Translator

Click the **Translate** button to translate the entire text in the **Text Area**. The translated results appear in the bottom half of the **Text Area** (Figure 3.38). Click the **Save** button to save the translated (English) results. Click the **Clear** button to clear all the contents in the **Text Area**.

You can use the sentence translation function separately from scanning and recognition. You can take Chinese text obtained from other applications and paste them into the **Text Area** here and translate them using TransEYE. For example, you can do scanning and editing in a Notepad window using miniScanEYE II, and then copy and paste the text to TransEYE for translation. You can also copy text from a web page while browsing a website, and paste that to the TransEYE. These usages completely bypass the scanning and recognition function of the TransEYE, and use only the translation feature of the program.

Figure 3.38 TransEYE—Sentence Translator—Translation results

On the other hand, if we are not satisfied with the translator provided by TransEYE, we can always use the pen scanner merely as a scanner and an OCR program. The scanned output of the miniScanEYE II program can be fed to just about any Windows application that accepts input to a text area. This works with Notepad, WordPad, Microsoft Word, and all the translation and dictionary programs which take inputs from a text box.

4. Chinese OCR Software

In this chapter, we will look at details of various Chinese OCR software products. These are the tools for converting scanned Chinese text images into the actual codes that represent characters. Only after obtaining the encoded text will you be able to use them in the MT (Machine Translation) or other programs, such as a word processor or a web browser. However, this tool is needed in the Chinese reading process only for extracting text from printed materials. If all the text you wish to read is already in electronic format, then you will not need the OCR. If this happens to be the case you can skip reading of this entire chapter.

I have worked with Chinese OCR products since the Windows 98 era. They are mainly used for scanning text from forms, converting documents into electronic format, archiving materials from books, etc. In the past twelve months, I have focused on seeking products that can be used by people who arc unfamiliar with the language. This is challenging, because most these OCR programs are designed exclusively for local language users. Some products may have good recognition rates, but unfortunately their user interfaces (UI) and manuals are in Chinese only. Other programs only work with Chinese versions of Windows, or even require special language framework to run on. Another consideration is that the software should be affordable for individual users, and easy to buy internationally. After an exhaustive search, I was able to find three products that fit these criteria. Hopefully, with the introduction of this book, we will start to see more foreigner users for this type of software, and vendors will begin offering products with English UI and manuals.

4.1 Presto! MaxReader 5

Presto! MaxReader 5, aka DanChing 5, is an OCR product made by the Taiwan-based company NewSoft Technology Corporation (力新國際). The name NewSoft may not sound familiar, but if you have used scanners before, you must have heard of the trademark "Presto!." Presto! PageManager has been bundled in numerous products from companies like Canon, HP, Epson, UMAX, Brother, etc. Their OCR software is also very popular in Taiwan and China. They have used the name 丹青 (DanChing) from the start. They added an English user interface to version 5, and also named it MaxReader, for easy to use by International users. This new name is used together with the name DanChing.

The website of NewSoft is located at http://www.newsoftinc.com and they have a trial version of MaxReader 5.0 that can be downloaded for free. This trial version can be used for 30 days, but all the save functions are disabled. You can't get around this by copying results to Windows Clipboard or sending the outputs using e-mail either, because all those functions are disabled as well. Basically, it gives you no way of using its outputs other than to view them on screen. This is pretty slick, but I can't complain. So far, it is the only Chinese OCR software product I know that offers a trial version.

The newer versions of Presto! PageManager, which are bundled with some scanners, may also include the Chinese OCR feature. Nevertheless, the OCR in this program is very simple, with fewer functions than MaxReader 5 and with inferior recognition abilities. I will give more descriptions of this bundled Chinese OCR in Chapter 4.4. NewSoft also has another stand-alone OCR product called Presto! OCR Pro that does not recognize Chinese at all. There is also a completely different software product made by another company that happens to have the same name "MaxReader." Please be aware of these similarly named products when you look for information from the Internet.

One thing I would like to mention up front is that MaxReader 5 is a very fine product and I consider it the best among all the relevant Chinese OCR software. However, I did run into some issues when testing the software. Don't be discouraged by them. The glitches exist in the trial version only, and they are minor. I will describe workarounds for them below.

4.1.1 Installation

When the setup program of MaxReader 5 (trial version) is first started, it shows some strange looking characters and buttons with unreadable symbols. You should ignore these messages and not to press any button. Wait for the self-extracting part of the installation to finish. After that, you will start to see regular screens in English. Follow the instructions on the screen to complete the setup.

After the setup is completed, proceed to the Windows **Start** menu, select the program group **NewSoft**, select **MaxReader 5**, and then click **MaxReader 5** again to start the MaxReader 5 program. Each startup of the program begins with a splash screen containing three buttons with unreadable text. It is my guess that the vendor had added an additional page to remind people of the number of days remaining in the trial version, but forgot to fix the UI part of it. The important thing is, just remember to click the top button. Once you get by that, the rest of the display will be in English, or the default language setting in your Windows system. The application is supposed to automatically detect your system's language setting and present the UI in that, which can be in English, simplified Chinese, traditional Chinese, or Japanese. If for whatever reason this automatic feature doesn't work, you can use a separate utility to set the UI language manually. To do this, close the MaxReader program, go to Windows **Start** menu, look for the program group **NewSoft**, and select **MaxReader 5**. There should be three program items listed in there. Click on the item with an icon that says **MUI**. This will bring up the **Multilingual User Interface settings** dialog for you to select the language for the UI.

Again, these glitches only appear in the trial version. When I installed the real version, everything came up smoothly without any issue.

4.1.2 Acquiring Inputs

Select **MaxReader 5** from the **NewSoft – MaxReader 5** program group to start the application. Figure 4.1 shows the Main window of MaxReader 5. At the center of the Main window is the Working area, which displays the image and recognized results. On top of the Working area is the **Display Toolbox**. This contains a dropdown box for adjusting the zoom of the view. It also has three buttons for selecting the different modes for the Working area: Image Mode, Page Mode, and Proof Mode. In Image Mode, the Working area contains the image of the selected page. In Page Mode, the Working area shows the recognized results. In Proof Mode, the image and recognized results are displayed together in two windows side-by-side, for comparing and fixing misrecognized characters. When a page is first opened, the only mode available is the Image Mode. At this time, the buttons for the other two modes are grayed, as shown in Figure 4.1. The Page Mode and Proof Mode become available only after the recognition.

MaxReader 5 acquires inputs either from a scanner (or any TWAIN compatible image capturing device) or image files. To get input from a scanner, choose **Select Source** from the **File** menu and specify the preferred image device first. This image source selection will be remembered by the software so you only need to do it once. The next step is to select **Acquire** from the **File** menu. This brings up the screen provided by the low level TWAIN device driver, and you can control your image device from there to complete the image capture. The detailed descriptions of the scanner and the TWAIN interface can be found in Chapter 3.5.

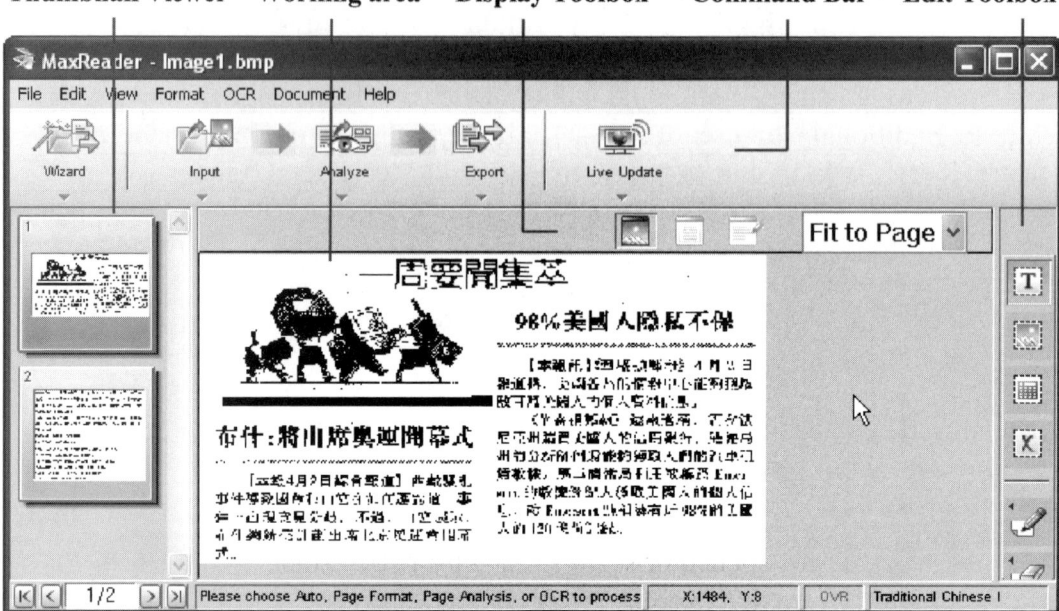

Figure 4.1 MaxReader 5 Main window

To use image files as the input source, click **File**, click **Open Image File**, and then select a file or files from there. MaxReader 5 supports various image file formats, including TIF, PCX, BMP and JPG. These are more than sufficient for our needs. Even though MaxReader 5 supports the recognition of text from color images, I recommend using color images only when the colors are simple and the contrast of text to the background is high. Otherwise, it is better to manually convert the color images into black and white (B/W) before recognition (refer to the description in Chapter 3.7.3 for details).

MaxReader can take the mixing of multiple images, from the scanner and/or preexisting files. It adds all the pages to a project and initially arranges them according to the order of opening. After a page is opened or scanned from a device, it appears in the Working area and also in the Thumbnail Viewer. The Thumbnail Viewer shows a thumbnail view of all the pages in the project and you can navigate to different pages from there.

When you click the thumbnail icon of a page, the page will be selected and brought to the Working area. Use the dropdown box in the **Display Toolbox** to adjust the zoom setting for viewing the image. You can rearrange the sequence of pages in the project by dragging a thumbnail to another place. Select **Image Information** from the **Document** menu to get basic information regarding width, length, resolution, and file size of the selected image. MaxReader also comes with basic processing functions that can be used to fix up images. These functions include rotation, touching, cropping, and inverting the color of the image. MaxReader cannot recognize white (light) text on black (dark) background. For images of this nature, you must reverse the color using the inverting function prior to the recognition. Note that the inverting function provided here only allows you to invert the whole page. You must perform extra processing in a situation where an image contains both white text on black and black text on white. Cut out the region with regular text into the Windows Clipboard, do the inverting to the rest of the page, and then paste the region back. The other way is to use the GIMP 2 image editor software discussed in Chapter 3.7.

4.1.3 Settings

After all the pages are opened or scanned, and properly arranged in the project, the next thing is to check the settings and make adjustments if needed. A critical setting is the selection of the Chinese character sets. Click **Format** from the main menu, select **Set Character Set**, and then make the selection of traditional or simplified character set from there. The OCR will not work properly if this selection in incorrect. There are two choices for traditional Chinese settings. The **Traditional Chinese I** is suitable for common everyday documents, while the **Traditional Chinese II** is to be used with documents composed of ancient words or characters that appear in old poetry or literature, etc. You cannot mix pages with text from different character sets. If there are multiple documents within one project, all the text must come from the same character set. The setting of character set stays in effect until it is changed.

Select **OCR** on the main menu and then click **Recognition Preferences** to open the **Recognition Preferences** dialog window. This dialog allows you to adjust source document related properties. Certain types of block layout are interpreted by the program as multiple text tracts. The **Force to Single Column** in the **Page Layout Property** section is used to force them to be recognized as single column. My recommendation is not to use it, as this usually causes problems when you view results and perform proofreading. The **Form** section allows you to select whether the document contains forms or tables. The **Text Alignment** section allows you to select the printing direction of the text. The selections in these two sections should be self-explanatory. In the **Data Type** section, select all the text types, including Chinese, alphabetic and numeric characters, unless you are certain that some of the types will never appear in your source document. Leave the other three sections on **Auto** to let the software determine their properties for you. Click the **Set as Default** button to apply these settings. These default settings will stay in effect until you change them. If you only want to change some settings temporarily, select **Format** from the main menu and then select the **Page Format** to open the **Page Format Setting** dialog. From there you can make the same adjustments described above, but any changes made only apply to the next recognition.

MaxReader 5 can recognize many different Chinese fonts, including Song (宋), Hei (黑), Kai (楷), FongSong (仿宋), Yuan (圆), and even Li (隶书). Texts of different fonts can be mixed on a page, and the program will automatically recognize all the fonts that it supports. There is no setting or configuration to be adjusted for this.

4.1.4 Analysis

The layout of a source document may be complex at times. It can contain graphics, tables, and text arranged in different blocks. Before OCR program starts the recognition process, it needs to perform another step called "analysis." This process distinguishes graphics from text, and identifies different text blocks based on the different fonts, sizes and printing directions. You can either do the analysis manually or have the software do it for you.

To manually analyze a selected page, first click the **Block Marking Tool** icon from the **Edit Toolbox** (Figure 4.1) to specify that you want to mark text blocks. Drag the mouse cursor to form a rectangle around the characters that belong together. They will be enclosed by a blue rectangle outline with black dots at the four corners. You can drag the black dots to resize the area, or drag the inside of the rectangle to move it as a whole. Create a new rectangle for each block of text that needs to be identified separately. Areas that are not enclosed will not go through recognition.

One interesting thing is that sometimes, even if you specify an area as one block, the software may get wise and decide to separate it into parts during the recognition process. This can happen when the program detects things like the spacing between two text rows being larger than normal. To prevent this, you can highlight the block and then select **Keep Block Intact** from the **Format** menu.

When a page contains graphics, you should mark these regions out as image blocks. This can be done in a similar way as marking a text block, but you should click the **Image Selection Tool** icon from the **Edit Toolbox** before drawing the rectangles. Image blocks are enclosed in a red rectangle frame, and will be passed during the recognition process.

To have the software do the analysis automatically (without doing recognition), you can either click the **Analyze** icon below the menu bar, or select **Analyze Pages** from the **OCR** menu. After the analysis, you will see blocks enclosed in blue or red rectangular outlines. A blue rectangle identifies a text block and a red rectangle identifies an image block. After the automatic analysis, you can do some editing to separate a block into two or to join two blocks together using the tools in the **Edit Toolbox**. You can also change the attribute of blocks from image to text or vice versa, or rearrange the order of blocks.

The automatic analysis function is quite reliable. Usually, you can do recognition without having to do analysis separately. The program will kick off the analysis process first and then follow with recognition automatically. After recognition, if the analysis is incorrect, you can either fix or discard the analysis results and redo the recognition.

There are certain circumstances where the automatic analysis does not perform well. One is when text comes too close to a graphic area and the software treats them as one image block. If this occurs, you will need to manually separate the text from the graphics. Sometimes an entire text block may be wrongly identified as an image block, or vice versa. This can be fixed by right clicking on the block, and then selecting **Change Block Attributes** to change the attribute of the block. There are also times when the program analyzes the running direction of the text (i.e., the horizontal vs. vertical) incorrectly. In cases such as these, you need to change the text alignment attribute. You can do this by right clicking on the block, selecting **Change Block Attributes**, selecting **advanced Attribute Settings** and then changing the selection in the **Text Alignment** option.

Another common mistake is that the software divides an area into two or more blocks where it really should be just one block. To correct this, you should select the **Connect Blocks** tool from the **Edit Toolbox**, and drag the mouse cursor to enclose the whole area that is intended to be one single block. After that, the whole area should be enclosed by a single rectangle frame. To prevent a block from being split after performing a manual identification, you need to select a block and then select the **Keep Block Intact** from the **Format** menu. This will mark your block in double blue lines and prevent the software from separating it.

4.1.5 Recognition

To begin the recognition, select the **OCR** menu and then click either **Recognize Current Page** to process the selected page, or **Recognize All Pages** to process all the pages in the project. If the selected pages have not been analyzed yet, MaxReader will do the automatic analysis first and then the recognition. When MaxReader 5 is performing the recognition, you will see an animation of the process shown on the screen.

After the recognition, you can use the tools in the **Edit Toolbox** again to combine, separate, change attributes, or rearrange the orders of blocks. These tools are used to group or split the recognized results for saving, or to fix the blocks so you can redo the recognition. To redo recognition on certain blocks, click the **Page Mode** icon from the **Display Toolbox** to set the program to Page Mode. Click a block or blocks to make them turn yellow. After that, click the **Re-OCR block** from the **OCR** menu. This will make the program redo recognition on all the selected (yellow) blocks. Sometimes, it is easier and more efficient to just redo the entire page after a poor recognition. You can do this by right clicking the page and selecting **Discard Current Page OCR Results** while in the Page Mode. It can also be done by selecting **Discard OCR Result of Current Page** from the **OCR** menu. This will wipe out all the recognized results on the current page, including analyzed blocks, either automatically created or manually drawn, and give you a completely fresh start.

4.1.6 Proofreading

When the recognition process is finished, the **Page Mode** and the **Proof Mode** icons will become accessible for the selected page. Depending on the setting made from the **Preferences** dialog, the software can be made to automatically enter Page Mode or Proof Mode after certain processes. Page Mode shows recognized results and contains tools to proofread and fix errors from the recognition. Clicking the **Verify Text Tool** icon from the **Edit Toolbox** show the recognized text, with suspected characters highlighted in yellow color and blue background. MaxReader highlights characters to show that it is not very sure that the recognition is correct. In normal conditions, you should see less than 10% of characters in a page marked as suspicious. If you see a figure much higher than that, then you should suspect that something is wrong. It may be either that the wrong character set is used, or a problem with image quality. For normal results, even if a character is marked as suspicious, it is more than likely just a false alarm.

The rationale is to be conservative and always flag a character unless the program is very certain that the character is correct. I think an adjustable setting for the threshold level would be a useful feature.

Other than viewing suspected characters in the OCR result, proofreading involves comparing the recognized text with the original source and making corrections when necessary. This will not be easy for someone who doesn't know Chinese. As such, most of the information provided in the rest of this section is for the purpose of completeness only. In reality, you will not need to use most of the functions described here—at least not on a regular basis.

When using the **Verify Text Tool** in Page Mode, as you click on a character, a small **Verify Text** window pops up and shows you the image of the character with a list of candidate characters that look similar (see Figure 4.2). You can use this tool to select a character from the list to replace the one on the page. One problem with this tool is that the characters in the list are too small to read. Another problem is that the characters from the candidate list are always displayed using the Song font, which may not be consistent with the font used in the image. I suppose the root cause of the second problem is the same as the first—space is too limited so it can only use the simplest font. I just do not understand why they have to make the pop-up window so small in the first place. It seems to me there is plenty of space to make the window much bigger.

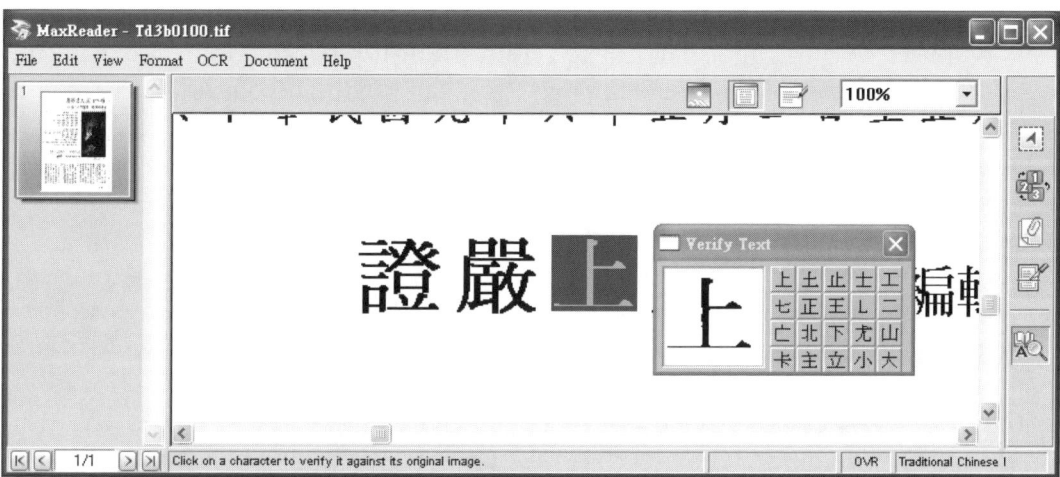

Figure 4.2 MaxReader 5—**Verify Text Tool**

You can set two option items for using the **Verify Text Tool**. They can be selected from a pull-down menu, activated by clicking the icon at the top left corner of the **Verify Text Tool** window (see Figure 4.3). The first option is called **Fix the Window Position**. When you have this checked, the pop-up window always shows up at a fixed place instead of a location relative to the character that you are checking. The second option is **Quick Browse the Character Image**. When this option is turned on, you no longer need to click the mouse button to show the pop-up window. The window pops up and its contents change automatically as you move your mouse cursor over different characters.

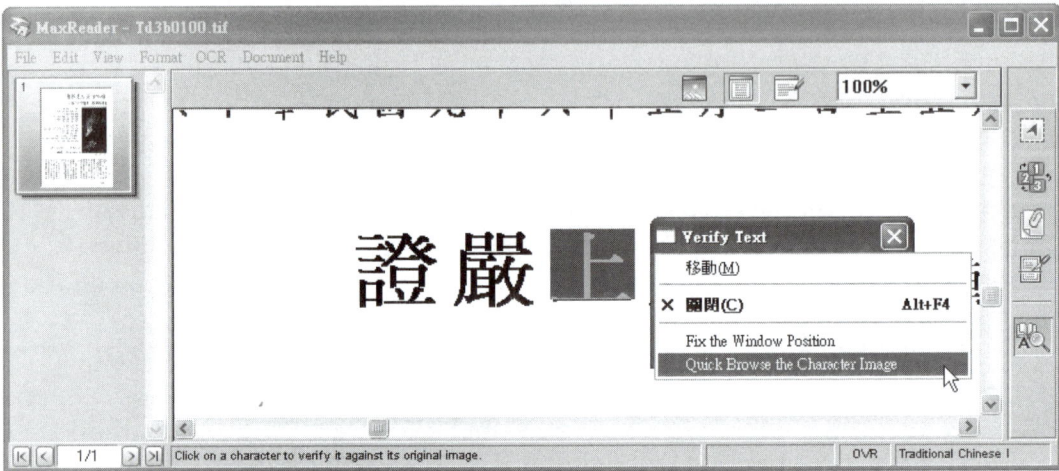

Figure 4.3 MaxReader 5—change options in **Verify Text Tool**

After recognition, the program can operate in Proof Mode. This allows you to proofread and make corrections to the recognized results. Figure 4.4 shows the MaxReader 5 screen when it operates in Proof Mode. The Working area is divided into four quadrants. The **Page Thumbnail** (top left quadrant) displays the overall image layout of the selected page. You can see the layout of all the blocks on the page, with the currently selected block highlighted in blue outline. The **Blocks Menu** (bottom left quadrant) shows a list of blocks with the first few recognized characters from each block. You can change the block selection from either the **Page Thumbnail** or the **Blocks Menu**. The **Text Viewer** (top right quadrant) displays the recognized text in the block, with questionable characters shown in blue. The bottom right quadrant is further divided into three areas. The main area is called **Character Image pane** and it contains a close-up view of the part of the image that you are looking at. You can navigate to a different location within a block by clicking on a different character from the **Text Viewer**. As you do this, the image in the **Character Image pane** is also changed accordingly. The red rectangle outline in there indicates the location of the character that you are currently working on. On the bottom of the **Character Image pane** is the **Suggested Characters toolbar**. It consists of a list candidate characters that may replace the character that you are working on. When you click on a character in the **Suggested Characters toolbar**, the character in the **Text Viewer** will be replaced with the character you picked.

Page Thumbnail   **Text Viewer**

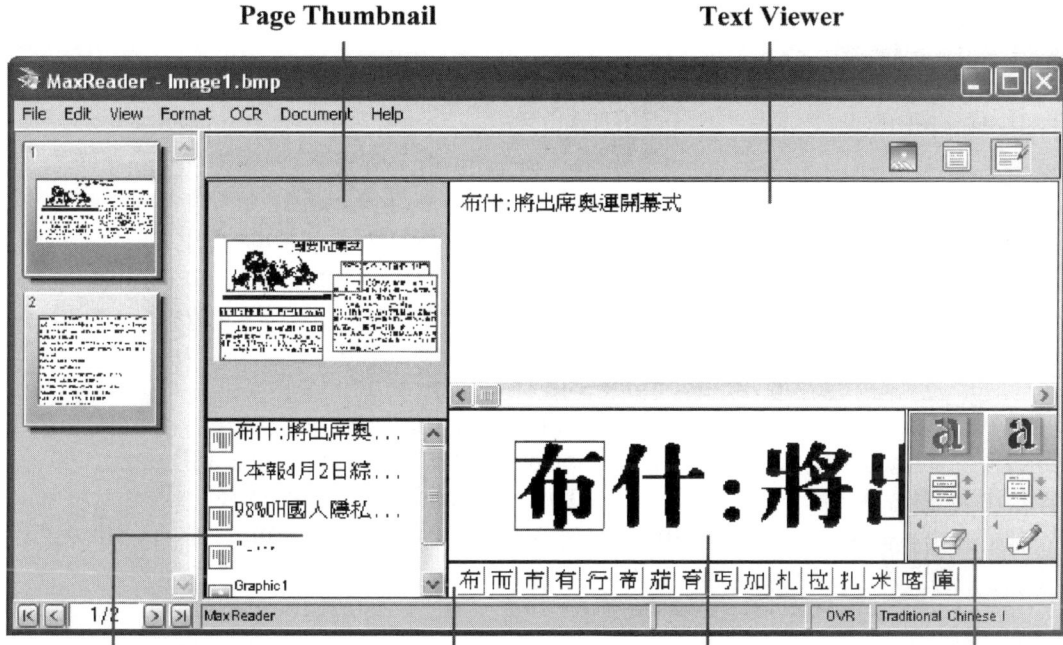

Blocks Menu   Suggested Characters toolbar   Character Image pane   Re-OCR toolbar

Figure 4.4 MaxReader 5—Proof Mode

On the right of the **Character Image pane** is the **Re-OCR toolbar** (Figure 4.4).
This tool can fix certain types of errors and have the software redo the OCR on
the fly. To use the functions of this tool, you must first put the cursor on the
recognized character that you wish to work on, by clicking the character from the
Text Viewer. As you doing this, the corresponding character image will be
highlighted (enclosed in a red rectangle) in the **Character Image pane**. The
Divide character and Recognize tool allows you to divide a character into two.
It is used when the software has mistakenly recognized two separate characters as
one. You will probably notice this kind of error as you see the red enclosures in
the **Character Image pane** showing up abnormally wide or long (depending on
whether the text goes horizontally or vertically). To use this tool, click the knife-
like cursor at the position where the separation should be made in the **Character
Image pane**. When you do this, the program will make the separation, redo the
recognition and give you the new recognition results right away. The **Connect
characters and Recognize tool** allows you to join two characters into one. This is
used when the software has mistakenly recognized one character as two. This can
be noticed by characters being abnormally skinny or short. To use this, drag the
mouse cursor to enclose the entire character in the **Character Image pane**. As
you do this, the software will make the join, redo the recognition, and give you
the new results right away.

The idea behind the **Divide a line and Recognize tool** is similar to the dividing of a character, except it applies to a whole row (or column) of characters. It allows you to divide a row or column of characters, depending on the running direction, into two rows or columns. I suppose this is useful when the software has mistakenly identified two separate rows or columns of texts as one. I can't imagine how that can happen, but this sure reduces my confidence in the OCR technology. Anyway, use this tool similarly to the **Divide character and Recognize tool**. By the same token, the **Connect lines and Recognize tool** is similar to **Connect characters and Recognize tool** except now it works on an entire row or column of characters. Sometimes, recognition is incorrect because there are dirty spots on the document. In such a situation, you can use the **Erase and Recognize tool** to swipe the area and erase the speckles. After erasing, just click anywhere outside the red frame or press the **<Enter>** key and the software will redo the OCR on the fly. The **Draw Line and Recognize tool** is for retouching missing areas and unclear spots. When noticing some areas with light spots or breaking strokes, you can use this tool to touch up the image. The program will redo the OCR on the fly when you click outside the red frame or press the **<Enter>** key.

As we have seen earlier, the **Suggested Characters toolbar** (Figure 4.4) contains a list of candidate characters for replacing the recognized character. The characters in the list are obtained in two ways: similarity and association. Similarity means characters that look similar in shape that the OCR may be confused with. Association denotes characters that are associated with the previous or the next characters of the current position. When we say two characters are "associated," it means that they form a valid Chinese word when used together. Assume that we click the mouse cursor on one character in the **Text Viewer**. The character that is currently highlighted (selected) is the current character. The character ahead of the current one is the previous character and the character behind the current one is the next character. When checking for associations, the program assumes that the previous and next characters are the correct characters at their positions. Based on this assumption, the software will look for all the Chinese words from its dictionary and come up with a list of characters that can be used in the current position.

Let's look at an example in Figure 4.5. Assume we are selecting the character 峡. The software is going to include characters that look similar to 峡, including 陕, 恢, 挟, etc. It also looks at the one character in front of 峡, which is 大. It looks for any character that can be placed after 大 to form a meaningful word, for example, 班, 跌, 阪, etc. It also looks at the character after 峡, which is 谷. It then looks for any character that can be placed before 谷 to form a meaningful word, for example, 山, 峽, 曼, etc. One problem with the **Suggested Characters toolbar** is that its width is limited, and there is no scrollbar available. If there are more characters than it can hold, then those ones that can't fit are dropped. The associated characters can be selectively included in the **Suggest Characters toolbar**. Select the **File**, and then click **Preferences** to open the **Preferences** dialog window. In the **Suggest Characters** section there are two checkboxes: **Include All Characters Related to Previous Character** and **Include all Characters Related to Next Character**. These two settings allow you to determine whether you want the associated characters to appear in the list in the **Suggest Characters toolbar**.

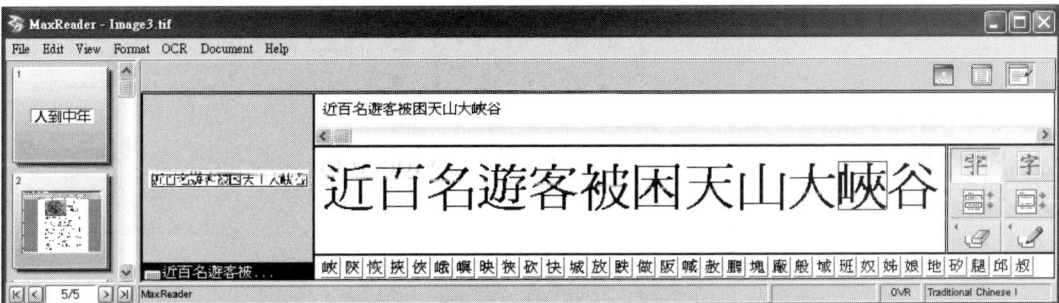

Figure 4.5 MaxReader 5—**Suggested Characters toolbar**

4.1.7 Outputs

After all the misrecognized characters are corrected, you can click **Copy** from the **Edit** menu to copy the output to Windows Clipboard, and use it directly from another application, such as a translation program. You can also save the output to a file by selecting **Save OCR Result** or **Save all OCR Results** from the **File** menu.

MaxReader 5 supports saving into different file formats, including Word document (DOC), Rich Text Format (RTF), HTML, plain text (TXT), Excel (XLS), Comma Separated Values (CSV), and Symbolic Link file (SLK). When saving to a Word document, RTF, or HTML file, the pictures, text fonts and direction information are preserved, but the page layout information is lost. Instead of seeing the document as shown in the Page Mode, you actually only get sequentially appended blocks. Luckily for our text reading purposes, the layout of the output text is not important. When you choose to save the output as a plain text file, the selection shows **Text File (ASCII)**. Note the wording "ASCII" in here is incorrect because the text will be saved in UTF-8 (Unicode), not ASCII.

4.1.8 Using the OCR Wizard

MaxReader 5 has an **OCR Wizard** function. However, it does not work like those wizards you normally see in other programs, which ask questions and then let you choose options you wish to use. The OCR Wizard in this program works like an "easy button." When clicked, it executes some predefined steps to make the executing of routine tasks simpler.

Click the downward triangle below the **Wizard** button to open a pull-down menu. From there you can choose one of the four predefined tasks you wish to perform when the **Wizard** button is pressed. These tasks are the four combinations of getting an input source from the scanner or a file, with the option of saving the outputs. For example, let's say you assign the **Wizard** button with the **Open >> Recognize>>Export** steps. When the **Wizard** button is pressed, the program will execute these three steps automatically. It will first present you with the **Open Image** dialog window for you to select an image file to open. After that, it will start the automatic recognition (including the analysis) process. When that is finished, it will export the results to a text file and open it in Notepad.

4.1.9 Conclusion

There are some rough edges with the MaxReader 5 program. The **Recognition Preferences** dialog window only partially displays some text because the spaces have not been made large enough. The steps for analysis and re-recognition are not intuitive. The places for setting the program options are very confusing. Users must change settings in four different places, and some of them are redundant. The character size used for proofreading is too small and the font does not match what is actually being used in the source image. The candidate list in the proofreading tool cannot be displayed completely if there are too many characters available. The user manual is not helpful in setting out essential explanations. Most of these are minor issues, and the vendor should be able to fix them easily.

I feel that the analysis side of MaxReader 5 can be improved. Occasionally I noticed that it mistakenly treats one character as two without any valid reason. This happens even though the layout of the text is very simple, with all of characters of the same size and uniform spacing. To me, this misrecognition seemed more like a defect in the code.

With more interactions between people that use different character sets, we are starting to see the mixed use of traditional and simplified Chinese characters within the same piece of writing. One improvement really needed is the removal of the limitation of having to choose either character set. Since the OCR output of the text is in Unicode, this kind of constraint does not make sense at all. The system should be made to recognize characters from both character sets at the same time.

Overall, I found MaxReader 5 to be a comprehensive Chinese OCR program with excellent recognition quality. It is of no doubt the best OCR program that suits our needs.

4.2 IRIS Readiris Pro 11 Asian

Readiris is an OCR product from I.R.I.S., a Belgium-based company. Their website is located at: http://www.irislink.com.

The latest release of Readiris is version 11, introduced in 2006. The product supports 120 core languages, and it has various editions and additional language packs. The two editions that fit our needs are the Readiris Pro 11 Home Edition Asian and Readiris Pro 11 Corporate Edition Asian. The Asian edition has the support for the three Asian languages: Chinese, Japanese and Korean, which is outside of the 120 core languages.

4.2.1 Installation

When I started out with the setup program, it asked me which languages to install. I picked only languages that I needed: simplified Chinese, traditional Chinese, and English. I suppose you can also install all the languages first and disable those you don't need later.

After installing and starting the software for the first time, it asked me for a serial number and refused to proceed without one. Since the serial number I found on the package did not work, I had to call the technical support number. The support person was very responsive and gave me a new serial number over the phone right away. However, I tried the new serial number and it still didn't work. The support person then realized I had purchased an Asian edition so he gave me another number, which finally worked. I think they were a little confused themselves, with so many different editions and versions of products.

Compared with other Chinese OCR products, Readiris Pro 11 is relatively simple and easy to use. This is mainly due to the fact that it lacks proofreading and correction functionality. The software includes an OCR Wizard that can guide you through the scanning, file opening and recognition processes. Unlike the Wizard in MaxReader 5, which works like an easy button, the Wizard in Readiris actually asks you questions and walks you through the process. This can be helpful in the beginning when you are not familiar with the operations. I will discuss using the Wizard first. When you are more familiar with the program, you can begin to use the menus and controls by yourself.

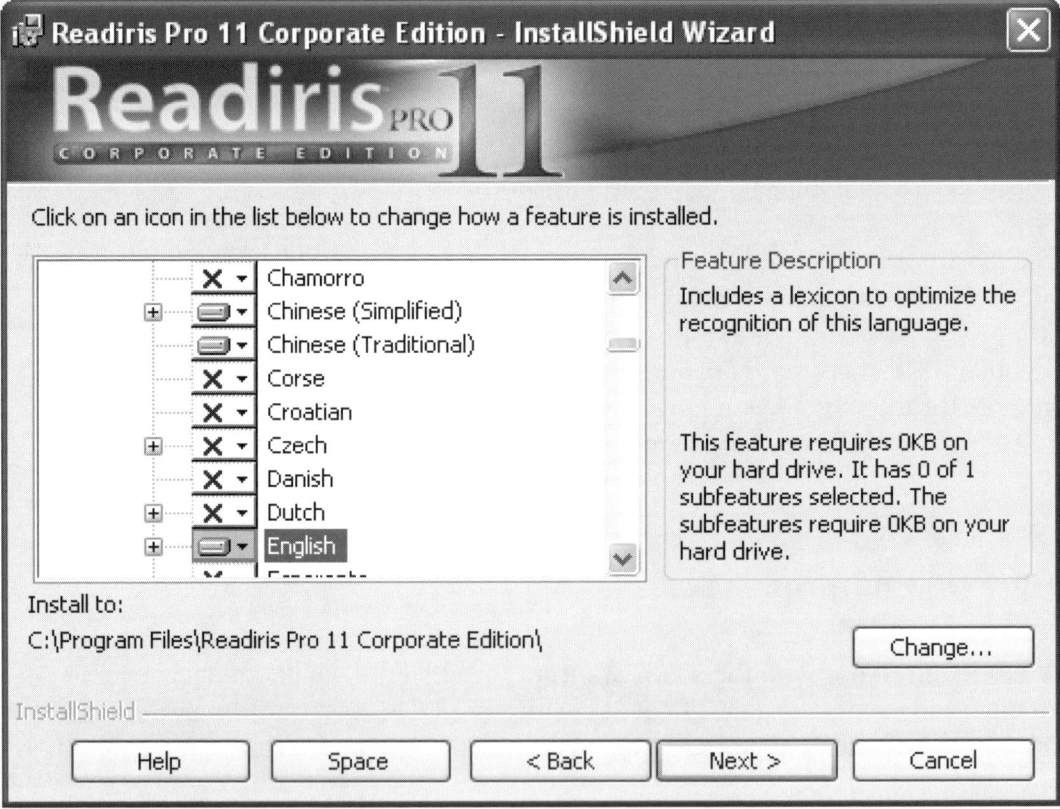

Figure 4.6 Readiris installation—select installed languages.

4.2.2 Using the OCR Wizard

The Wizard can be started by clicking the **OCR Wizard** button located on the top left corner of the Main window. The first time you use Readiris, the Wizard comes up automatically. You can disable this automatic starting up option from the first screen of the Wizard.

After the initial screen, the first question it asks you is to select the document type. You should click the **Text Pages** radio button for a regular document, unless you are scanning a business card, in which case you should use one of the other two options. The next step is to choose the image source. This can be either a scanner or an image file. Check both the **Detect Page Orientation** and the **Page Deskewing** selections to enable these options. The **Detect Page Orientation** option allows the program to rotate a page automatically when it is placed sideway or upside down. The **Page Deskewing** option is designed to straighten a page if it is not aligned properly during scanning. I experimented with these two options for a while. The first option worked in some situations, but the second one did not seem to have any effect whatsoever. As I have mentioned previously, always align the material as straight as possible on the scanner and do not rely on the software to fix such things. My suggestion is to just leave these options on, unless of course if they work against you. One of the situations I can think of to not have the **Detect Page Orientation** on is when several blocks of text are printed on a page and they face different directions. This rarely occurs, but I think it does get used once in a while. For example, the answer to a quiz is sometimes printed upside down.

If you chose the image source to come from a scanner, the next dialog will let you choose some settings for scanning. Click the **Change** button to open the **Scanner** dialog window and specify the scanner settings from there (see Figure 4.7).

This **Scanner** dialog gives you a simple and generic way of specifying scanning settings. You have the choice of using the settings in either this dialog or the TWAIN dialog provided by the scanner vendor. Click the **Configure** button to display a list of TWAIN sources and select the one you wish to use. Click the **Scanner Model** button to display a list of the make and model of scanners, and select your scanner from there. Since the Canon CanoScan 4400F I am using is not on the list, I just choose the generic model **<Twain> <other models>**. If you wish to use the TWAIN dialog provided by the scanner vendor to specify the settings, do so via **<Twain> <other models> (user interface)**. By choosing that, you will be presented with the vendor's TWAIN dialog window later on (before the scanning). If you choose this option, you don't need to bother specifying the other settings, i.e., **Resolution** and **Black-and-white/Greyscale/Color** from this window.

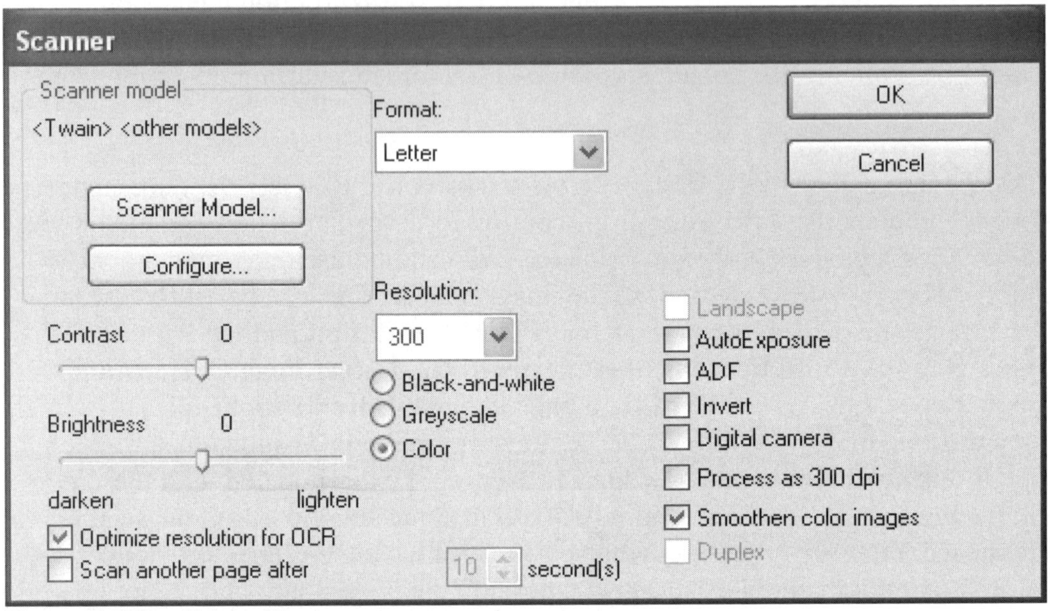

Figure 4.7 Readiris—Change scanner settings

There are a few interesting options you can find in the **Scanner** dialog. The **Digital camera** selection is used for giving special treatment for low resolution images. Since the resolutions of digital cameras are lower than scanners, the quality of the image will not be as good. When this option is on, the software will use special recognition routines that are optimized for low-resolution images. I performed a few experiments using images from a digital camera and also images scanned using low resolution, from 150 to 200 DPI. With the tests I have done, it is hard to conclude that turning the option on produces better recognition results. All I can say is that it did produce different results than without using the option. Another option is **Process as 300 dpi**. When this option is selected, if your image resolution is not at 300 DPI, the software changes its size accordingly to make it 300 DPI. For instance, say your image is scanned using the resolution of 150 DPI. This means a character of one inch height will contain 150 dots. After applying this option, 150 dots will now become only 0.5 inch, and all the characters will be shrunk in half. The **AutoExposure** option allows the software to adjust the color and intensity of your images automatically.

The next screen presented by the Wizard allows you to select the language(s) used in the source document. To make changes, click the **Change** button to open the **Language** dialog. Select either the **Chinese (Traditional)** or the **Chinese**

(Simplified) from the dropdown box, depending on the contents of the source text. You shouldn't worry about the **Secondary languages** selection. You can either leave this blank, or check **English** and/or **British English**. I found that with or without the selection of English in the Secondary languages section, the OCR always recognizes the mix of Chinese, English, and numeric characters correctly. You can consider English alphabets to be a subset of Chinese characters in here.

The next step asks you what to do with the recognized results. The outputs can be put to Windows Clipboard, saved to a file, or opened from an application. Readiris supports saving to various file formats, including PDF, RTF, HTML, XML, WPS, and TXT. Since some formats can preserve the original document layout and item properties, there are additional things you can specify in here. Click the **Change** button at this step to bring up the **Text Format** dialog (see Figure 4.8), and make changes from there.

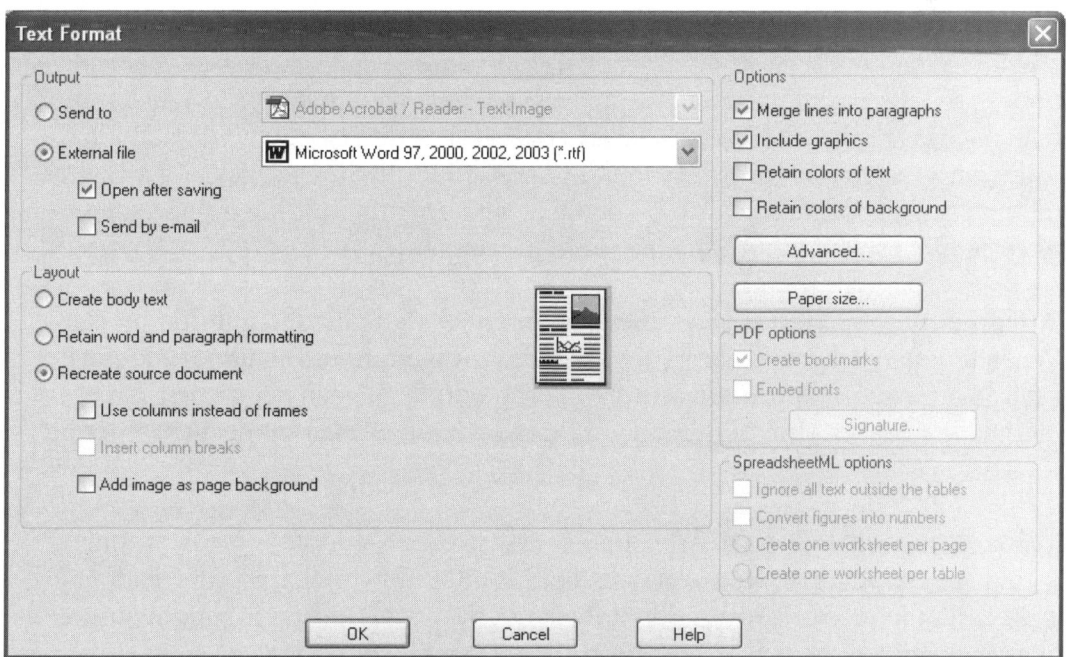

Figure 4.8 Readiris—**Text Format** dialog

The **Output** section allows you to specify the file format you wish to save, with an option to open it from the related application after the saving. You can specify the file type by using either **Send to** or **External file**. These two selections actually say the same thing. Basically, they come down to picking one of the output file types supported by Readiris. The **Clipboard** selection in the **Send to** list allows for sending the output to Windows Clipboard. For all other file formats, you will need to specify the filename of the output file later on.

The **Layout** section in the dialog lets you control the layout of the text in the output. The **Create body text** option allows you to create plain text with no formatting. The **Retain word and paragraph formatting** option preserves some format information such as fonts, sizes, etc., but does not retain the page layout. The blocks are written one after the other, and their relative positions on the page are not preserved. If you wish to preserve the original layout of a page, you must use the **Recreate source document** option. There are other advanced options here, allowing you to retain the text color or the background color, etc. I won't describe these advanced options because they are irrelevant for our purposes. Please refer to the Help manual of the product if you want to get more detailed information on these topics.

After these steps, the software will now start scanning if the source is from the scanner. If image files have been chosen to be the source, you must specify the names of the files in the next step, which shows an **Input** dialog. Readiris supports many different image formats, including TIF, JPEG, BMP and a few other less commonly used ones. The **Digital camera** and **Process as 300 dpi** options we discussed previously apply in the same way in here. To select more than one image file, hold down the **<Ctrl>** or the **<Shift>** key while making the selections. As you do this, the program opens multiple image files and arranges them in sequence automatically. The OCR results from multiple image source pages will be saved to multiple pages in the output file.

After the sources are specified, the program now starts the recognition process. When that is finished, the program asks you for the output filename, and then saves the recognition results to that file. The output file can be opened automatically according to the option that you have chosen in the **Text Format** dialog.

This concludes the Wizard steps. Unlike MaxReader 5 or other OCR products from Chinese vendors, Readiris does not have the functions for proofreading or correcting the recognized results. It does not have a feature to highlight suspicious characters either. To do the proofreading manually, you will need to open the original image file and the output file (produced using the **Recreate source document** option) together, and place them side-by-side for comparison.

4.2.3 Using OCR Functions Manually

There are relatively few steps involved in using Readiris. Once you know what to do, you no longer need to rely on the Wizard. Doing these steps manually is much faster and gives you more controls.

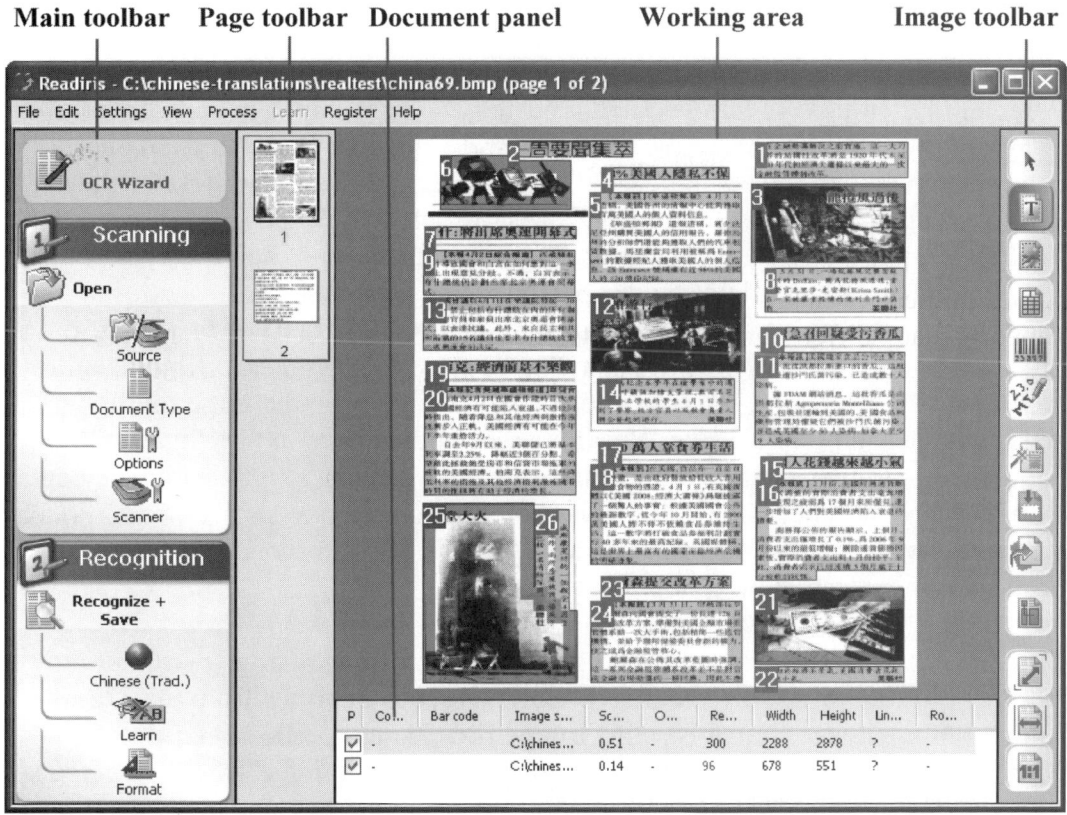

Figure 4.9 Readiris Main window

Figure 4.9 shows the Main window of Readiris Pro 11. First, make sure that all the settings are correct. From the **Settings** menu, select the **Document Type** submenu to verify the setting is correct. Select **Language** from the same **Settings** menu to verify and set the source language. The selection in the dropdown box should be set to **Chinese (Traditional)** or **Chinese (Simplified)**, depending on your source document. Check the **Page Deskewing** and **Detect Page Orientation** options from the **Settings** menu to let the software adjust for misaligned images, and those with incorrect orientation. Refer to the descriptions from the previous section for more detail on these two selections. Check the **Page Analysis** option for the software to automatically analyze the pages. The program will distinguish graphics from text and identify different text blocks based on different fonts, font sizes and running directions. When this option is turned off, you must mark each block manually before sending it for recognition. During recognition, only blocks that are marked (identified) are processed.

Select **Text Format** from the **Settings** menu to open the **Text Format** dialog. From there, you can verify or change the output file format and other related settings. Refer to the descriptions in the previous section if you need more information.

After all the settings are checked and adjusted, the next step is to open or scan the images. To use image files as the source, select **File**, then **Open** to open one or more files. You can choose multiple files by holding down the **<Ctrl>** or the **<Shift>** button while selecting. Another way to select multiple files is just to use the **File – Open** command repeatedly. The software assigns each file opened with a page number and adds it to the project. You can see a thumbnail view of all the pages in the project from the **Page toolbar** (see Figure 4.9). The **Document panel** gives a list of the image files with some basic information on each file, including the filename, image size, resolution, etc. Click a page from the **Page toolbar** to select a page and bring it to the Working area. Click a page in the **Page toolbar** using the right mouse button to rearrange the page sequence or to exclude a page from the project. Select **File – New Document** to start a new project from scratch. Be careful with this command because it will void all your work in the current project, without saving or giving any warning.

The **File – Acquire** command allows you to acquire images from a scanner. Before doing so, make sure the image source is set to **Scanner** from the **Main toolbar**. If the image source is set to **Image files**, then the **File – Acquire** command works the same as **File – Open**. Also, make sure the TWAIN source is set to the one that you wish to use, in case there is more than one image source on the system. This can be done by using the **File – Select Source** command.

Readiris allows you to enter multiple pages from a mix of image files and images obtained from the scanner in one project. All you need to do is to keep on adding pages using the **File – Open** or the **File – Acquire** command. Note that when you enter these commands for the second time, the program will prompt you with a dialog box saying: "Are you ready to delete the current document?" Answer "No" to tell the program to append the page to the project instead of starting a new project. Be aware that all the pages you opened must use the same Chinese character set, either simplified Chinese or traditional Chinese, not both.

When the **Page Analysis** option is turned on, the software will analyze the page and identify blocks automatically. Each identified block will be enclosed by a thick outline border. There are five different block types used by Readiris. A Text block is marked using the dark brown color. A Graphic block is marked in purple. A Table block is marked in cyan. A Bar code block is marked in green, and a Hand printing block is marked in blue. The Bar code block is irrelevant for our purposes, and the hand printing recognition is for Latin-based characters only. There is no description on hand printing recognition for Asian languages in the manual. I experimented with hand-written Chinese characters, and did not find any difference between using Text block and Hand printing block. Besides, the results from the recognition of hand-written Chinese character are too poor for our purposes.

To manually analyze a page or edit the automatic analyzed result, you need to select the page into the Working area by clicking it in the **Page toolbar**. To mark a block on a page, select one of the five block types by clicking its respective icon from the **Image toolbar** first. After the proper type is selected, use the mouse to drag the rectangle area where you want the block to be, and you will see the block enclosed with the respective color. If a region cannot be enclosed using a simple rectangle, you can draw multiple overlapping rectangles to cover it. To select a block, click the **Select window** icon first, and then click inside of the block. When a block is selected, you should see a thin outline drawn on the outside of the thick color outline. You will also see square-like dots on the corners and center on every side of the block where you can drag and change the size. You can delete a block with the **<Del>** key when it is in selection. You can change the block type by right clicking a block to bring up a pop-up window (Figure 4.10). After that, click **Window**, **Type**, and select one of the five types from the menu.

After all the blocks are selected, you can click **Recognize** from the **Process** menu for the software to start the recognition. When the recognition finishes, the program will present the **Output File** dialog for you to specify a filename to save the results. Check **Open after saving** option from there to have the associated Windows application open the file after it is saved.

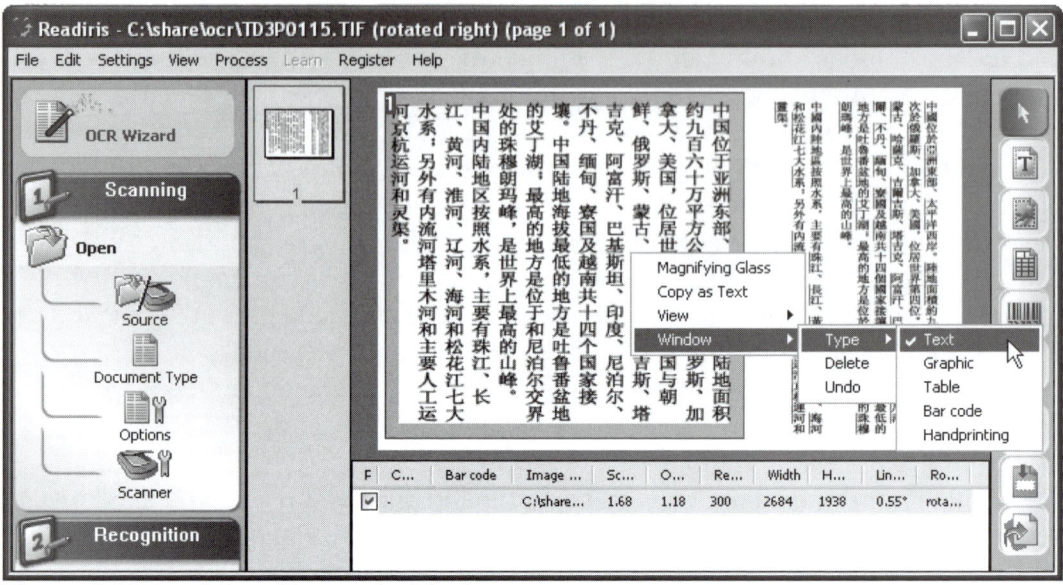

Figure 4.10 Readiris—Change the block type

4.2.4 Conclusion

Readiris was originally designed for Latin-based languages. It provided the Asian language recognition as an add-on product only in the last few versions. There are certain features from the core language product that are not available for Chinese. These include learning, speed-accuracy trade off, and hand printing recognition. I do not know where the program got its Chinese OCR engine from, but the recognition quality is reasonably good. My concern with this software is that it lacks the abilities to proofread and edit the recognized results. It also does not give you hints on characters that may be misrecognized. I believe the reason is because the software was not specifically designed for Chinese, and such functionalities are just not applicable for Latin-based languages.

On the other hand, this program has been updated more frequently than other products I have evaluated. It has a few features that are more advanced than its competitors. For example, it is able to handle inverted image automatically. It also has the option of preserving the original layout in the output file.

4.3 PenPower OCR Pro 3.1

PenPower OCR Pro 3.1d is the third Chinese OCR program I evaluated. From the information I got on the Internet, it seems they have not updated this software in quite a while, so I was a little reluctant to try it at first. However, one of my classmates from college had recommended it to me. The other reason is that the founder of the company is from one of the best colleges both in Taiwan and China —the Chiao Tung University (交通大學). Because this happens to be the same college that I graduated from, I decided to give it a shot.

Both the installation program and the application itself have UI (user interface) in both English and Chinese, so there is no problem of operating it by English speaking users. However, if you plan to use this product, let me warn you first that there is no English version of the user manual. Apparently, they did not target this product for non-Chinese speaking users.

I have carefully tested and documented in this book all the details a user needs to know for our purposes. I did experience a couple of minor technical difficulties that I need to share with you. Overall, I think this program is of very good quality and can stand up to any other competition. I do hope that they update this product a little more frequently, even though they do not plan on putting major investments into it any more.

4.3.1 Installation

The installation program of PenPower OCR Pro is located in the "ppocrpro" folder of the program CD-ROM. If the installation does not run automatically when you insert the CD-ROM to the CD-ROM drive, you can start it manually by running "setup.exe" in the "ppocrpro" folder. You can do this by selecting **Run** from Windows **Start** menu, navigate to the "ppocrpro" folder, and then run **setup.exe** from there.

Figure 4.11 shows the first screen of the installation program. Make sure the **Use English Message** is selected if that checkbox is accessible. For the Language section, just choose any language for now. Click the **Continue** button and then follow the instructions on screen to complete the installation.

Figure 4.11 Installation of PenPower OCR Pro

The program CD contains two applications: PenPower OCR Pro and PenPower OCR Pro Jr. PenPower OCR Pro Jr. is a less comprehensive version of PenPower OCR Pro. The setup program will install both applications and place them under the **PenPower OCR PRO 3.1** program group. The operation of PenPower OCR Pro Jr. is almost identical to PenPower OCR Pro. In this book, I will only cover PenPower OCR Pro.

Before starting the program, there is one important thing you must do first. PenPower OCR Pro 3.1d is an older application, and it does not use Unicode for displaying Chinese text. To use this program in our (US version) Windows system, you need to set an option in the Windows for it to support non-Unicode Windows applications. Depending on whether you are going to work on traditional or simplified Chinese characters, the selection in the **Language for non-Unicode programs** section (in Windows system) needs to be set accordingly. Please refer to chapter 3.2 for detailed instructions on setting this option. If this option is not set, you will get a message "Error Loading DLL file" when starting the PenPower OCR Pro program, and it will not run at all.

4.3.2 Using the OCR Wizard

Select **PenPower OCR PRO** from the **PenPower OCR PRO 3.1** program group to start the application. Figure 4.12 shows the Main window of PenPower OCR PRO. The program comes with a Wizard that gives step-by-step guidance with the processes. You should start by using this Wizard first. After you are familiar with the process, you can do things manually, which is faster and gives you more control.

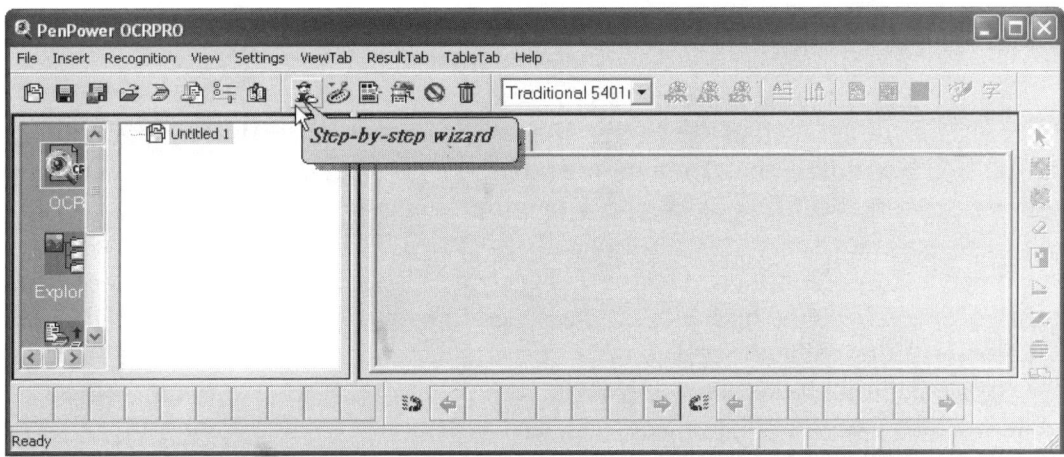

Figure 4.12 PenPower OCR Pro—Selecting the wizard from the Main window

Select **Step-by-step wizard** from the **Recognition** menu or click the **Step-by-step wizard** button from the **OCR Toolbar** to start the Wizard. The first step is to select the image source (Figure 4.13).

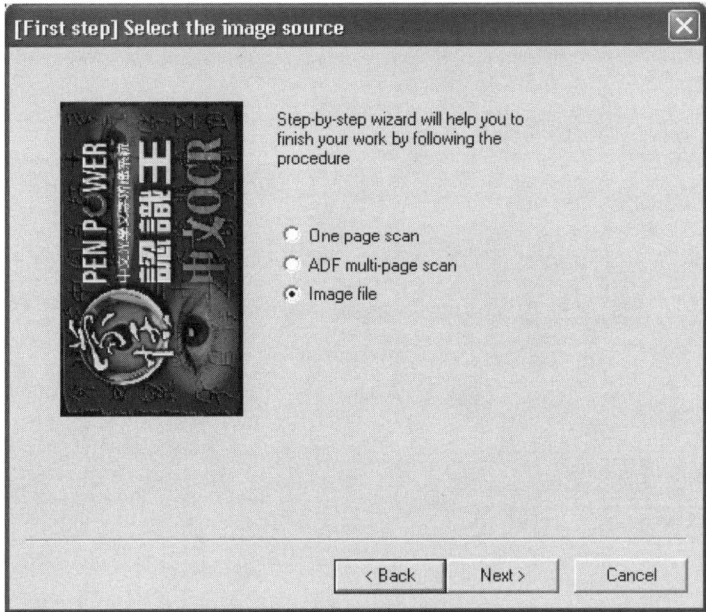

Figure 4.13 PenPower OCR Pro Wizard—Selecting the image source

Like other OCR programs, PenPower OCR Pro allows you to select inputs from a TWAIN-compatible scanner, or from image files. The **ADF multi-page scan** option is for scanning multiple pages from a scanner with ADF (Automatic Document Feeder). Note that some scanners may have a multi-scan mode that supports ADF even though they don't really have the feeder. When selecting the input source from a regular (non-ADF) scanner, you can only scan one page a time using the Wizard.

To open image files, select the **Image file** option on this page. When you do this, the next screen will be the **Open** dialog window. You can select multiple files by holding down the **<Shift>** or **<Ctrl>** key while doing the selection. PenPower OCR Pro supports many image formats, including TIF, PCX, BMP, JPG and a few other less frequently used formats. These are more than sufficient for our needs. However, I have noticed that the program has trouble opening certain kinds of color TIF files. When that occurs, it gives an "Error Loading File." message. To work around it, you can use GIMP to convert the TIF file to another format, such as BMP. Please refer to Chapter 3.7.2 for details.

In the next step, you need to specify the source character set, recognition result encoding, and some miscellaneous settings (Figure 4.14).

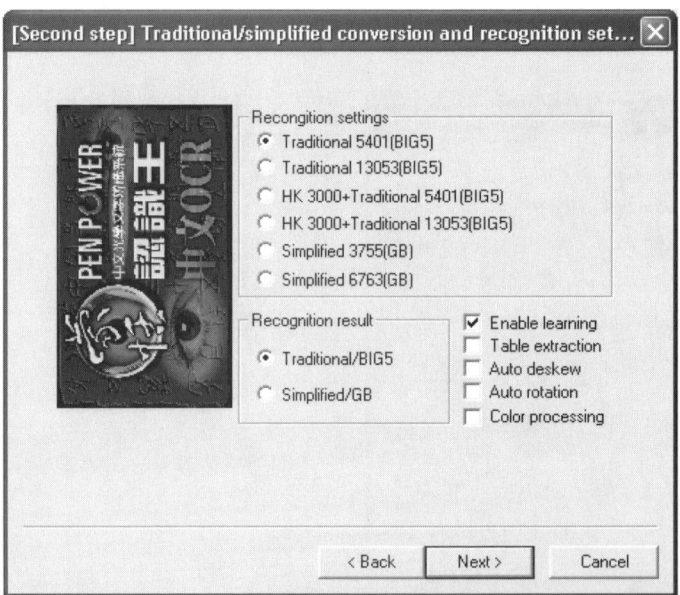

Figure 4.14 PenPower OCR Pro Wizard—Miscellaneous settings

The **Recognition settings** section specifies the character set that the OCR is based on for recognition. If the source document contains traditional Chinese text, select the **HK 3000+Traditional 13053(BIG5)**. If the source contains simplified Chinese text, select the **Simplified 6763(GB)**. The **Recognition result** specifies the character set (encoding format) used for producing the output. Choose **Traditional/BIG5** or **Simplified/GB**, based on the output format you want, which should normally agree with the source character set. This is a separate choice from the source (the selection in **Recognition settings**) because you can actually recognize documents written in traditional Chinese and then output the results with simplified text using the GB encoding, or vice versa. I do not recommend such a practice. At a later stage you may need to visually compare the recognized results with the original text image. It will not be easy when the recognized characters are written differently from their sources.

Be aware that the output text produced by this program is encoded in Big5 or GB, not in Unicode. When the **Recognition result** says **Traditional/BIG5**, it means the output character is in traditional Chinese characters, and the encoding system is Big5. The Big5 or GB encoded text cannot be opened directly by applications without setting up for non-Unicode support in the Windows system. Even though non-Unicode support in the Windows system takes care of the problem, you are limited by having to choose either traditional or simplified Chinese, but not both. To resolve this issue once and for all, you should convert the outputs into Unicode encoded text. We will cover this topic at the end of this section. For now, let us focus on getting the documents recognized.

There are a few other options selectable from the screen. The **Enable learning** option allows the corrections from the previous learning results to be applied to future recognitions. The **Table extraction** option allows the program to recognize text in tables and forms. The outlines of tables and forms are preserved when saving certain types of file (.doc, .xls and .htm). If the output goes to a pure text (.txt) file, then only the text contents are saved. If this option is not selected, any table or form on the page will be treated as graphics and not recognized.

Auto deskew allows the software to adjust for some minor distortions in the document due to misalignment. The **Auto rotation** option allows the OCR to rotate the document in 90 or 180 degrees when it detects incorrect orientation. The reason for using this option is that sometimes you place the document sideways for scanning because of the layout of the document. I did some tests with this **Auto rotation**, but found that it doesn't work too well. My recommendation is to not use this option. You should always place the document in its correct orientation on the scanner if it is going to feed to the OCR directly. With image files, use the GIMP image editor to rotate the image if it is placed sideways or upside down.

This program is able to open and recognize text from color images. The **Color processing** option will supposedly enhance its ability to extract text from color backgrounds, but its effectiveness is very questionable. Generally speaking, you should use color images only when all the text areas have dark text on simple and light colored backgrounds. In cases where the background colors are too complex, or the contrast is not high enough, it is better to manually convert the image into B/W before sending it for recognition (refer to the descriptions in Chapter 3.7.3 for details).

The next dialog screen asks you how you want the results to be saved. You have the choice of not saving, saving to a single file with multiple pages, or saving to multiple files. If you plan on copying the results to Windows Clipboard and using them directly from a translator program, you can choose not saving. When you do this, the OCR will stop after performing the recognition. You should also choose that if you plan to proofread and edit the results after the recognition, because proofreading is not a part of the Wizard's steps. When the Wizard process is done, manually do the proofreading and editing, and then manually save the results after that.

The other two options can be used if you do not plan to do proofreading. When those two options are chosen, the Wizard will show a **Save File** dialog window for you to specify the output file. You can give the filename, file type and a couple of options for the output file in that dialog window. PenPower OCR Pro supports saving to a few different file types. The TEXT (.txt) is the pure text file with no formatting. The WORD (.doc) is the Microsoft Word document type, and the HTML (.htm) is the Hyper Text Markup Language document. When Word or HTML file types are used, some of the format and layout information in the source is preserved. Such information includes text fonts, text sizes, graphics, tables, and the layout of blocks. The other output format is the Excel (.xls), the Microsoft Excel document type. It is commonly used for saving information in tables and forms.

When choosing the output file formats, you should use either text (.txt) or an HTML (.htm) if you plan to convert the output files into Unicode encoded files. The **Keep the original format** option preserves the block layout information. The **Auto wrap around option** is for removing the line feed information within blocks. When the source contains multiple pages, the output can be saved to either a single file with multiple pages or multiple files. If you choose to save the output as multiple files, the program will append a sequence number to the filename you provided to form new filenames.

This concludes the Wizard steps. After that, the OCR program starts the analysis and recognition automatically, and then saves the results to a file or files, if that is what you have chosen in your last step.

Figure 4.15 shows an example of the OCR program screen after the recognition. The program identifies different blocks in a page based on different fonts, sizes, layouts of the text. It shows results with different blocks and automatic assigned block names.

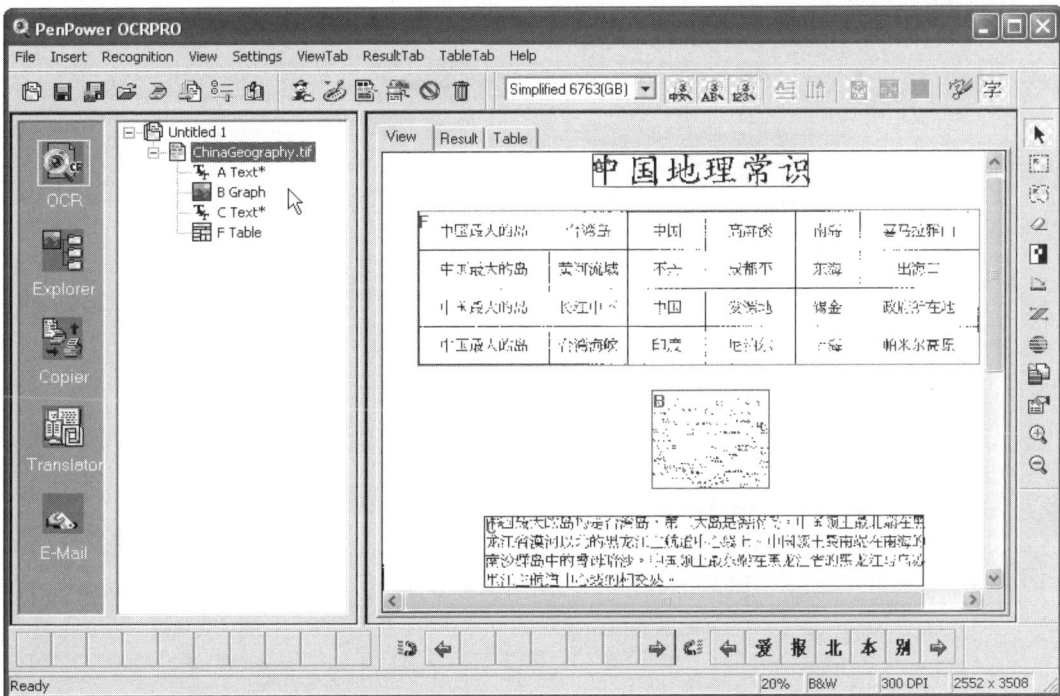

Figure 4.15 PenPower OCR Pro—image view with identified blocks

In this example, I have opened an image file with the name ChinaGeography.tif. The page contains two text blocks, one table and one picture. The first text block contains a large size text going horizontally in one row. The second text block contains small size text running horizontally in multiple rows. As shown in the **Tree view area**, the OCR program had created a project "Untitled 1" and placed the image file under the project. In this example, there is only one page "ChinaGeography.tif" listed under the name "Untitled 1." In case there are multiple images, you will see multiple pages listed underneath the project. There are four blocks listed under this page. Block "A" and "C" are Text blocks. Block "B" is a Graph block, and Block "F" is a Table block. In the Working area, you can see the identified blocks enclosed by colored outlines, with the block name shown at the top left corner. Text, Graph, and Table blocks are identified by blue, red, and green respectively. If a block is incorrectly identified, you can manually fix its attributes and then redo the recognition. I will describe the details of this topic in the next section.

Since we will be using some of the tools for verifying and editing the recognized results, let us become familiar with the layout of the Main window first (Figure 4.16).

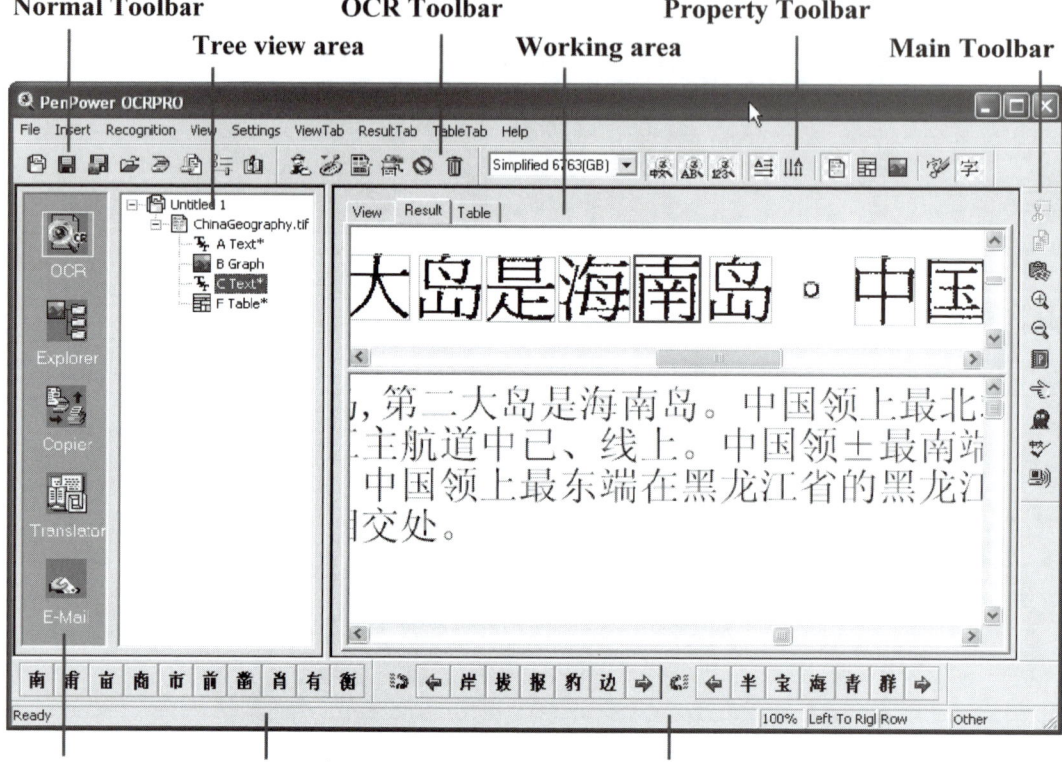

Figure 4.16 PenPower OCR Pro—Working area showing recognized results

Tools on the Main window are grouped into toolbars. You can hide an unneeded toolbar by unselecting it from the **View** menu. On the very left-hand side of the main window is the **Function Bar** that contains a vertical column of icons including **OCR**, **Explorer**, etc. This allows you to navigate to other functions provided by the software. The **Normal Toolbar** contains functions such as to open or save files. Naturally, the **OCR Toolbar** operates the OCR. The Main window has two panes in the center. The one on the left is the **Tree view area**, which contains a tree (hierarchy) view of the projects. The one on the right is the Working area, which contains three tabs: **View**, **Result**, and **Table**. The **View** tab shows the original image of the page. The **Result** tab shows the recognized result of Text blocks. The **Table** tab shows the layout and recognized contents of Table blocks. On the bottom of the Main window there are the **Candidate Toolbar** and the **Associated Phrase Toolbar**. These two toolbars are used for editing recognized results.

4.3.3 Proofreading

After the recognition, you can proofread the result and make changes if necessary. The program has provided tools for this task, but they are not included in the Wizard steps.

Proofreading involves comparing the recognized text with the original source and making corrections when necessary. This will not be easy for someone who doesn't know Chinese. As such, most of the information provided in this section is for the purpose of completeness only. In reality, you will not need to use most of the functions described here —at least not on a regular basis.

To verify the result, go to the **Tree view area** and expand one image (page) at a time under the project. In our example, you should click "ChinaGeography.tif" to select the page, and then click the small "+" icon in front of the name "ChinaGeography.tif" to expand the tree and get a list of all the blocks in there. The Working area shows the information related to the currently selected page. Select the **View** tab to see the original image with recognized blocks enclosed in rectangles. Sometimes you may find that the program has identified some blocks incorrectly or identified a dirty spot on the image as a block. To remove an extra block, select it from the **Tree view area** and press the **<Del>** button. In case you were wondering where the "D" and "E" blocks in the example went, you now know the answer.

Most of the work of using Chinese OCR software is in proofreading recognized text. To verify recognized results, you need to visually compare the characters in the source image with the result text. Select a Text block from the **Tree view area** and select the **Result** tab in the Working area (Figure 4.16). The program automatically separates the **Result View area** into two windows. Depending on the orientation of the text in the block, the program arranges the two windows on top of each other or side-by-side. In our example, the text goes horizontally, so we see two windows arranged on top of each other. The top window contains the source image and the bottom window contains the recognized result. As you select a character from either window, the software highlights the character in the image window by enclosing it with a red rectangle, and also places a blinking cursor at the corresponding location in the recognized window. One important thing in comparing these characters is that you need to set up the proper text Font for showing the results. If the traditional/simplified character set for the text font is used incorrectly, you may find characters in there that are totally wrong.

To select the text font for displaying in the recognized text window, you need to go to the **Settings** menu and select the **Fonts** from there (Figure 4.17). From the **Font** dialog, you need to find fonts that show the proper script—either CHINESE_BIG5 or CHINESE_GB2312, depending on whether you are showing traditional or simplified text. You should also pick a font that closely resembles the type face used in the source, so the characters displayed in the two windows can look alike. Please refer to Appendix C for more information on where to get and how to install additional Chinese fonts on your system. From this dialog, you can also change the setting of the text color, size, etc. to be used in the display.

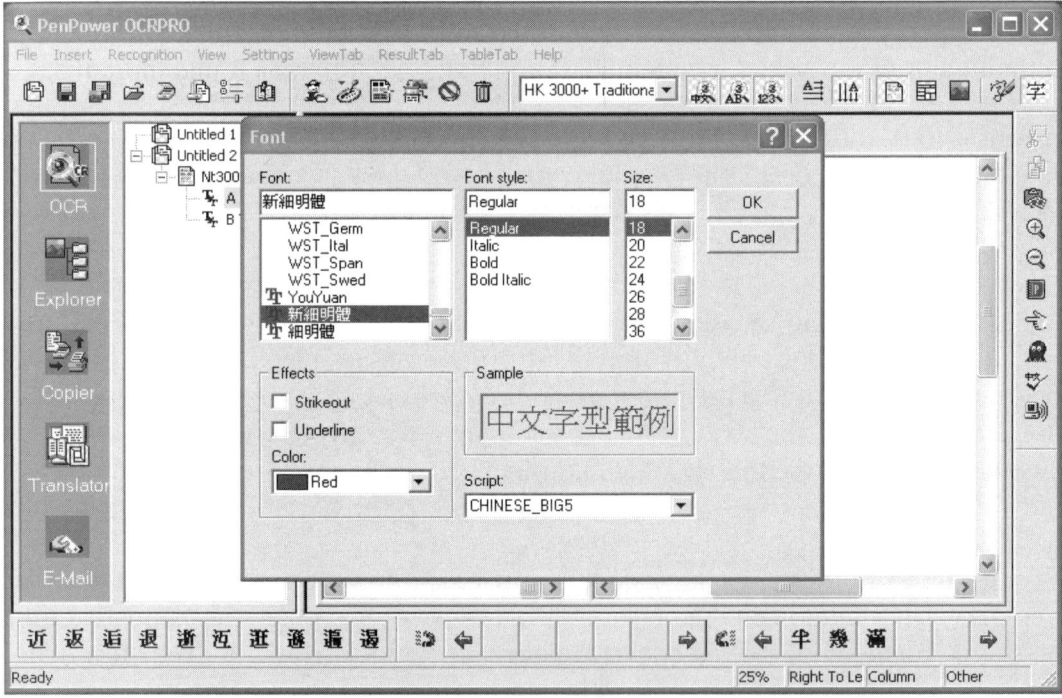

Figure 4.17 PenPower OCR Pro—setting the proper text font for displaying text

As you navigate through each character in the Working area, a list of replacement candidates for the recognized character will appear in the two toolbars located at the bottom of the Main window. The **Candidate Toolbar** contains the recognized character and a list of similar looking characters. The **Associated Phrase Toolbar** has two parts: the pre associated and the post associated. When we say two characters are "associated," we mean that they form a valid Chinese word when used together. Whenever you highlight one character in the Working area, the selected character is the current character. The character ahead of the current one is the previous character and the character behind it is the next character. When looking for associations, the software assumes that the previous and next characters are correct at their positions. Based on this assumption, it will look for all the Chinese words from its dictionary and come up with a list of characters that may possibly fit the current position. This is how the list of associated characters is derived. In our example in Figure 4.16, the currently selected character is 南 and the previous character is 海. There are a number of characters that will form meaningful words when they are used after the character 海. These words include 海岸, 海拔, 海报, 海豹 and 海边. As such, the **Pre Associated Phrase Toolbar** displays the characters 岸, 拔, 报, 豹 and 边. The **Post Associated Phrase Toolbar** works in a similar way, but is for the association with the character after the current selected one.

The arrow-shaped icons in the **Associated Phrase Toolbar**s are for scrolling through the lists of candidates. In our example, the software has found more than five characters that can be associated with the previous character, but it only has enough space to show five at a time. To display more characters from the list, click on the two arrow icons to scroll through the list. When you spot an incorrectly recognized character during the comparison, if the correct character appears in these toolbars, you can click it from there to replace the misrecognized one.

Proofreading a Table block is similar to what we have described above, except that you will be using the **Table** tab instead of the **Result** tab in the Working area.

A very important note is that the "support non-Unicode" Windows system setting needs to match the character set you are using, otherwise the characters in the **Candidate Toolbar** and the **Associated Phrase Toolbar** will not show up correctly. When reading traditional Chinese characters, you need to make sure the "support non-Unicode" Windows system setting is set to traditional Chinese, and vice versa. Refer to Chapter 3.2 for detailed instructions on adjusting the "support non-Unicode" Windows system setting.

4.3.4 Outputs

After all the misrecognized characters are corrected, you can highlight a block of text and click **<Ctrl> C** to copy the output to Windows Clipboard, and use it directly from a translation program. You can also save the results by selecting

Save Document from the **File** menu or clicking the **Save recognition results** button from the **Normal Toolbar**. There is one thing you need to know before proceeding with the file saving. The files produced by this program contain characters encoded in Big5/GB instead of Unicode. To use such files in other applications, you will always need to set the "support non-Unicode" Windows system option to the matching code (either Big5 or GB, but not both). To resolve this problem once and for all, you can convert the files generated from this program into Unicode encoded files. Once doing that, you no longer need to rely on the "support non-Unicode" Windows setting to handle the Big5/GB coding. You can even have files containing both simplified and traditional Chinese characters.

To convert files into Unicode, save the results to either a text (.txt) file or an HTML (.htm) file and then use the conversion software (Internet Explorer) to convert the file into a Unicode encoded text or HTML file. You cannot save the output as a Microsoft Word (.doc) or Excel (.xls) document file because Internet Explorer is not able to open these files.

There is one last trick concerning saving the output files. This is about a defect in the PenPower OCR Pro program. This defect affects the HTML file with GB encoding. In Chapter 3.3 when talking about HTML files, we looked at the encoding method meta tag in HTML. This is a meta tag for the web browser program to automatically determine the encoding method used in the HTML file. PenPower OCR Pro has a defect: it always puts the "big5" tag in the HTML file, regardless of the actual encoding method. To work around this problem, just remember that when you open a GB encoded HTML file from the web browser, you need to manually select the encoding method to use "GB."

For more information on the conversion process, the encoding tags, and the manual selection of encoding methods, please refer to Chapter 3.3.

4.3.5 Using OCR Functions Manually

Now that you are familiar with the operation of the program, let's look at ways of doing things manually. This will be faster, and gives you more control than using the Wizard. Here are the basic steps to follow:

Step 1: Adjust the OCR settings

Select **Options** from the **Settings** menu or click the **Options** button from the **Normal Toolbar** to open the **Options** dialog. You have seen most of these items in the previous section. The selections from the **learning correction** tab are for applying the corrections to use in other places in the future. When the **Enable learning** option is checked, a correction made to a misrecognized character will be learned by the software and used at other places. When the **Current block** in the **Scope** section is selected, the software will apply its current "lesson" to other places within the block. In this case, the **Direction** option specifies whether this is going to apply to the characters before or after the current position.

It is important to make sure that the traditional/simplified character set selection in the **Recognition settings** and the **Recognition results** sections match what you have in the source document. They also need to agree with the "non-Unicode" Windows system setting, as well as the selected text font in the **Font** dialog.

The **Thumbnails** tab is for adjusting the thumbnail icon size when in Explorer mode. This is irrelevant to the OCR process.

Step 2: Add pages to the project
When you first start the program, a new project "Untitled 1" is added automatically. Select that project from the **Tree view area** and click the right mouse button to open a pop-up menu (Figure 4.18). Select **Open Image File** to open from a file or select **Acquire** or **ADF Acquire** to acquire images from scanner. After a page is opened or acquired, it will show up in the Working area, and its name will be added under the project in the **Tree view area**. For scanned pages, the software will assign names to them automatically. Repeat this step to add more pages as needed. You can drag the pages around in the **Tree view area** to rearrange their sequences.

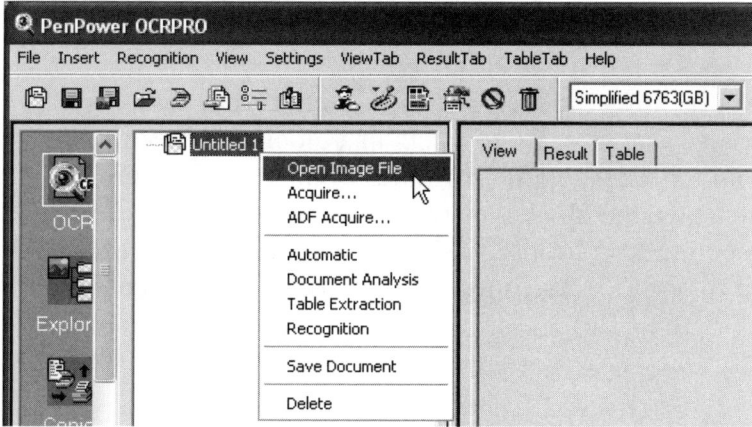

Figure 4.18 PenPower OCR Pro—Pop-up menu for adding image sources to a project

Step 3: Analyze pages

Click the right mouse button on the project name from the **Tree view area** to open the pop-up menu again. Select **Document Analysis** to allow the software to analyze all the images in the project. Note that if the selection is on a page or a block when you do this, the program will analyze the page or the block only, so make sure to select on the project. The program will identify different block types (Text, Graph, or Table) and distinguish Text blocks based on different fonts, sizes and printing directions. Click the "+" sign in front of an image name in the **Tree view area** to expand the tree view under each image. You can see a list of all the identified blocks under that image. For the example in Figure 4.19, as you expand the image "Geography1.tif" in the **Tree view area**, you see five blocks listed under it.

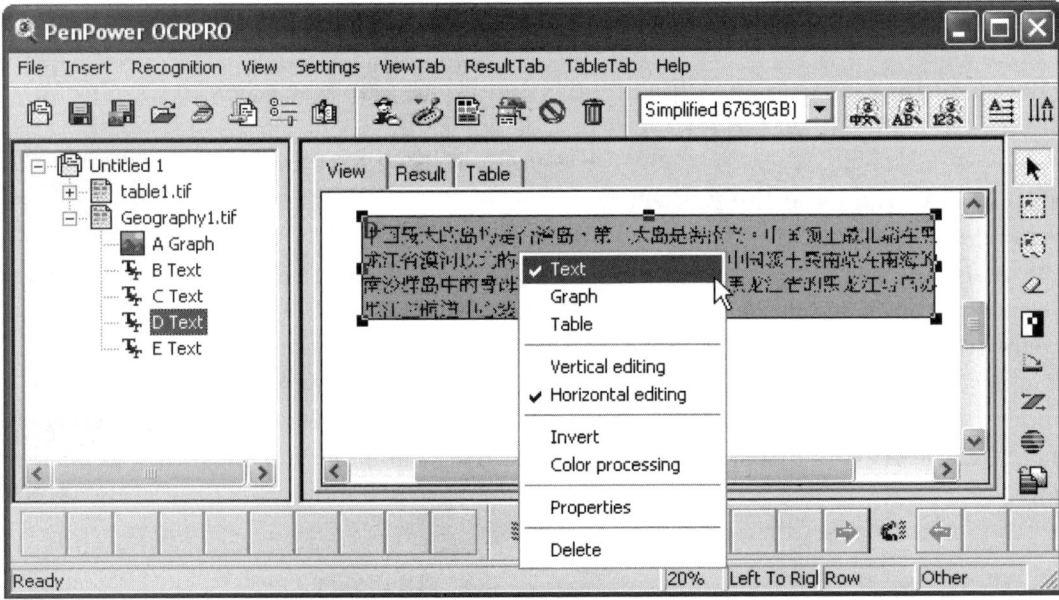

Figure 4.19 PenPower OCR Pro—Pop-up menu for changing block attributes

The Working area (**View** tab) shows the image of the selected page, with identified blocks enclosed in rectangles. Right-click on a block in the Working area to open a pop-up menu for adjusting the attributes of the block (Figure 4.19). From that menu, you can change the block type or the printing direction of a Text block. You can invert the color, do color processing, or delete the block. Select the **Properties** menu item to open the **Settings for block** dialog for specifying other details of the block (Figure 4.20).

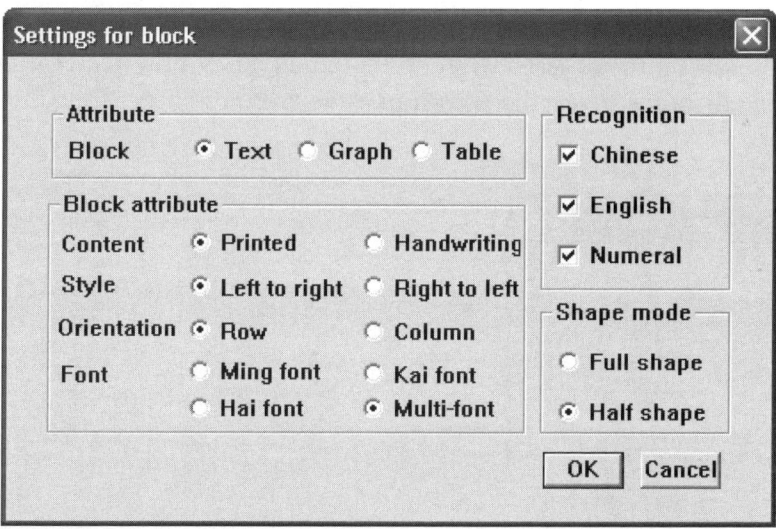

Figure 4.20 PenPower OCR Pro—Detailed block attributes

Most of the items in Figure 4.20 should be self explanatory. The **Font** section selects the printed fonts used in the source. You should leave the setting on **Muti-font** to specify that there are different fonts used in the source, and let the program determine that. The **Shape mode** section is used to specify the encoding method for alphanumeric characters used in non-Unicode encoding. You should leave the setting on the **Half shape** selection.

You can manually add new blocks by using the **Select the rectangle block** or the **Select the polygon block** icon from the **Main Toolbar**. When using the **Select the polygon block** tool, click the vertexes around a polygon region, and then do a double click at the last vertex. You can change the shape of a block by dragging the nodes on its outline. When you add a new block, the program assigns a new name to it, and adds that under the page in the **Tree view area** automatically.

There is a **Settings for document** dialog window (Figure 4.21) that is similar to the **Settings for block** dialog. This dialog can be opened by clicking the right mouse button while selecting an image in the **Tree view area**. Most selections in here are the same as the selections in the **Settings for block** dialog, except these apply to the whole page. The **Attribute** selection (**Newspaper**, **Magazine**, and **Others**) is for compensation for image quality, with the assumption that the Newspaper printings contain more specks. For most situations you can just choose **Others**.

One last thing I would like to mention is that step 3 (analyzing pages) is not mandatory. You can skip this step and go directly to step 4 (recognition). As you do this, the software will do the analysis and then perform the recognition automatically. If the recognition result is incorrect due to analysis problems, you can come back to fix the attributes using the techniques described in here, then redo the recognition.

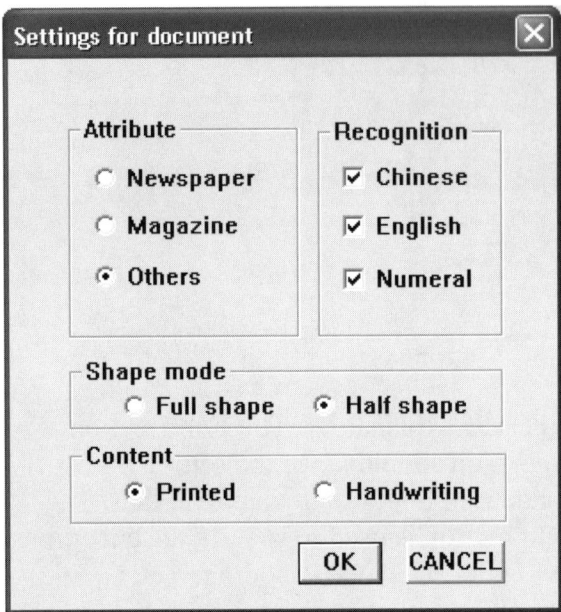

Figure 4.21 PenPower OCR Pro—document attributes

Step 4: Start the recognition
Click the right mouse button on the project name from the **Tree view area** to open the pop-up menu. Select **Recognition** to recognize every page in the project. Note that if the selection is on a page or a block when you do this, it will recognize the page or the block only, so make sure to select on the project. After the recognition, the blocks that have been recognized will be marked by an asterisk (*) in the **Tree view area**.

Step 5: Redo the recognition (if needed)
Sometimes you may need to adjust the properties of a block after verifying its results. In such cases, you need to redo the recognition. This can be done by right mouse clicking on the block from the **Tree view area** and selecting **Recognize** from the pop-up menu. When doing this, only the selected block will be re-recognized.

Step 6: Proofread the results
We have already covered this when describing the Wizard process in the last section.

Step 7: Save the results
This topic has also been described in the last section.

4.3.6 PenPower OCR Pro Translator

PenPower OCR Pro has a special translator function that you may find useful.
This tool is actually a Chinese to English dictionary. After a block is recognized,
you can select it from **Tree view area** and then choose **Translator** from the **View**
menu. This puts the software in Translator mode and the program will show the
Translator window, which has three panes (Figure 4.22).

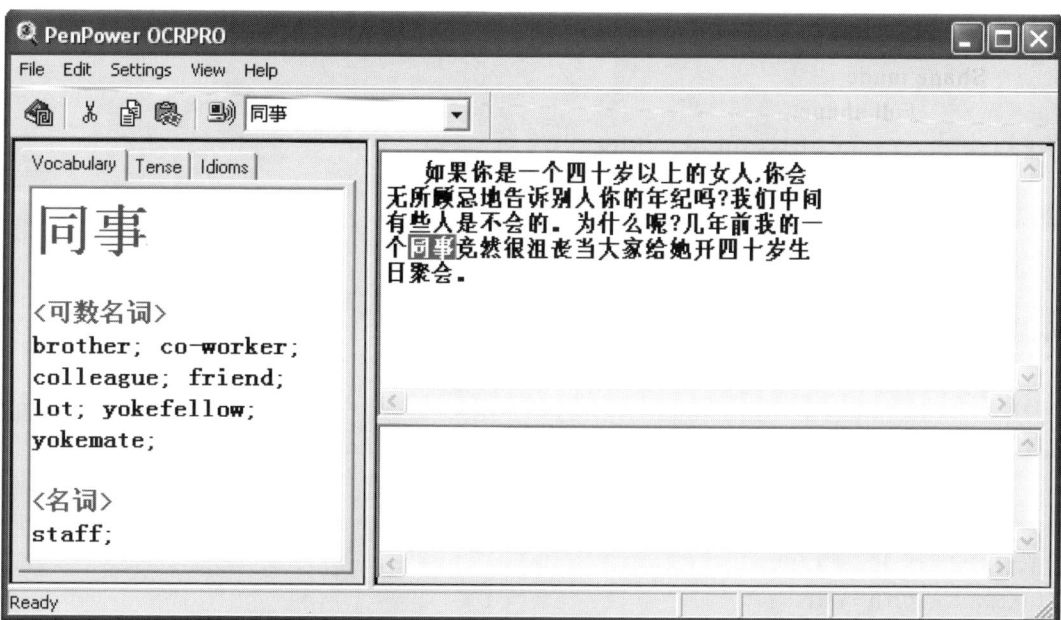

Figure 4.22 PenPower OCR Pro—Translator mode

The pane on the top right displays the recognized text. This area is just a regular
text box window. In essence, you can paste any Chinese text in here to use this
translator function, not just the OCR output. The left pane shows the lookup
results from the dictionary. As you click on or highlight a word in the top right
pane, the dictionary looks up the results and puts them in the left pane.

The translator can also translate a whole paragraph of text. It uses the bottom right
pane to display the translated result. The whole paragraph translation only works
from English to Chinese, so it's not useful for our purposes.

Choose **OCR** from the **View** menu to switch back to OCR mode.

4.3.7 Conclusion

PenPower OCR Pro is an older software product. Its recognition quality is compatible with other new Chinese OCR products, but a major inconvenience is that it is a non-Unicode program. It needs to use the "non-Unicode" Windows system setting for running in the US version of Windows, and the outputs produced by it are not in Unicode either.

It has a few minor problems, such as having trouble opening certain types of color TIF files, and producing wrong encoding tags when saving GB encoded HTML files.

In general, it is a full-featured Chinese OCR program, and the operations are smooth.

4.4 Other Chinese OCR Software

In the rest of this chapter, I will briefly go over some of the other Chinese OCR software products I have evaluated. I have displayed test data of these products on our supporting website (http://www.georgekung.com/ocr.html), but I won't give detailed descriptions here. These products either do not have the English UI (user interface), or have other limitations. Some of these products are also hard to buy outside Eastern Asia.

4.4.1 Microsoft Office Document Imaging

Microsoft Office 2003 and Office 2007 bundle a suite of software called Microsoft Office Tools. One of the tools in the bundle is called "Microsoft Office Document Imaging" (MODI), and it contains OCR functions. Unfortunately, the OCR in the US version of Microsoft Office only recognizes text from a few western languages including English, French, and Spanish. To have the Chinese recognition function, you need the Chinese version of Microsoft Office. The

Chinese OCR recognition engine in MODI comes from the company that makes TH-OCR (see Chapter 4.4.2), and the quality of the recognition is very good.

The OCR from the traditional and simplified Chinese versions of MS Office recognizes traditional and simplified Chinese respectively, but not both. Another deficiency of this software is that it does not have tools for proofreading and correcting results. If your images contain very simple text layout, and you are not planning on using the proofreading tools, then it works fine. This tool looks more like a teaser program to me. I suppose with such a setup, Microsoft can claim more functionality with its Office software, the OCR engine maker gets large exposure without losing actual sales, and end users get extra things for free, so on the surface, it looks like a win-win-win situation.

4.4.2 TH-OCR 9

TH-OCR (清华紫光 or 清华文通) is a Chinese OCR program developed by Tsing-Hua University (清华大学). This is also one of the best colleges in both Taiwan and China. Other than the stand-alone TH-OCR 9.0 program that I tried, the TH-OCR core software is bundled into many scanners and also marketed as OEM (Original Equipment Manufacturer) products under other names. The quality of the TH-OCR is among the top of all the Chinese OCR products.

Unfortunately, the end user application TH-OCR 9.0 does not have an edition with an English UI (user interface). The product is not targeted for international users, nor is it easy to buy from outside Eastern Asia.

4.4.3 Han Wang 6

Han Wang (漢王) is another of the numerous Chinese OCR programs I have tried. The version I tested is Han Wang 6.0. This OCR does not have an English UI. The quality of the recognition is average.

4.4.4 ShangShu 7

ShangShu (尚書) is yet another Chinese OCR product I have tested. The version I tried is ShangShu 7.0. This OCR does not have an English UI. The quality of the recognition is marginal.

4.4.5 Presto! PageManager 7

Presto! PageManager (version 7.15.14) is a program bundled with my CanoScan 4400F scanner. The OCR tool in there actually recognizes both traditional and simplified Chinese text as well as text from nineteen other languages. This is a very simple OCR with no option to select other than to choose the languages. It can get its input from a scanner or an image file and produce outputs such as an RTF, HTML, or PDF.

There are no functions for proofreading or correction, but it does mark suspicious characters. The flagship Chinese OCR product from Presto! is MaxReader 5 which I described earlier. This OCR tool in PageManager looks like a stripped down version with fewer functions and inferior recognition quality.

4.5 Improving OCR Results

OCR vendors like to advertise their products as having "greater than 9x% recognition rate," or being "the most accurate," "super accurate," etc. The truth is that OCR recognized results are usually not completely correct on a page. To ensure that OCR outputs are free from error, we need humans to verify and correct mistakes. This can be an issue for us, because we cannot rely on the translation software to find problems in its source (i.e., the output from OCR) for us. If the source is not perfect, then we may get unexpected results.

I recently encountered a translated result saying: "Chinese continent is new and free." This is very different from the "Mainland China news" I was expecting. When looking more closely into the source text 中國大陸新聞, I realized that the problem was that the OCR has misrecognized the character 聞 as 閑, because these two characters look alike. The character 新 means "new," the character 聞 means "hear," and the word 新聞 means "news." The character 閑 means "idle;"

"free," and there is no such word 新閒 in Chinese. The translation software has tried its best to come up with a character-by-character interpretation: "new and free."

While reading a translated sentence like this, you would probably have noticed that something was wrong, so in reality, such an error would not go undetected. I am using this example to show that even a very slight mistake from the recognized output can make the translated result completely unusable. To make the process work, you should do as much as you can to improve the recognition accuracy before sending the OCR output for translation.

When examining commonly seen problems from OCR, I came up with a list of reasons as to why OCR programs could give incorrect results. I also listed things you can do to avoid, identify or fix these problems.

1. Image quality issues
OCR software works well only when fed with very clean images, with high enough resolution and contrast between the text and the background. Refer to Chapter 3.5, 3.6 and 3.7 for tips on how to obtain good quality images.

2. Incorrect software settings
It is easy to end up with a few incorrect settings when switching back and forth between the simplified and traditional character sets, different scanning directions, etc. These errors are usually easy to identify because the recognized results will be mostly wrong and look very different from the image source. To actually find the incorrect setting and fix it can take longer, because some programs have settings at various places, and some settings are even in the Windows system. It will require familiarity with the programs to resolve these kinds of issues.

3. Problems with punctuation, alphanumeric or other symbols
Sometimes OCR is confused at places where Chinese characters are mixed with special symbols such as English letters, numbers, punctuation marks, etc. Pay special attention to the characters near these symbols when utilizing the proofreading tools. If alphanumeric or punctuation characters are mistaken as Chinese characters, you can manually remove the incorrect characters and type the alphanumeric or punctuation characters in there, which is a simple task. If it is the other way around, then it may be more difficult to fix. If you spot an error but are unable to correct it using the proofreading tool, you may need to adjust the software settings for recognizing alphanumeric characters to see if that will avoid the problem. Another trick is to exclude the symbols from the block, or to split the block into two at the trouble spot to steer away from it. If this also fails to work,

you may need to use the image editor (GIMP 2) to remove the alphanumeric symbols, but this is a last resort.

4. Incorrect Analysis

Sometimes, OCR may incorrectly identify the orientation of the printing. This can happen if spacing between two characters is about the same as the spacing between two rows (or columns). This is usually easy to detect once you familiarize yourself with the software program. The output will look very strange and sometimes contains only one or two characters, etc. Most software allows you to manually set the direction of the text in a block, so fixing this should be easy.

5. Problems with identifying characters

Sometimes, OCR may incorrectly identify two characters as one or one character as two. This kind of problem occurs more often than I originally thought, which is somewhat beyond me. My thinking is that printed characters are always enclosed by same-sized rectangles, and the spacing between them is also uniform. Different characters should be easily distinguishable even without knowing them. In reality, once in a while an OCR program stubbornly splits characters in its own ways, almost like it is showing off its ability to view these ideographs differently. Such problems can be identified using the proofreading tool but this is tedious, because you need to navigate through all the characters. Most OCR programs with proofreading ability also include some special tools to join or split characters.

6. Similar-looking characters

Some Chinese characters look alike and may be mistaken for others for various reasons. Sometimes this problem is caused by specks or faint printings in the images. This can also happen when the OCR misses part of the character, or includes a part from another close-by character. This kind of problem is harder to identify, because you need to do a character-by-character comparison between the result and the source image. You can utilize help from the proofreading tools to compare and replace characters from the candidate list, but navigating through all the characters is very tedious.

Figure 4.23 shows some examples of Chinese characters that can be easily mistaken because of their similarities. These are obviously just a small portion of similar looking Chinese characters, and not meant to be a complete list. It is provided only to show you how closely some different characters may look alike in Chinese.

人入
日曰
犬大太
己已巳
午牛
工土士
主王玉五
天夫夭元无
鳥烏
聞閗開間問

Figure 4.23 Examples of similar looking Chinese characters

7. Problems related to source image layout

Characters near graphics or page borders may sometimes be misinterpreted by the OCR. To fix this you can use the image editor (GIMP 2) to remove the graphics or increase the canvas size of the page. Some pages contain complex layouts of text blocks with text jumping from one place to another. This can cause confusion for the OCR during analysis and recognition. In some cases, you may need to manually do the analysis and mark or set the block types. Sometimes you may even need to use the image editor to move blocks around to simplify them.

8. Uncommon fonts

When text is written using some uncommon fonts, or when they are unusually fat or skinny, they may not get recognized correctly. The OCR will try its best to come up with something, but sometimes that doesn't help. Once in a while, when I encounter this situation, I compared the source image with the recognized characters and couldn't help but wonder where they came from. Sometimes, I just wish there was a setting I could use to tell the OCR to stop pretending that it recognizes something when it really doesn't have a clue. Anyway, problems like these are usually easy to identify, but there is no good solution to fix them. If the text font looks big, fat, or thin, try isolating and resizing that area using the image editor and see if that helps.

9. Issues with color images
Even though many OCR products can take color images, they usually don't handle them too well. The best practice is to convert color images into B/W before sending the file to the OCR for recognition. Refer to Chapter 3.7.2 and some earlier sections in this chapter for the discussion of color images.

4.6 Comparison of OCR Programs

In an effort to help readers see how different OCR products stand up against each other, I have conducted some basic tests to compare the quality of their recognition results. Please be advised that these data are merely suggestive. The comparison results are rudimentary, and serve as educational purpose only.

The results of these tests can be found on our supporting website at:

http://www.georgekung.com/ocr.html

5. Translation Software

This chapter covers the core product used for our process: the translation (and dictionary) software. After all the hard work spent setting up the system and preparing your materials, now finally comes the exciting moment of feeding the data to the translation software to view the results you are waiting for.

There are three kinds of translator programs: web-based, stand-alone, and the hybrid type. Web-based translators are usually offered free of charge by vendors who make translation or other language-related software for product demonstration. Sometimes they are offered by companies that provide professional translation services as a way of enticing businesses. They can also be put out by companies such as Yahoo! and Google, who offer a whole suite of services on their websites. Web-based translators are accessible by navigating to the websites that provide such services. You can either navigate to the URLs from the web browser directly or activate them from the browser's toolbars. These toolbars are add-on controls that get installed into your web browser. Both Yahoo! and Google have their own toolbars, allowing you to add the translation function. By using the toolbar, web-based translation is just one click away.

A web-based translator usually has two text boxes, one holding the source text and the other holding the translated results. To use it, copy the Chinese text from the source document and paste it to the source text box of the translator. After that, hit a "Translate" button to view the translated English text in the other text box. The number of characters allowed in the source text box is usually quite limited, so you can only translate a few sentences at a time. In addition to using text boxes, some translators allow you to enter the URL of a Chinese web page to translate the whole page. The translated results are displayed in a separate window. A special note: some of the "free" products are actually demo programs put out by vendors, with the hope that people will buy the software from them. Although I have categorized all of them as web-based translators, the demo products should be treated differently from truly free services, such as those offered on Yahoo! or Google. Depending on their purposes, I suppose we can make judgment on whether to use them on a regular basis.

The second type of product I call stand-alone or desktop-based translators. Instead of using them from a web browser, you need to install these products on your PC. One advantage of stand-alone translators is that you do not need an Internet connection to operate them. This can be useful when the source materials already exist locally in your computer, or when you plan to use a scanning device and OCR to get these materials. Another advantage of a stand-alone translator is that it is faster. For web-based translators, you need to send the source out to another machine on the Internet, wait for the translation, and then get the results back. One other thing about web-based tools is that you need to do things through the web browser, which usually has limited user interface (UI) functions. The stand-alone tools are usually more responsive and easier to use. They may also have special features such as integrating directly with other applications like word processors or e-mail clients.

Unlike free web-based translators, which usually take a one size fits all approach, stand-alone translators give you more control over handling the translation. It may give you options for adapting to different styles of materials. Some products include specialty dictionaries to improve translation accuracy when the contents in the source are related to some specific categories, such as business, medical, etc. Some translators even allow you to define your own dictionaries. Stand-alone translators may offer more choices of other things, such as the file formats for input and output. Technically, I should not say that the advantages mentioned in here are what stand-alone translators offer over their web-based counterparts. It is also possible for web-based translators to add such features in their products. In fact, the web-based translator from WorldLingo that I shall describe allows the use of specialized dictionaries as well. It just so happens that the web-based products I am going to discuss are either offered as free services or used for demonstrations. As such, you do not see too many fancy features included.

There is a third type of translator, which is a hybrid of web-based and stand-alone software. This type of tool uses its own user interface to interact with users, but the translation engine is located somewhere on the Internet. To do translation, it sends out the source text to a server that handles translation on the Internet and gets the results back from there to present to the user.

5.1 Yahoo! Babel Fish Translator

Yahoo! has a web-based translation tool named "Babel Fish." It is located at the following web address:

http://babelfish.yahoo.com

When navigating to this web page, you see the translator (Figure 5.1) displayed on your web browser screen.

Figure 5.1 Yahoo! Babel Fish translator

This tool can translate either a block of text or a web page. The usage of the tool is pretty much self explanatory. To translate a block of text, select the appropriate language option from the dropdown box under the text box first. In our case, you need to select either the **Chinese-simp to English** or **Chinese-trad to English**, depending on whether you are translating simplified or traditional Chinese text. You need to copy a block of Chinese text into Windows Clipboard from your source document, paste it into the text box, then hit the **Translate** button. After that, the tool will show another text box on top of the original text box and put the translated results in this new text box. There is a limit on the number of words you can put in the source text box for translation. For Chinese to English translation, you can enter a maximum of about 2,500 to 3,000 Chinese characters. When the number of characters reaches the limit, the translation results may be incomplete. To be on the safe side, it is better to limit the source characters to under 2,500 Chinese characters.

To translate a Chinese web page, you must use the controls in the bottom (**Translate a web page**) section on the screen. Select the appropriate language options from the dropdown box, enter the URL address of the web page to be translated in the one line text box, and then hit the **Translate** button. The tool will directly display the translated web page in the browser window. Graphics, tables, forms and layout information of the source page are cloned on the translated page. They may become a little displaced in some places, because it is hard to maintain the exact layout when Chinese text is replaced with English.

Entering web URL addresses in a text box is cumbersome. It would be easier to just navigate to a web page in a normal way, and press a button to activate the translation when it is needed. To allow for this, you need the Yahoo! Toolbar on your browser, with the Babel Fish button on it. If you do not have the Yahoo! Toolbar on the browser yet, you need to install the toolbar first by clicking the **Download Yahoo! Toolbar** link from the Babel Fish web translator page as shown in Figure 5.1. Follow the instructions there to complete installing the toolbar. After that, you need to revisit the Babel Fish web translator page. As you do that, the link in that page will now show **Add Babel Fish to your Yahoo! Toolbar**. Click that link and then follow the instructions in there again to add the Babel Fish translation button to the toolbar.

Babel Fish is a free, simple, general-purpose translation tool. It does not provide special dictionaries, and it lacks any customization functionalities. The translator is powered by the translation engine from SYSTRAN, a leading supplier of language translation software. SYSTRAN's website is located at:

http://www.systransoft.com

SYSTRAN makes its own translation software, and also has a web-based translation tool for demonstration purposes. I will describe them later in this chapter.

5.2 Google Translator

Google has a web-based translation tool just like Babel Fish. It is located at the following address:

http://www.google.com/language_tools

http://translate.google.com/translate_t?langpair=zh|en

The first URL address brings you a general form of the tool where you need to select source and target languages. The second URL address gives you the same tool with the language pair already set to **Chinese to English**.

Figure 5.2 shows the screen of the Google Translator. This is almost identical to Yahoo! Babel Fish. It can translate either a block of text or a web page. One convenient thing about this tool is that you don't need to choose between the simplified and traditional character set. It not only automatically identifies the character set in the source, but also allows for the mixing of characters from both sets. This should really become a standard feature for the next generation of Chinese OCR software and translation software.

Figure 5.2 Google Translator

The usage of the tool is pretty much self explanatory. To translate a block of text, first make sure the **Chinese to English** language option is selected from the dropdown box under the text box. You need to copy a block of Chinese text into Windows Clipboard from your source Windows application, and paste it into the text box before hitting the **Translate** button. The tool will display the translated results in the right-hand area. The tool handles up to roughly 10,000 source characters at a time, which is more than enough for regular needs.

One special note about Google Translator is that it always treats a new line as the beginning of a new sentence. You need to make sure not to have extra new line characters in the text. Some OCR programs may add new line characters to the output, to make it appear the same as the source document. Remember to remove them if you wish to use Google Translator.

To translate a Chinese web page, make sure the **Chinese to English** language option is selected from the dropdown box in the **Translate a Web Page** section. Enter the URL address of the web page in the single-line text box in that section, and then press the **Translate** button. The tool will display the translated web page directly in the browser window. Graphics, tables, forms and layout information of the source page are cloned on the translated page. They may become displaced in some places because it is hard to maintain the exact layout when Chinese texts are replaced with English.

As with Babel Fish, entering web URL addresses in the Google Translator's text box is cumbersome. It would be easier to just navigate to a web page in a normal way, and press a button to activate the translation when it is needed. To allow for this, you need the Google Toolbar on your browser, and have the Translation button on the Toolbar. If you do not have the Google Toolbar on the browser yet, you need to install it first. The Google Toolbar can be found on the following website:

http://toolbar.google.com

Follow the instructions there to install the Google Toolbar. At the end of the Toolbar installation, you will see a link that says **Add buttons to the Toolbar**. Follow that link to find the button for the Translation Tool, and add that button to the Toolbar. After the button is added, select **Settings** on the Toolbar, select **Options**, and check the checkbox of the Translation tool to enable it on the Toolbar. The **Translate** button on the Google Toolbar is actually a pull down menu. Select the **Translate Page into English** from the pull down menu to translate the page you are currently viewing into English. The other item in the menu is a toggle switch for enabling or disabling the WordTranslator. The WordTranslator is a mouse-over dictionary tool that gives you descriptions of a word when your mouse is placed over a word in the web browser. It works only from English to Chinese, and not the other way around. As such, this tool is not useful for our purposes.

At the time this book is written, the Chinese to English translator is in the Beta version. From the stories I have read on the Internet, it appears that Google originally used the translation engine from SYSTRAN, but now they have decided to have their own translation engine.

The impression I got from using the tool is that it does not give consistent results. At times, it gives excellent translations, but other times it is substantially off. I figure they are in the process of improving the core engine as well as building up the dictionaries, which may take some time to complete.

5.3 WorldLingo Translator Website

WorldLingo Translations LLC makes translation software. They also provide translation-related services, such as human translation and localizations of software. The company's web-based demonstration tools showing its translation software are at the following URLs:

http://www.worldlingo.com/en/products_services/worldlingo_translator.html

http://www.worldlingo.com/en/websites/url_translator.html

http://www.worldlingo.com/en/products/email_translator_form.html

The first two links are the Text Translator and the Website Translator respectively, which are similar to the Babel Fish Translator and the Google Translator. The third tool is an Email Translator. It lets you translate a block of text and send the translated results by e-mail. These three tools are integrated into a single page and the three different functions are selectable from a tab control (Figure 5.3).

One special feature of the translation tools at the WorldLingo website is that they have an advanced option called **Subject Glossary**. Here, you can pick from one of twenty categories to optimize translation results. The twenty categories are: Automotive, Aviation/Space, Chemistry, Colloquial, Computers/IT, Earth Sciences, Economics/Business, Electronics, Food Science, Legal, Life Sciences, Mathematics, Mechanical Engineering, Medicine, Metallurgy, Military Science, Naval/Maritime, Photography/Optics, Physics/Atomic Energy, and Political Science.

Click the **Text Translator** tab to translate a block of text. Select **Chinese Simplified** or **Chinese Traditional** from the dropdown box on the left for the source language. Select **English** from the dropdown box on the right for the target language. Copy a block of Chinese text into Windows Clipboard from your source Windows application, paste it into the text box and then hit the **Translate** button. The tool will add another text box on top of the original one and put the translated results in the new text box. The maximum number of source characters it allows for is only 150, which is very limited.

Click the **Show Advanced Options** link to access the **Subject Glossary** dropdown box for the selection of a special category. The default selection is set to **General**, which does not specify any category. You can pick from one of the twenty categories that you feel appropriate for the contents of your text. This supposedly improves the accuracy of the translation, since the translator will use a dictionary to look up special words used in that category.

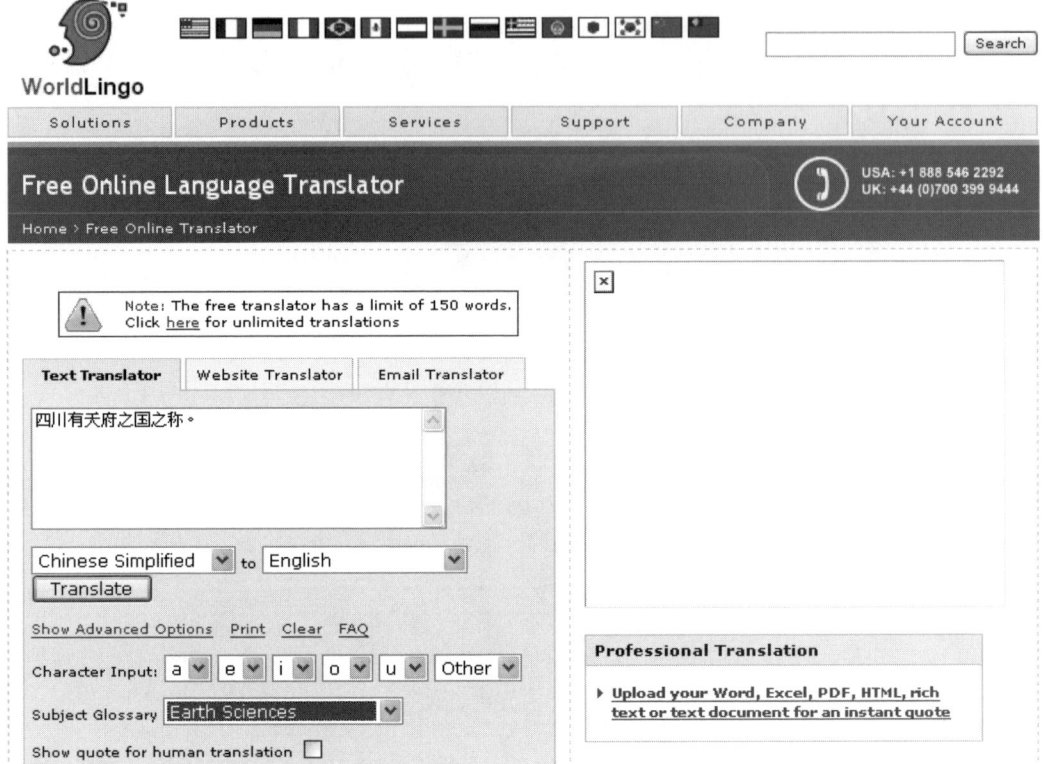

Figure 5.3 WorldLingo Free Online Language Translator website

The operations of the Website Translator and Email Translator are self-explanatory, so I am not going to give more descriptions here. The tools in this website are provided for demonstration purposes only. The Website translator only translates a few hundred characters on a web page, which is way too ungenerous. When testing with the home pages of Yahoo! China and Yahoo! Taiwan, it only translated a small portion of those pages into English and left others in Chinese, which looks funny. The worst thing is that on some pages, none of the characters in the URL links are translated. I was unable to determine which parts of the untranslated text have been left due to the actual limitation of the tool as opposed to the limitation set for demonstration. I do not consider this demo version of the tool satisfactory for the purpose of a valid demonstration, let alone of any practical use for our application. As for the Email Translator, we will not require such a function.

5.4 Microsoft Word Integrated Translator

The translation function from MS Word 2003 (including Word 2007) uses a hybrid approach. The application integrates a web-based translation service provided by WorldLingo Translations LLC. When a user initiates the translation from the Word application, the source text is sent to the translation server over the Internet, gets translated, and then sent back for display.

To use this translator, you will need the (US version) of Word 2003 or 2007. I am assuming that readers who wish to use this already have the application installed, so I am not going to describe it here. To get started you can use Word to open a Word document or a plain text file with Chinese text. The other common way is to start a new document, copy Chinese text from the source application to Windows Clipboard, and then paste the text into the new document.

When opening a plain text file, Word will ask you to confirm the encoding method of the file (Figure 5.4). Most of the time, Word is smart enough to select the correct encoding method, so all you need to do is to click the **OK** button to accept.

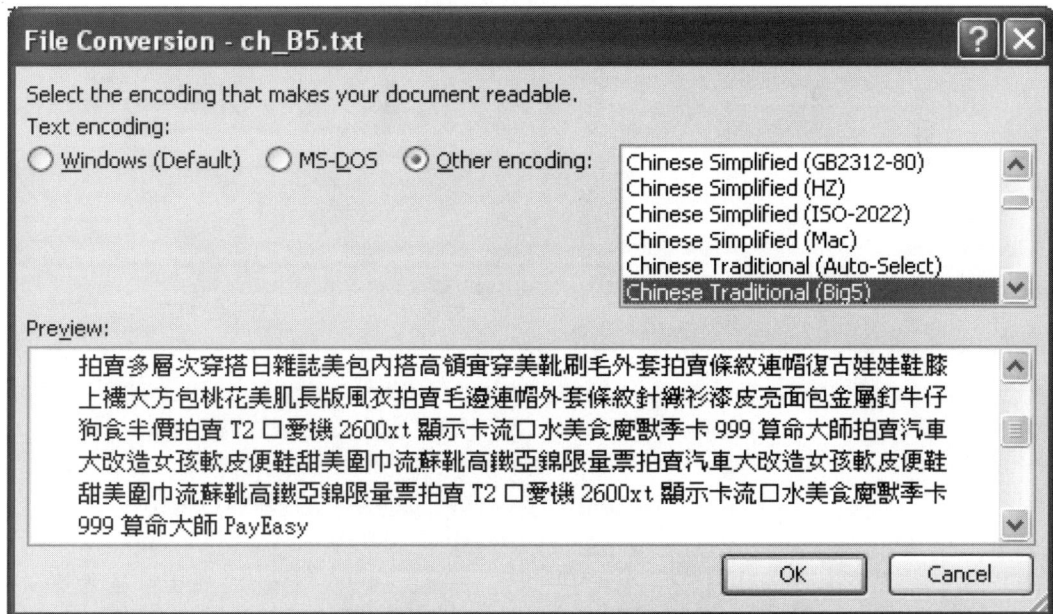

Figure 5.4 Microsoft Word—Confirm text encoding method

After the source text is opened in the Word window, select **Tools** from the main menu, select **Language**, and then select **Translate** to display the Translation window (Figure 5.5).

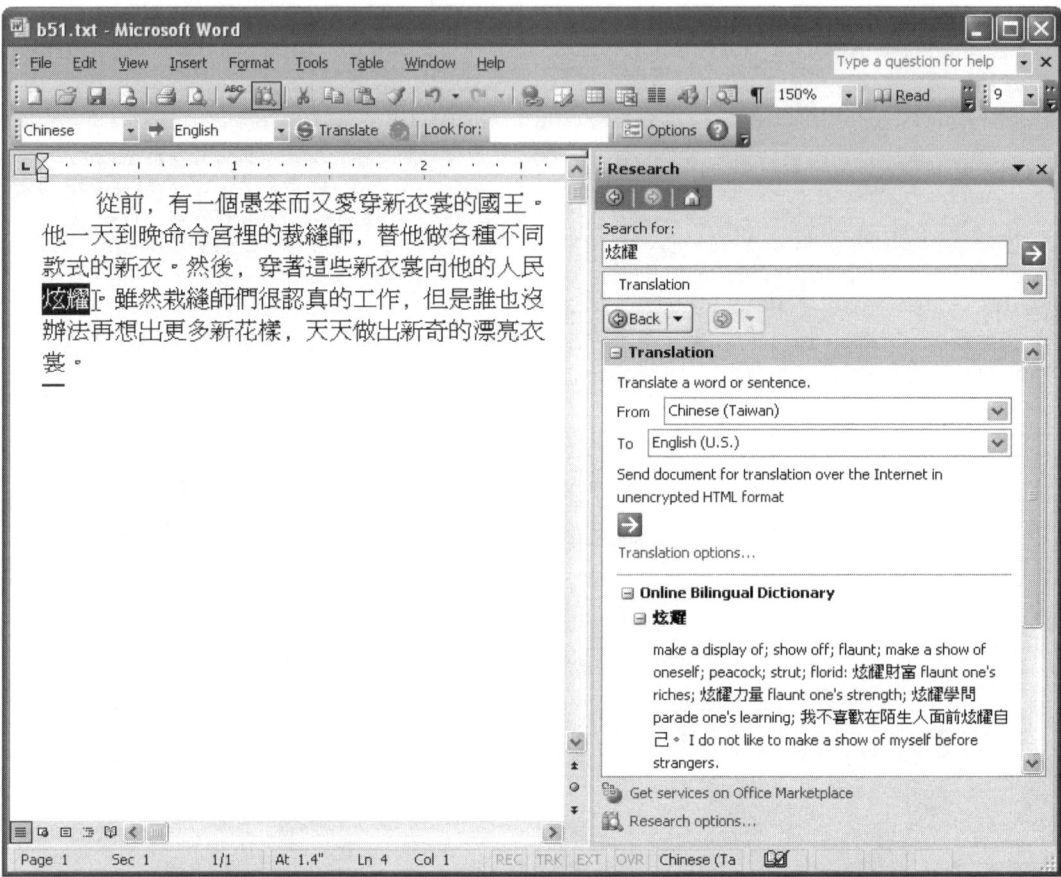

Figure 5.5 Microsoft Word 2003—**Translation** window

Select the appropriate source and target language pair from the two dropdown boxes first. Translation can be performed on a word, a sentence, or the whole document. To translate a word or a phrase, highlight these characters by selecting them using the mouse, hold down the **<Alt>** key and then click the mouse button. The selected characters will appear in the **Search for** text box, and the translated results will appear in the bottom of the **Translation** window. If no character is selected, as you hold down the **<Alt>** and click on a character, the software will translate the closest phrase or sentence near the character.

To translate the whole document, click the arrow-shaped icon above the line of text that says "Translation options…" The software will translate the whole document, return the results as an HTML file, and open that in a web browser window (Figure 5.6).

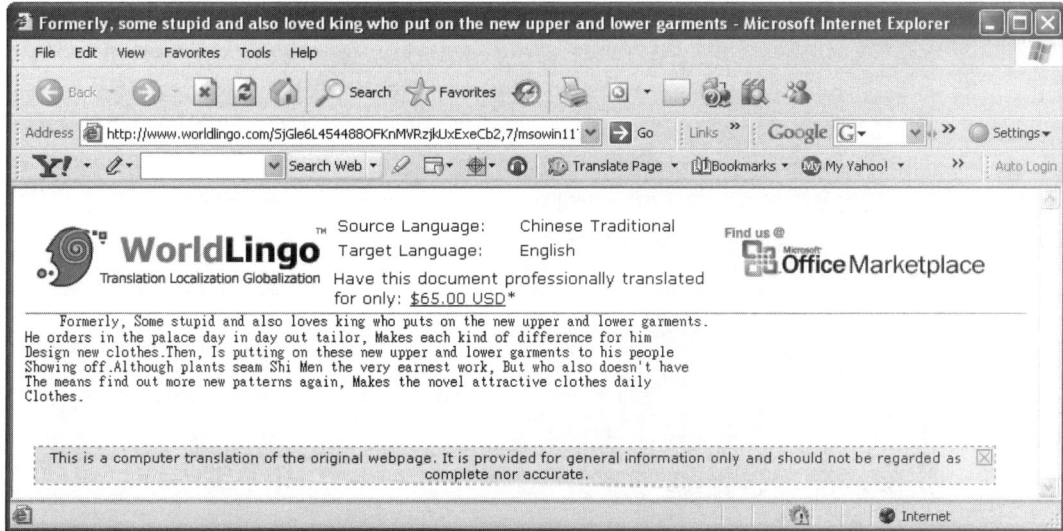

Figure 5.6 Microsoft Word—Whole document on-line translation

There is a problem with using the translation function in the MS Word. When the non-Unicode support is set up in the Window system to handle Chinese (see Chapter 3.2 for details), the translation function in MS Word will no longer work. The non-Unicode support feature is provided by Windows to allow non-Unicode applications to show Chinese texts under Windows. Normally, it should not interfere with Unicode applications, but in this case it actually makes the translated results coming back from WorldLingo show up totally wrong. To get around this, you need to make sure **English (United States)** is selected in the non-Unicode display setting for your Windows system when you need to use the translator function in Word.

5.5 SYSTRAN Translator Website

SYSTRAN Software, Inc. is a leading supplier of language translation software. The company has an entire family of translation-related products. Yahoo! Babel Fish is powered by the translation engine from SYSTRAN. You can find more information about their products from their website at:

http://www.systransoft.com

SYSTRAN has a website demonstrating its translator located at:

http://www.systransoft.com/desktop.html

The demonstration tool (Figure 5.7) operates in two modes: Text mode that translates a block of text, and URL mode that translates a web page. You can switch between the two modes by pressing the **Text** or the **URL** button. Specify **Chinese** as the source language in the dropdown box on the left, and **English** as the target language from the dropdown box on the right. Similar to Google translator, this tool allows for the mixed use of simplified and traditional Chinese characters.

Figure 5.7 SYSTRAN demonstration website

In Text mode, paste the Chinese text in the text box on the left and the translated results appear automatically in the text box on the right. In URL mode, enter the URL address of a web page to the one line text box area where it says "http://" and then hit the **Translate** button. The software will start translating and then put the translated results into a new browser window.

In Text mode, the maximum number of source characters allowed is around 500. The other limitation is that the translated results only appear in the target text box for about twenty seconds. After that the target text box starts to show advertisements like "Special Offer!" To see the translation again, you can always repeat the process. A better way is to copy the contents in the target text box to Windows Clipboard before it disappears, and paste it into Notepad to view the results.

5.6 SYSTRAN Translator 6

SYSTRAN Translator is a stand-alone language translation software product. Version 6 is the latest release, introduced in 2007. The product has five editions, going from low to high: Web, Home, Office, Business, and Premium. In addition to the different editions, they also market the products with different "language packs." To translate Chinese, you need to get either the Asian Pack (includes Chinese, Japanese, and Korean) or the World Pack (includes all the languages they have).

I obtained an electronic version of the Office edition. Instead of getting a CD through the mail, I downloaded the file directly from their website. The download file is a self-extracting EXE of about 700 MB in size. The EXE file expands itself to a temporary installation directory. After that, I ran **setup.exe** from there and followed the instructions to complete the installation. The installation program created a **SYSTRAN** Program Group and added two applications in there. The **SYSTRAN Toolbar** is the main application, and the **SYSTRAN Dictionary Manager** is an application for managing and editing dictionaries.

5.6.1 SYSTRAN Toolbar

Select the **SYSTRAN** program group from the Windows **Start** menu and then select **SYSTRAN Toolbar** to start the application. When started, the program displays the main window and adds an icon to the Windows Taskbar. The application has two main functions: Translate and Lookup. The Translate function translates a paragraph of text, and the Lookup function gives explanations for a word. These two functions can be manually activated from the main window.

Select the appropriate source and target languages from the dropdown boxes first. To translate a paragraph of text, select the **Translate** tab, paste the text to the left panel and hit the **Translate** button to see the translated results show up on the right panel (Figure 5.8).

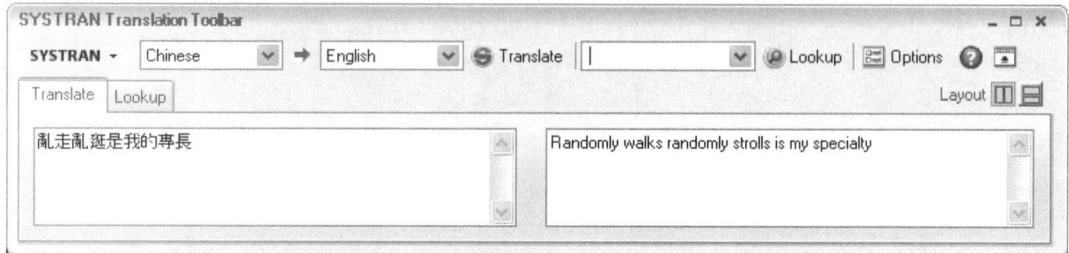

Figure 5.8 SYSTRAN Translation Toolbar main window—Translate function

To look up the definition of a character or a word, choose the **Lookup** tab, paste the character or word into the dropdown box in front of the **Lookup** button and then hit the **Lookup** button. The lookup results will appear in the panel as shown in Figure 5.9.

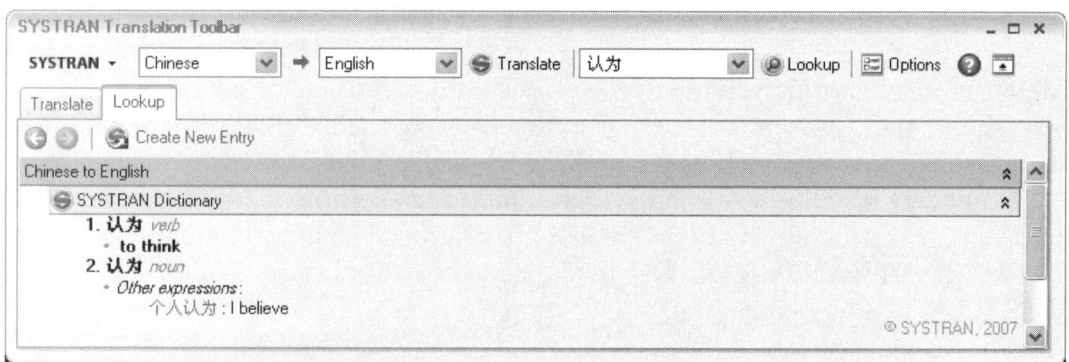

Figure 5.9 SYSTRAN Translation Toolbar main window—Lookup function

There is actually an easier way to operate SYSTRAN Translation Toolbar—using hot keys. This allows you to translate text while working in another application. Say you are using WordPad or Notepad to open a file with Chinese content. You can activate a shortcut (press a hot key) in your application to tell SYSTRAN to translate a block of text or to look up the definition of a word. A hot key is a special keystroke combination used to activate the translation or lookup function while working in another application. The default hot key for translation is **<Ctrl> T** and for lookup is **<Ctrl> L**. If these keys conflict with any existing functions used by the application, you need to reassign these functions with some other keys from the **SYSTRAN Global Options** window. This can be selected by clicking the **Options** button on the main window.

In some editions of the SYSTRAN, the **SYSTRAN Toolbar** can be added to the **Toolbars** section in MS Office products (Word, Excel, Outlook and PowerPoint). For example, when you are working on MS Word, the **SYSTRAN Toolbar** can be used for operating the translation functions (Figure 5.10).

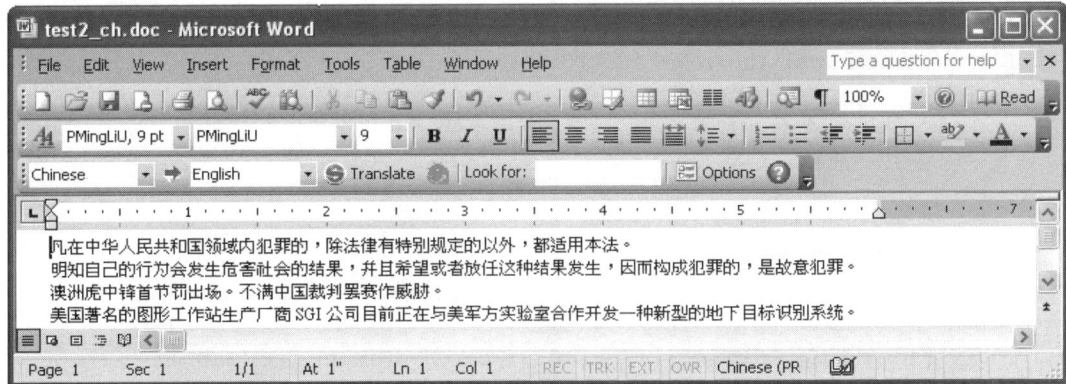

Figure 5.10 SYSTRAN toolbar in Microsoft Word

The **SYSTRAN Toolbar** can also be added to the **Toolbars** section of Internet Explorer and Firefox web browsers. When you click the **Translate** button as you browse a Chinese web page, SYSTRAN displays the translated results in another window and shows it side-by-side with the window of the original text, as shown in Figure 5.11. This is a neat feature, but unfortunately the scrolling of the two pages cannot be synchronized automatically.

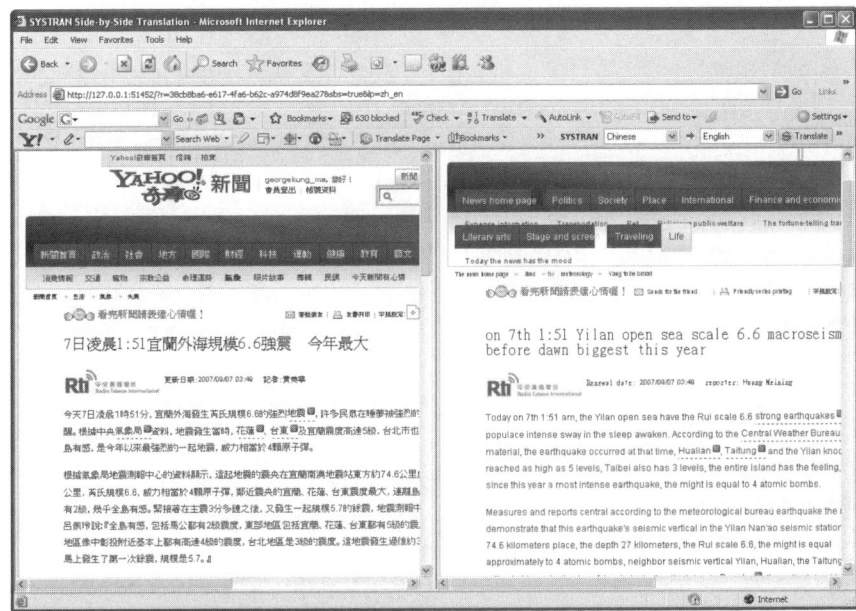

Figure 5.11 SYSTRAN side-by-side display of web pages

The web browser integration also has an option called Fluid Navigation. If this option is enabled, when you navigate from one web page to another following the URL links on the pages, SYSTRAN automatically translates the new web page so you don't need to click the **Translate** button every time.

The Translate function automatically differentiates traditional Chinese from simplified Chinese and translates accordingly. The Lookup function only works with simplified Chinese, which looks like a defect to me. When looking up words in traditional Chinese, it always comes back with a "No information found" message.

The Office edition and other two lower end editions of the product lack any additional dictionaries. Only the core dictionary comes with the purchase, but the Office edition and the Home edition do allow you to create a user-defined dictionary. I have run some tests with the Office edition and compared the results with the outputs from the demonstration tool of their website, and they look identical. The quality of the translation is better than the results from Yahoo! Babel Fish, which claims to be powered by SYSTRAN. I suspect Babel Fish either uses a previous version of the translation engine or was given an older or crippled core dictionary.

5.6.2 SYSTRAN Dictionary Manager

SYSTRAN Dictionary Manager (SDM) is the application used to manage and edit dictionaries that can be used in addition to the core dictionary. The two higher end product editions include additional dictionaries, and they allow more flexibility in editing user-defined dictionaries. For the Office Edition, there is only one user dictionary available to use for each language pair. The other thing I do not like is that it only allows 200 entries in the user-defined dictionary. Even though I have not tested the product extensively with the user-defined dictionary, this number feels too low for any practical use.

Figure 5.12 shows the main window of the SDM. When the application is first started, you need to click the **Open** button under the main menu once. This will bring up the **Open Dictionary** panel at the right, which contains a list of dictionaries available for editing. You will see the "Personal Chinese to English Dictionary" displayed on the list. This is actually the one and only dictionary you can manage for Chinese to English translation in the Office edition. You need to select the dictionary first and then hit the **File Open** icon on the right panel to open the dictionary.

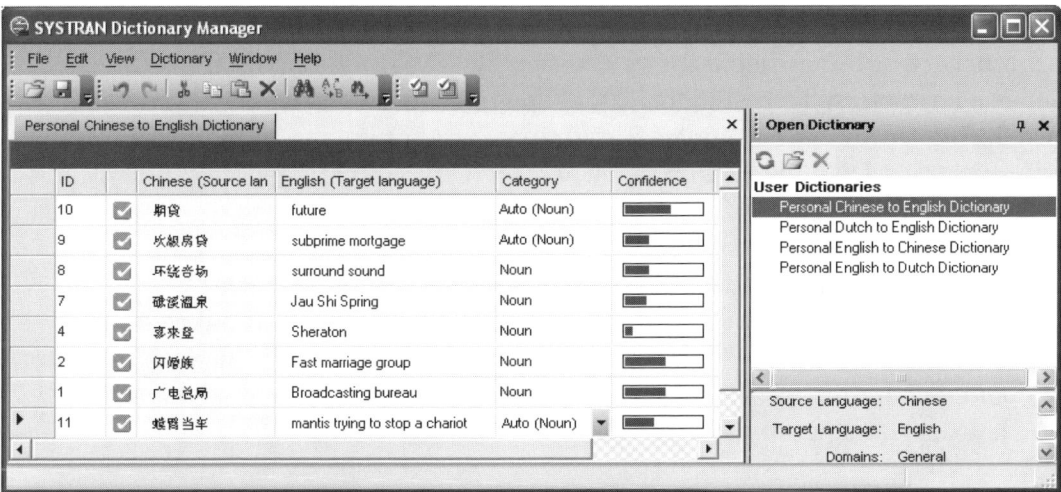

Figure 5.12 SYSTRAN Dictionary Manager (SDM)

The editing part is straight forward. For each entry, enter a Chinese word in the **Chinese (Source language)** text box, and its English translation in the **English (Target language)** text box. For the Chinese part, you can use either traditional or simplified Chinese characters. Use the **Category** field to specify the grammatical category of the word, such as Noun or Verb, etc. You can pick a selection from the dropdown box or just leave the choice as **Auto (Unknown)** for the program to decide. The **Confidence** field is read-only and not for editing. Keep on adding more entries as needed. After all entries are entered, click the **Code selection** or the **Code All** from the **Dictionary** menu to check the validity of the selected entries, or of all the entries. A green check mark indicates an entry is checked correctly and a red error mark flags an error. The **Confidence** field shows the level of confidence the program has in the accuracy of the information you entered. I suppose the program will look up characters from its own dictionaries and compare with the definition you entered. After all the entries pass the checking, you need to save the dictionary, and that will automatically put it in use.

A user dictionary entry can be used not only to supply a definition missing from the original (core) dictionary, but also to override an original definition. For example, the Chinese word 新华社 is originally translated to "Xinhua News Agency." If you add an entry in the dictionary saying that 新华社 should be translated to "Shinhua News" and put it to use, then the new definition "Shinhua News" dominates the original definition from the core dictionary.

There is a special entry type called DNT (Do not Translate) that you can assign to a word in a dictionary. When you do this, instead of translating the Chinese word into English definitions, the phonetic (Pinyin) information of that word will be used. Again, take 新华社 for example. If you assign it to DNT in the dictionary, the translator will translate it to "xinhuashe," which is the Pinyin of the three Chinese characters. To assign the DNT type to a word as you edit it, you can click the **Change entry type** from the **Dictionary** menu or do a right mouse click, and then select that from the pop-up menu.

SYSTRAN Toolbar allows you to bypass the SDM and add entries directly from its main window. From the **Lookup** tab, click the **Create New Entry** button to open the **New Dictionary entry** dialog window (Figure 5.13). Put the Chinese word in the **Source** text box and its English translation in the **Translation** text box, and then hit the **Save** button. As you do that, the new entry will be added to the dictionary and put to use right away.

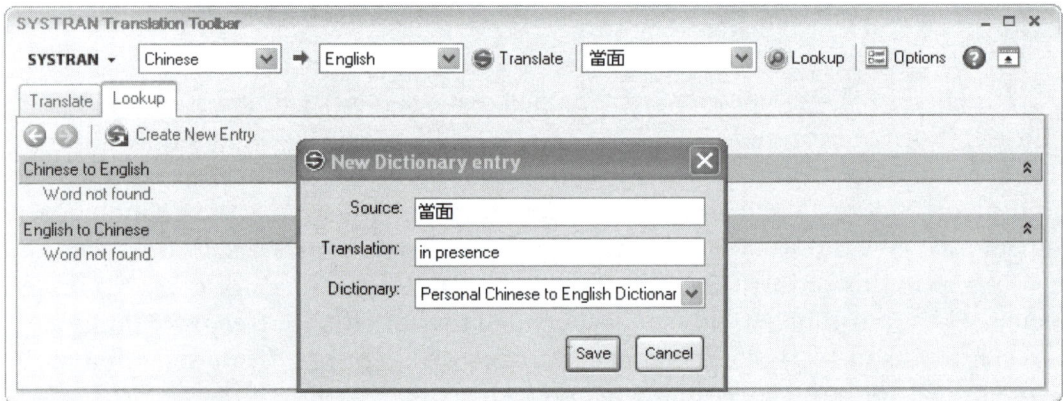

Figure 5.13 Add a new dictionary entry from the SYSTRAN main window

One thing that is unclear to me is how the category attribute of a word comes into play in translation. It would make sense that an entry should only be used when the translation engine determines that the category of the word matches the usage as it analyzes the grammatical structure of the sentence. As I cannot find descriptions in the user guide for this, I decided to do a small test just to see if the category attribute really makes any difference.

This test was very simple. I wrote the following Chinese sentence and told the SYSTRAN to translate:

新华社是中华人民共和国的国家通讯社

The software translated it into:

The Xinhua News Agency is the People's Republic of China National News agency.

This is fine. If the translator has the intelligence to analyze the grammatical category of words, then clearly it had treated the subject 新华社 correctly as a noun or a proper noun. Next, I added an entry to the dictionary which translates 新华社 into "Shinhua" and left the category as "Auto." SDM automatically picked "Noun" for me as the category and put into use. Now the translation becomes:

The Shinhua is the People's Republic of China National News agency.

This is fine so far. After that I started the real test and changed the category of the word 新华社 from "Auto (Noun)" into "Verb" to see if that made any difference. My thought is that the new definition "Shinhua" should only be used when the translator treats the word as a verb. In other situations it should still use the original definition "Xinhua News Agency."

The actual test results were not surprising. Regardless of which category I chose for the word, the translation still used the new definition. This suggests that the category information has not been used in choosing words for mapping from Chinese to English. It is also some indication that there is no grammatical structure analysis on the Chinese sentence side of the translation.

The next thing I did was to change the definition of 新华社 into "communicate" and gave it the category of "Verb." After that, the translation becomes:

Communicating is the People's Republic of China National News agency.

The software changed the word "communicate" into "communicating" because it knows that the English sentence needs a noun there. However, this only tells me that the program does analyze the grammatical structure of the output (English) sentence. The category attribute of a word in the user-defined dictionary may have affected the constructing of output (English) sentences that way, but I doubt that is the case. The reason is that the program should have asked me for the noun-form of the word at the time I defined a verb. From what I can see, most likely the program knows that "communicate" is a verb from its internal dictionaries, and not from the definition I entered.

5.7 LEC Translator 2007

Language Engineering Company, LLC (LEC) is a premier translation software vendor. They used to mainly provide their software as Original Equipment Manufacture (OEM) products to other companies in the past, but now they have begun to offer a large range of titles on their own. The text translation part of Babylon 7 is powered by the LEC translation engine, which is actually a service offered directly from the server farm of the LEC.

LEC has a website for demonstrating their translator (Figure 5.14). It is located at: http://www.lec.com/w2/translate-demos.asp

Figure 5.14 LEC Translator demonstration website

This is a very simple translator that can be used for translating a block of text, and its usage is self-explanatory. This page is only made for demonstration purposes, and is not convenient for any practical use.

LEC has a few different editions of desktop (stand-alone) software for Chinese to English translation. From low to high are the Translate Personal, Translate Business, and Translate Pro. Translate Personal is the most basic translator with no additional technical dictionary. Translate Business includes the Business dictionary. Translate Pro includes all the technical dictionaries, including Business, Chemical, Civil Engineering, Computer, Electrical Engineering, Finance, Health, Law, Management, Mechanical Engineering, and Medicine dictionary.

LEC also offers a suite of translation software on a subscription basis called Translate DotNet. It include six different programs: LEC ClipTrans DotNet, LEC FileTrans DotNet, LEC LogoTrans DotNet, LEC MirrorTrans DotNet, LEC TransIt DotNet, and LEC Translate DotNet.These software products use what I called a hybrid approach. The programs are installed and run locally on the Windows desktop for interacting with users. To do translation, they send out source texts to LEC's server on the Internet and get the results back to display.

You can find more information, including a 7-day free trial of Translate DotNet from the following website address:

http://www.lec.com/w2/translate-dotnet.asp

ClipTrans DotNet translates the contents of the Windows Clipboard. Figure 5.15 shows the main window of ClipTrans DotNet.

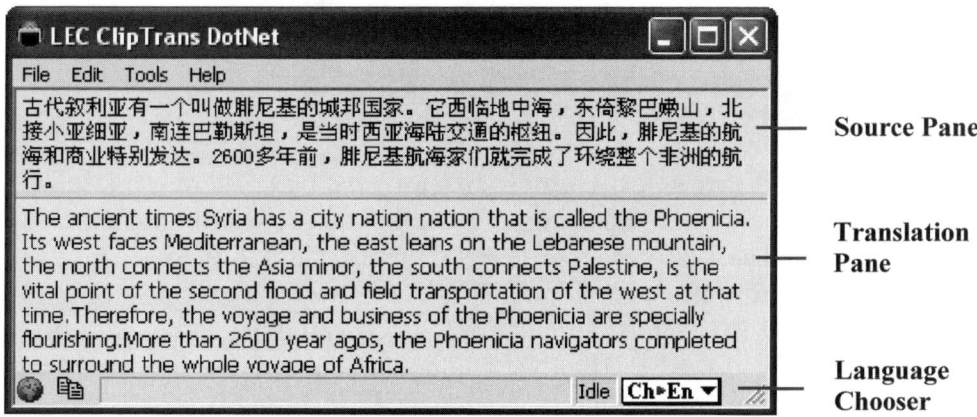

Figure 5.15 LEC ClipTrans DotNet

You need to adjust a few settings before using it for translation. The first is the language pair. Click the **Language Chooser** icon at the lower right corner of the main window to set **Chinese to English** as the language pair. The second setting is to choose the traditional or simplified Chinese character set. To make the adjustment, select **Tools** on the main menu, and click **Options** to open up the **Settings for LEC ClipTrans DotNet** dialog window (Figure 5.16).

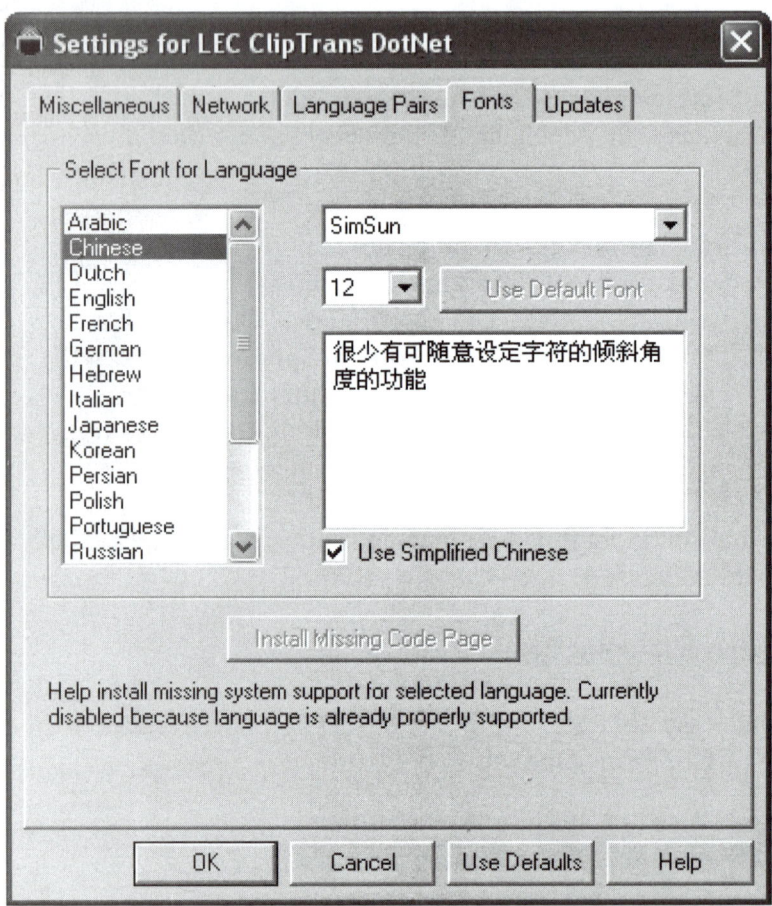

Figure 5.16 Set Simplified or Traditional Chinese in LEC DotNet

Select the **Fonts** tab, and then select **Chinese** from the list box. There is a **Use Simplified Chinese** checkbox in the center. Check this box to use simplified Chinese, or leave it unchecked to use traditional Chinese. Click **OK** to accept the changes. Note that this simplified/traditional Chinese option is a global setting, which applies to all six LEC DotNet applications. Once you make the change of this option from any one of the LEC DotNet applications, it affects all other LEC DotNet applications. On the other hand, the language pair setting is per application, and you need to make the adjustment separately in each application.

To use ClipTrans DotNet, you can either leave its main window on the desktop, or have it minimized. You will work on the Chinese text from another application, such as a web browser to view a web page, or using a word processor to view a file. When you want to translate some text, select the block of text from your main application and copy it into Windows Clipboard. As soon as you do that, ClipTrans DotNet automatically copies the contents in the Clipboard into its **Source pane**, starts the translation, and displays the results in its **Translation pane**. If the main window of ClipTrans was minimized initially, it will be expanded.

LEC FileTrans DotNet translates the entire content in a file and saves the translated result into a new file. Figure 5.17 shows its main window. The program does not need to display the source text and/or translated results so there is no need for a large window. First you need to make sure the language pair and simplified/traditional Chinese settings are correct, using similar methods that you used in setting up ClipTrans DotNet. To tell FileTrans DotNet application to translate a file, you either drag-and-drop the source file to its main window, or click the **Translate** button and then navigate to the source file. As you do that, the program will open the source file, do the translation, generate a new filename and save the translated results to a new file automatically.

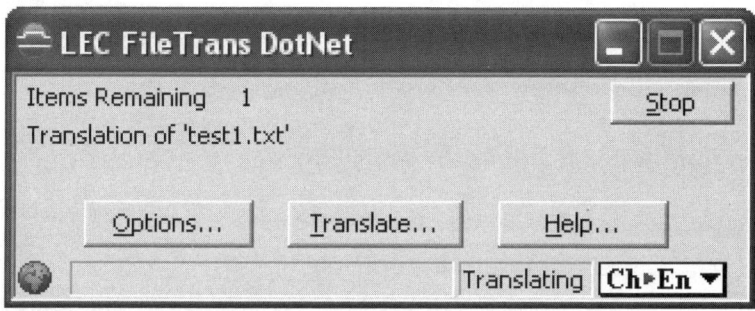

Figure 5.17 LEC FileTrans DotNet

The types of files allowed by the application actually depend on the version of your subscription. The regular subscription only supports plain text (.txt) and HTML files. The premium subscription supports additional file types including MS Word document (.doc) and Adobe Acrobat (.pdf) files.

The LEC LogoTrans DotNet gives you a window to enter texts and translates the contents as you type. This application is not useful for our purposes.

The LEC MirrorTrans DotNet clones the layout of another window (the front end application) and translates the contents in there to display in the clone window

(Figure 5.18). This can be useful when the front end application contains text and graphics, as it allows you to easily correlate the source text with its translation.

Figure 5.18 LEC MirrorTrans DotNet

To use MirrorTrans DotNet, first make sure the language pair and simplified/traditional Chinese settings are correct. Next, associate MirrorTrans with the source window, i.e., the window to be cloned. To do this, drag the **Window Chooser Icon** located at the bottom left corner of the MirrorTrans DotNet, and drop it into the source window. After the association is established, MirrorTrans is now supposed to translate and refresh its contents whenever the source window changes.

It appears that the MirrorTrans DotNet only works with a small number of Windows applications. I briefly tested the program with some commonly used applications, including Windows Notepad, Internet Explorer 6, Mozilla Firefox 2, Microsoft Word 2003, Microsoft Publisher 2003, and Microsoft PowerPoint 2003. I found that the program is able to work properly only with Notepad and Internet Explorer 6. Even with those two applications, sometimes the real time update did not work and other times the program just crashed. Apparently, more work needs to be done to improve the stability of the program.

LEC TransIt DotNet translates words, phrases, and short sentences (Figure 5.19). You operate it by pasting Chinese text into the text box and then pressing the **<Enter>** key. The program will then translate and overwrite the text in the text box with the translation results. The program can also be configured to send the translated results to another window. The TransIt DotNet application is useful for someone who uses the Chat or IM (Instant Messaging) program. As you type text into the TransIt DotNet text box using the source language, it gets translated into the target language and sent to another window (Chat or IM program) directly. This is a neat gadget, but does not appear to be useful for our purposes.

Figure 5.19 LEC TransIt DotNet

LEC Translate DotNet works like a control center for all the LEC DotNet programs (Figure 5.20). You can use it for rapid access to other LEC DotNet applications. It also has a text box similar to the one in TransIt DotNet. When you type or paste text to it and press the **<Enter>** key, it will translate the text and replace the content in the text box with the translation results.

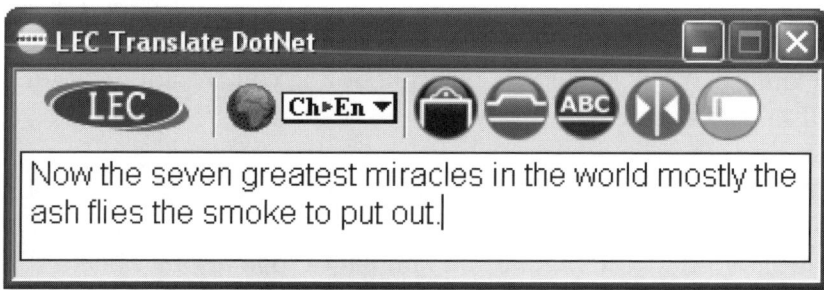
Figure 5.20 LEC Translate DotNet

One last thing I want to mention about the Language Engineering Company is that their customer service is excellent. They were very helpful and patient with all my questions, even though I had not actually purchased their product.

5.8 Babylon 7

Babylon is a dictionary and translation program with a few additional features, including a conversion utility, and writing aids. The dictionary look-up function can be used either on-line or locally. The full text translation function works only when connected to the Internet. Babylon started out as an electronic dictionary vendor, providing add-on contents to products from traditional dictionary and encyclopedia publishers. It began to offer full text translation only since version 6, which was introduced in April 2006. Babylon does not have its own translation engine and the translator part of the application is actually supported by the translator from LEC. When Babylon needs to have a block of text translated, it sends the source data to LEC's server over the Internet and then gets the results back to display. Even though the dictionary and translator are integrated under one Babylon application window, they are really separate pieces and do not work together. This is somewhat different from other translation-oriented software products, which have the dictionaries integrated into their translator engines. The dictionary part of the Babylon is very powerful because this is their core business. They have over 1,300 dictionaries that cover about 50 different languages. The translator is a separate item from the dictionary products, and is not able to take advantage of the large collection of dictionaries. You can also think of the translation feature in Babylon to be the same as one of its on-line dictionaries, with the ability to look up a whole paragraph of text.

There is a third component of the application, called "Conversions." This is a tool that converts between different currencies, units and time zones. The tool is capable of going on-line to retrieve the currency conversion rate information on the Internet everyday. I won't describe this further, since this feature is not relevant to reading Chinese. You can disable this function if you are not planning on using it. This will save you time and annoyance.

Unlike the desktop translator from SYSTRAN or LEC, Babylon does not market its software into many different levels or various language packs, which may cause occasional confusion. Babylon bundles all languages together into one product. They also offer a subscription deal that lets you subscribe to the latest version of the software for one year at less than half the price of purchasing a permanent edition. The Babylon software I have is a subscription edition. I started out by downloading a trial version of Babylon 6 and then purchased a subscription edition. When they released Babylon 7, I got the upgrade for free because with subscription you are eligible for the latest edition.

5.8.1 Installation

You can find trial edition of Babylon 7 at their website:

http://www.babylon.com

Click the giant **Download Now** button and download the self-extracting EXE file. You can either click the **Run** button to run the EXE directly, or click the **Save** to save it to a folder and then run it from there. Follow the instructions on the screen to finish the installation. One option you can choose during the installation is the hot key, used to initiate the translation or dictionary lookup. Similar to SYSTRAN Translation Toolbar, Babylon allows you to activate its lookup functions using a hot key while working from another application. Pressing the hot key in Babylon is known as doing a "Babylon click." You can choose a function key or the combination of a mouse button and the **<Ctrl>**, **<Shift>** or **<Alt>** key as the hot key. The default choice is the **<Ctrl>** key with the right mouse button. Don't worry if you have made a bad choice during the installation; it is easy to change this setting later.

5.8.2 Main Window

Figure 5.21 shows the main window of Babylon 7. On top of the main window are the **Toolbars** that contain some control buttons and a dropdown box (the **Term Box**) used for dictionary lookup. Below the **Toolbars** are the **Sidebar Pane** on the left, and the **Results Pane** on the right. The **Sidebar Pane** contains a list of active dictionaries (dictionaries that return results for the current word) and frequently used functions. The **Results Pane** displays the translation and lookup results. There is a **Show/Hide Sidebar** toggle button to hide or show the **Sidebar**. You can hide the **Sidebar** if you don't need to use the functions and information in there. This makes the **Results Pane** bigger.

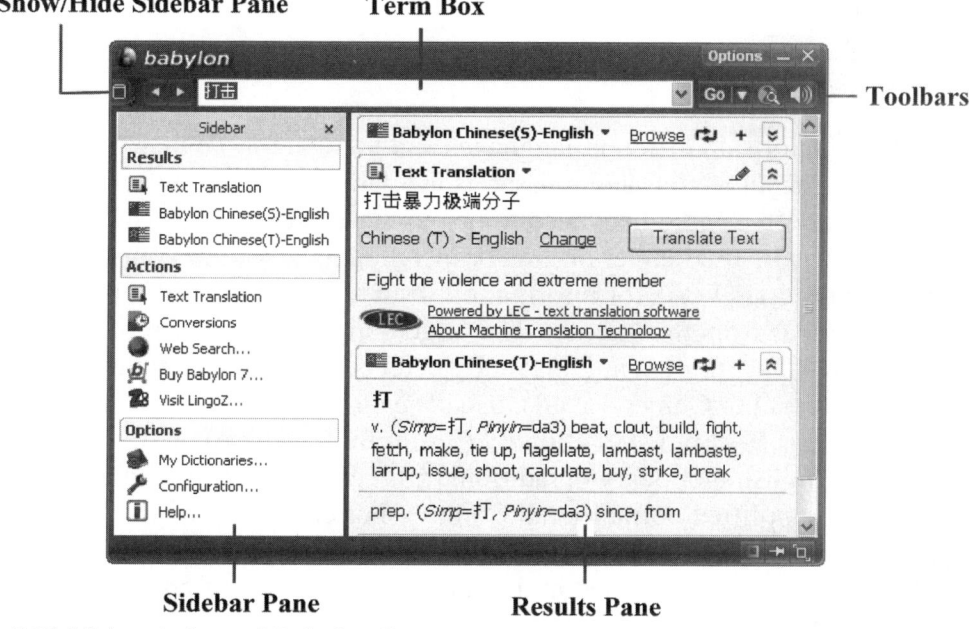

Figure 5.21 Main window of Babylon 7

Babylon is intended to be used while you are working from another application, such as a word processor, a web browser, etc. To look up a word, leave the mouse cursor near the Chinese text from your application and do the "Babylon click." Babylon puts the source word in the **Term Box**, does the lookup and puts the results in the **Results Pane**. The program is smart enough to look around the cursor to find characters make up a meaningful Chinese word as the source word for looking up. For example, the text 打击暴力极端分子 consists of four Chinese words: 打击, 暴力, 极端, and 分子. Users who do not read Chinese might have highlighted or left the cursor in front of the two characters that do not form a word, such as 击暴. In such a case, Babylon will look for the valid words and give you the translation of 打击 and 击, or 暴力 and 暴, depending on the proximity of the mouse cursor to the character 击 or 暴. If Babylon is not able to find a word that consists of more than one character in the vicinity, it will just give you the translation of a single character. Take the following Chinese sentence "若您想再买两个也行。" for example, each of these characters in there is used singly and does not form any word with the next character. In such a case, the program will just give the translation of each individual character. One glitch I noticed is that when a word contains multiple characters that span across two rows, they cannot be recognized as one word. This is certainly not the right behavior. In Chinese text, a multi-character word can start at the end of a line and continue on the next one.

5.8.3 Dictionaries

Babylon 7 supports 48 different languages and there are more than 1,300 dictionaries, encyclopedias and glossaries available for it to use. Some of the dictionaries are free and others need to be purchased separately. Many dictionaries can be used either on-line or installed locally onto your PC. By default, the program looks for information from all the dictionaries that it can find locally as well as from the Internet. The target language is chosen based on the configuration. The program automatically detects the source language based on the text contents. For Chinese words, usually you will get results from the Babylon Chinese(S)-English dictionary (Simplified Chinese) or Babylon Chinese(T)-English dictionary (Traditional Chinese), depending on whether the words are in simplified or traditional Chinese. For characters or words that are common in both sets, you will get results from both dictionaries. Since many Chinese characters are also used in the Japanese language, often you might also see results from Japanese-English dictionaries. This is of course undesirable, even though the meanings of Chinese characters are usually the same when they are used in Japanese. What makes things worse is that Japanese dictionaries always seem to precede Chinese dictionaries by default. To prevent this from happening, you need to set up a list of dictionaries ("My Dictionaries"), and then tell the program to look up results from dictionaries on that list only.

To set up My Dictionaries, click the **My Dictionaries** link located in the Sidebar Panel to open the **My Dictionaries** dialog (Figure 5.22).

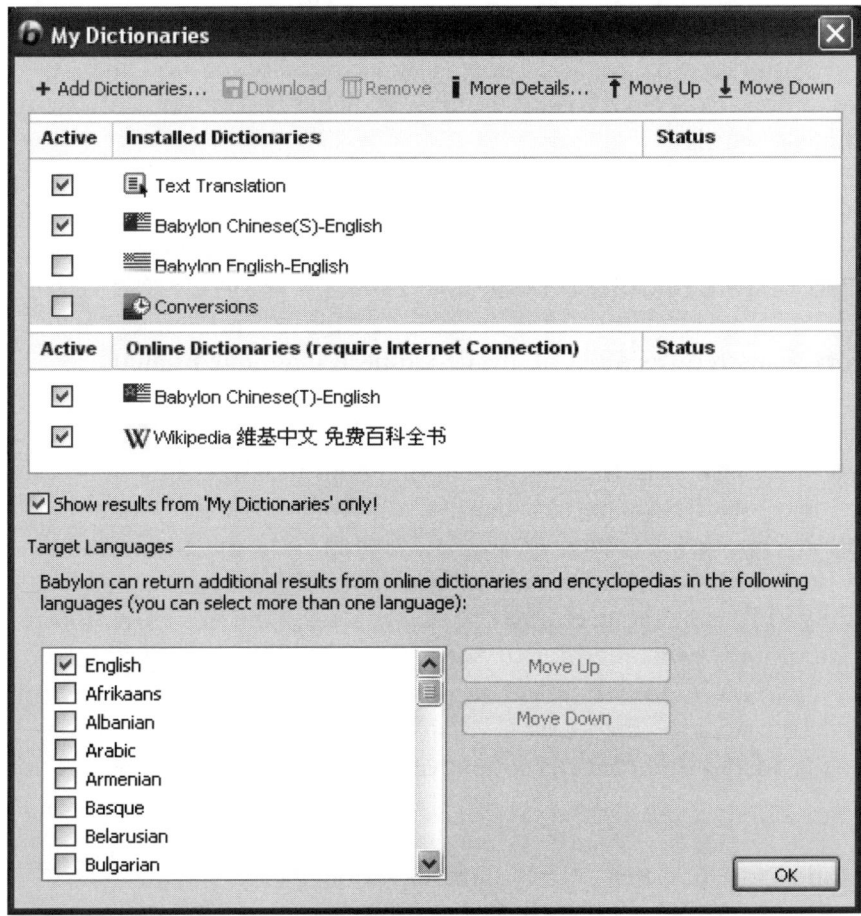

Figure 5.22 Babylon 7—**My Dictionaries** dialog

The top half of the dialog shows a list of all the entries currently in **My Dictionaries**. The dictionaries installed locally in the PC are listed first, under the **Installed Dictionaries** section. The dictionaries that need to be used on-line are listed next, under the **Online Dictionaries** section. Use the **Move Up** and **Move Down** buttons to adjust the order of the dictionaries. When lookup results are available from multiple dictionaries, the output results are displayed based on this order. Use the **Active** checkbox in front of each dictionary to enable or disable it. The Babylon program only retrieves results from dictionaries that are enabled. Check the **Show results from 'My Dictionaries' only** checkbox to avoid reference to unwanted dictionaries. The **Target Languages** section contains the selections of target languages to use.

When the Babylon program is initially installed, there are three dictionaries set up automatically: **Babylon English-English**, **Conversions**, and **Text Translation**. **Text Translation** is the full text translation function provided from LEC, used for translating text blocks. If you don't need the English-English dictionary or the Conversions utility, you can have those disabled. Because there are no Chinese dictionaries set up in here, you need to add them to your list before you can use it for looking up Chinese words.

To add dictionaries to your list, click the **Add Dictionaries** link at the top left corner. This brings you to a website with information and links to all the dictionaries and encyclopedias for use in Babylon. Look for the place that says "Free Dictionaries and Encyclopedias" and find the "Chinese" link under the Languages category. This returns a list of all the Chinese language related dictionaries and encyclopedias.

Click the link on a title to find out more information about it. Click the big **Download** button next to a dictionary to download and install the dictionary locally to your PC. If you wish to use it on-line only, then click the small link that says "Click Here To download on-line version." Certain dictionaries, such as Wikipedia, are allowed for on-line use only so you won't see the big **Download** button for them. Dictionaries installed locally on your PC will be accessed faster and can be used without an Internet connection. The disadvantage is that you will need to manually do the update when newer versions are released. My recommendation is to install them locally whenever possible, since updates do not happen that often.

I have found the following dictionaries to be useful for our purposes:

Babylon Chinese(S)-English
This is the main simplified Chinese to English dictionary. It contains 56,920 entries. You should download and install this locally and my recommendation is to place it as the first or second order on the list.

Babylon Chinese(T)-English

This is the main traditional Chinese to English dictionary. It contains 56,944 entries. You should install this locally and my recommendation is to place it as the first or second order on the list.

Babylon English-Chinese(S)
This is an English to simplified Chinese dictionary. It contains 70,919 entries. You can use this for Cross-translation (translating the translated results back to Chinese).

Babylon English-Chinese(T)
This is an English to traditional Chinese dictionary. It contains 67,721 entries. You can use this for Cross-translation (translating the translated results back to Chinese).

CEDIT Simp. Chinese-English
This is a Chinese to English dictionary and it has the Pinyin annotations for characters. It contains 23,496 entries of both simplified and traditional Chinese words. The name "Simp. Chinese-English" may be a misnomer. You should install this dictionary locally for complementary use.

Chinese idioms explained in English
This dictionary gives you English explanations of Chinese idioms. It contains 510 entries. It is useful, except there are too few entries. You should install this dictionary locally for reference.

Chinese-English Dictionary (T) Traditional Chinese Version
This is a traditional Chinese to English dictionary. It contains 29,144 entries. You should install this dictionary locally for complementary use.

URX ZHEN Chinese (Simpl.)-English English-Chinese (Simpl.) dictionary
This dictionary contains a total of 42,554 simplified Chinese to English and English to simplified Chinese entries. You should install this dictionary locally for complementary use.

5.8.4 Cross-Translation

One special thing about Babylon is its ability to perform Cross-translation. This is the process of looking up a result and then using it as the source to do a reverse lookup from a dictionary that translates from the opposite direction. When the results from the Cross-translation are close to the original source, they give you more confidence in the definition you've got from the original lookup. To do Cross-translation, click the **Cross-translation** icon located at the title section of the translated results (see Figure 5.23). Once you do that, the program will stay in the Cross-translation mode until you click the icon again to bring back the normal mode. Figure 5.23 shows the Babylon window in the Cross-translation mode. In here, the dictionary title shows "Babylon Chinese-English-Chinese (T)." For each entry, there is a list of explanations in English, and then for each English explanation there is a collection of explanations in Chinese.

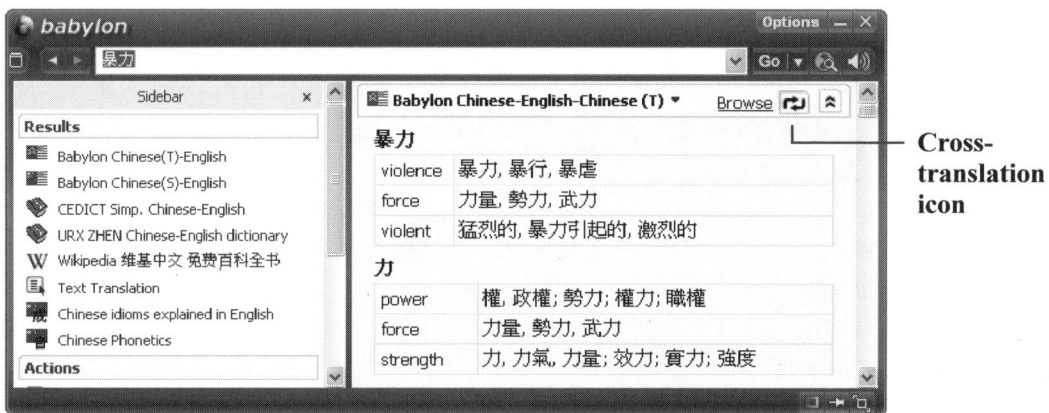

Figure 5.23 Babylon—Cross-translation mode

5.8.5 Text Translation

Text Translation is the component of Babylon that does the primary task that we are most interested in—the full text translation. As you do a Babylon click, the text in the vicinity of your cursor are automatically copied into a read-only text box in the **Text Translation** section in the **Results Pane** (Figure 5.24).

You need to make sure the source and target languages are set correctly, and then hit the **Translate Text** button. When the translated results come back, they will be shown in an area underneath the read-only text box. One problem I found with this function is that the block of text it automatically copies may not always be the desired text. Even if you explicitly highlight a block of text from your main application, Babylon may decide to pick something nearby. To have the exact block of text you want, you need to click the **Edit** icon (Figure 5.24) to make the read-only text box editable, and paste the desired text in there.

Figure 5.24 Babylon—Text Translation

The other thing I don't like about the translator is that it does not offer a way to specify the default source and target languages, and it does not remember the previously used selections either. I always choose either Chinese (T) or Chinese (S) as the source and English as target. For some reason it tends to change that and gives me Japanese as the source language the next time. Once in a while, it also has this strange habit of choosing German as the target language for me, and I have no idea where that comes from. When using this program for real tasks, this can become quite annoying after a while. According to the help manual, the program should remember the previous selections so this seems like a defect in the program. My overall experience with text translation in Babylon is that it is not the main focus of the product, so it has been somewhat ignored.

5.8.6 Text-to-Speech

There is a speaker-shaped icon on the top right corner of the main window. Clicking it tells the program to speak out the word in the **Term Box**. This is a text-to-speech (TTS) function, but it does not work for Chinese words. In fact, the TTS feature works for English only. When entering a German or French word, the program says something, but the pronunciation is still in English. Even though I don't speak German or French, I can tell this doesn't sound right. The quality of the machine pronunciation is not that good even for English words. I believe this is from the speech engine by Microsoft, which is in turn a technology acquired from a company called Lernout & Hauspie. The vendor claims their TTS to have superb quality, but I know for a fact that even ten years ago there were other TTS engines that sounded better than this. It is unfortunate that it is not always the better technology that wins the race in such games. I just hope that readers realize that the voice you are hearing here does not reflect the limitation of the TTS technology.

5.8.7 Conclusion

My general experience with Babylon is that the dictionary part provides results from rich resources, which is ideal in complementing the results from translators. The quality of the **Text Translation** function is there is inferior, and I would not recommend using it. What I hope to see is continuous improvement of the dictionaries, because as of today there are still too many commonly used words that I could not find in any of them. The other thing on my wish list is the mouse-over feature. For dictionary look up, I wish to move my mouse along a line of text quickly and browse their definition right away. The program should show the results when I leave the mouse cursor over a word for a certain amount of time, say one second. To avoid getting unwanted results, the mouse-over can be combined with the use of a key, say the **<Ctrl>** key. This way I don't need to keep on doing Babylon click, Babylon click…which becomes tiresome.

In the next section we are going to look at a program that looks very much like Babylon, and it allows the use of mouse-over UI.

5.9 Lingoes 2

Lingoes is a multi-language dictionary and translation software. The product is very similar to Babylon, only it is free and more powerful in doing our tasks. It is intended to be used while you are working from another application, such as a word processor, a web browser, etc. To look up the translation of a word, simply place and leave the mouse cursor near the Chinese text from your application and Lingoes will display the explanations of the word in a pop-up window.

The dictionary lookup function can be used either on-line or installed and run locally. The whole text translation function has to be performed on-line, and it allows selections from many different translation services. Unlike Babylon, which sends text to the translation server from LEC, Lingoes does not use a dedicated translation vendor. It works like a portal and allows you to connect to different translation service providers and get information from there. Imagine a human user who can manually go to all the free websites to get his or her text translated.

This software automatically does that for you behind the scenes, and provides an exquisitely designed user interface for doing so.

5.9.1 Installation

The main website of Lingoes is located at:

http://www.lingoes.net/

The Lingoes program is free and you can find a link from this website to download it. After downloading, run the self-extract EXE file and follow the instructions to complete the setup, which is very straight-forward. The version I have used is the 2.1.0 Beta version released at the end of 2007.

5.9.2 Main Window

Figure 5.25 shows the main window of Lingoes.

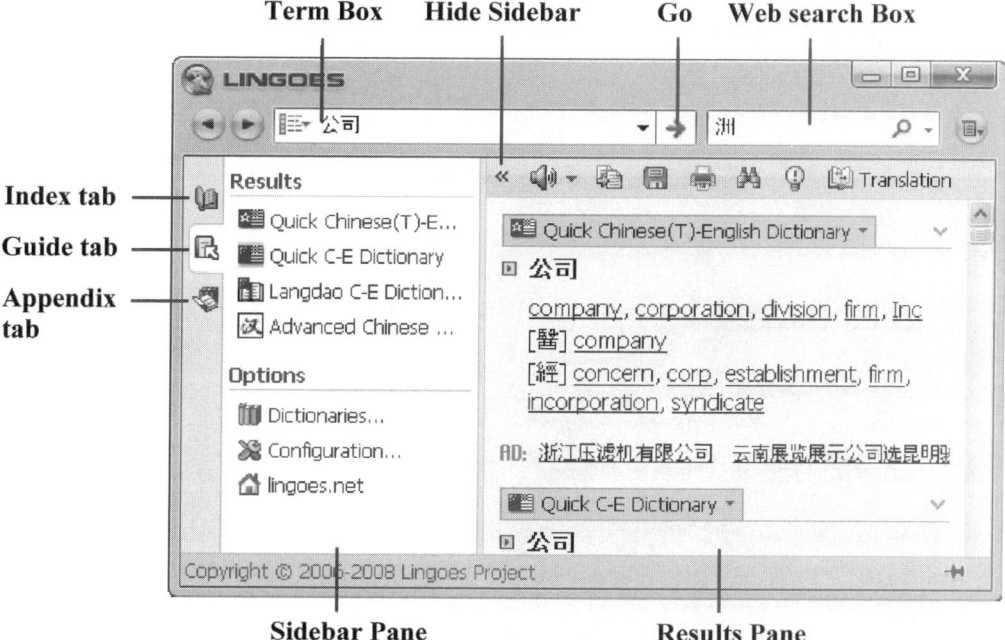

Figure 5.25 Lingoes main window

On top of the window are the **Term Box** for looking up words manually, and the **Web search Box** for searching things on the Internet. The main part of the window consists of the **Sidebar Pane** on the left and the **Results Pane** on the right. There are three tabs in the **Sidebar Pane**: **Index**, **Guide**, and **Appendix**. The **Index** tab shows a list of all the words from the selected dictionary. The **Guide** tab shows a list of currently active dictionaries (dictionaries that return results for the current word) and some frequently used functions. The **Appendix** tab is a new feature in version 2. It includes some miscellaneous tools and information, such as a calculator and a Periodic Table. It also has a utility for converting between the traditional and simplified Chinese characters. The **Results Pane** is for displaying the lookup and translated results of a selected word or block of text. There is a toolbar on top of the **Results Pane**. The left most icon on this toolbar allows you to hide and unhide the **Sidebar Pane**. Hiding the **Sidebar Pane** makes the **Results Pane** bigger.

5.9.3 Operations

In Lingoes, a word lookup can be initiated using mouse-over (placing the mouse cursor over a word). You may wish to configure Lingoes so it responds only to Chinese words and not to English words. You can't do this by simply not having any English dictionary installed, because the program still initiates the lookup whenever it sees a word. To set up for this, click the **Configuration** button from the **Guide** tab in the **Sidebar Pane**. This will open the **Configuration** dialog window (Figure 5.26).

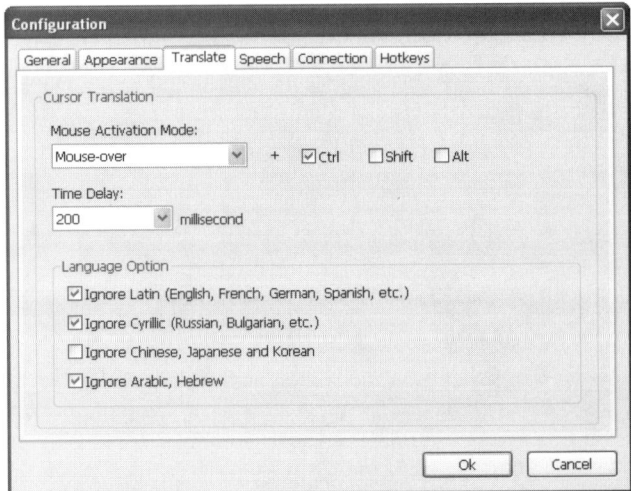

Figure 5.26 Lingoes—**Configuration** dialog window

Select the **Translate** tab from the **Configuration** dialog. In the **Language Option** section, check the respective checkboxes to disable languages that you want the software to ignore.

Lingoes does not have any Chinese dictionaries installed after the initial installation. To look up Chinese words, you have to download and install these dictionaries first. Unlike Babylon, Lingoes does not automatically search for results from on-line resources. Other than a few dictionaries that must be used on-line, most Lingoes dictionaries require you to download and install them locally. This is appropriate for Lingoes, as there will be noticeable delay when searching on-line, which will make the program less responsive. For Babylon, a delay feels less awkward because it requires a click (Babylon click) for any lookup, and people are used to a delay after clicking something. For a program that uses mouse-over, users expect a more prompt response.

You need to know a few special terms related to the operation of the program when setting up your dictionaries. Lingoes lets you manually enter a word into the **Term Box** and look up its definitions from a group of dictionaries. In Lingoes terminology, such an operation is called Index lookup. The group of dictionaries that are used for such an operation is called Index Group. As you enter (paste) a word in the **Term Box**, the software automatically looks up the word from the dictionaries in the Index Group, and displays the results from the top dictionary (the highest rank dictionary that returns results) in the **Results Pane**. If the **Sidebar Pane** is on, the program automatically selects the **Index** tab, and displays a list of entries from the top dictionary (Figure 5.27). The software also locates the word from the index list and highlights it automatically. You can use the scroll bar to scroll through the index of the dictionary and look up the explanations of other words by selecting other entries on the index list.

Press the **<Enter>** key or click the **Go** button to get alternative translations of the word in the **Term Box** from other dictionaries. Hitting the **<Enter>** key also puts the entry into the dropdown box (history list) of the **Term Box**. You can view previous results using either the history list or the two buttons in front of the **Term Box**. Note that when you hit the **<Enter>** key or select an entry from the history list of the **Term Box**, the operation is different from entering or pasting a word to the **Term Box** without hitting **<Enter>**. As you hit the **<Enter>** key, the operation becomes a regular lookup instead of an Index lookup. The lookup results now come from all the installed (and enabled) dictionaries, not just the dictionaries from the Index Group.

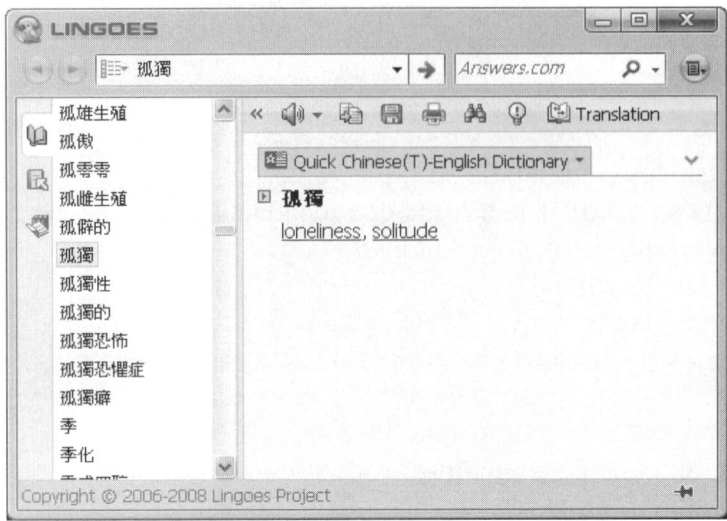

Figure 5.27 Lingoes—looking up from **Term Box**

Even though you can manually enter words like described above, it is not the usual way of operating the program. Lingoes is designed to look up words while you are working from another Windows application, such as a web browser or a text editor. When you wish to know the definition of a word, simply place your mouse cursor over the word and leave it there for a short period of time. Doing this will initiate the Lingoes program to do the lookup, and display the results in a pop-up window (Figure 5.28). In Lingoes' terminology, this operation is called Cursor Translation. The pop-up window is known as the **Cursor Translation** window. The group of dictionaries used for such purposes is called the Cursor Translator Group.

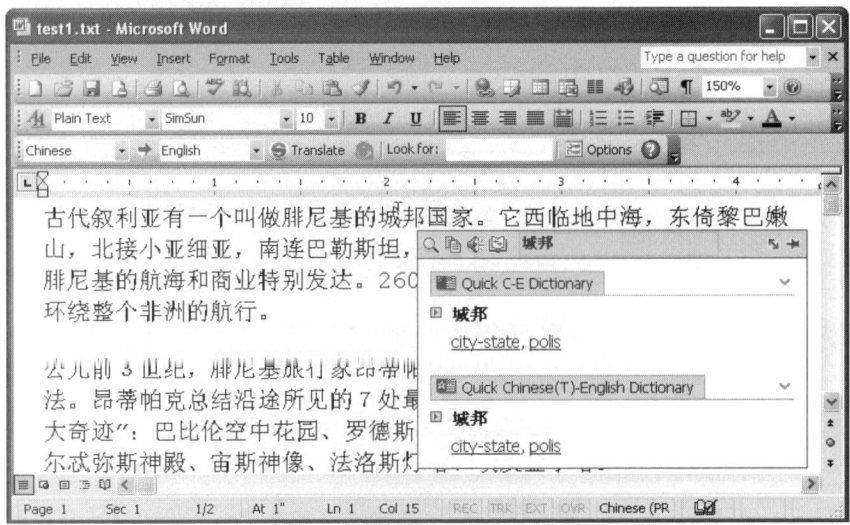

Figure 5.28 Lingoes—**Cursor Translation** window

There is a third way of operating the program, known as Clipboard translation. When this feature is enabled, whenever you paste a word into Windows Clipboard, the translated result will appear in a pop-up window (the **Cursor Translation** window). There is not a separate dictionary group used specifically for Clipboard translation, instead it just uses the dictionaries from the Cursor Translator Group.

The Clipboard translation feature is to be turned on and off by toggling the **<Alt> B** key (this key assignment is configurable). This is an awkward design, as I would expect a configurable option to turn on or off the function itself, not to select a key to toggle the function. I am also unable to find an indicator on the screen to tell me the on and off status of the function. Also, I don't like that the Clipboard translation feature is enabled initially after installation. This can cause confusion for users not aware of this feature, and also annoys people who don't want it.

5.9.4 Dictionaries

Now that you are familiar with the operations of the program, it is time to download and install the dictionaries. Be aware that some dictionaries have to be used on-line and cannot be installed locally. These on-line dictionaries can be used only for regular lookup—by manually entering words in the **Term Box** and hitting the **<Enter>** key. They cannot be used for Index lookup, Cursor Translation or Clipboard translation.

To install or set up dictionaries, go to the **Sidebar Pane**, click the **Guide** tab, and click **Dictionaries** to open the **Dictionary Options** dialog window (Figure 5.29).

Dictionary Options dialog contains functions for downloading, installing and uninstalling dictionaries. It also allows you to add, remove, enable, disable, and arrange the order of dictionaries in different groups.

Click the **Install From Lingoes** button to get to the Lingoes website where the dictionaries are located. This web page contains the information and download links for all the dictionaries used in Lingoes. Go to the bottom of the page and look for the places that say "Chinese(S) Dictionaries" and "Chinese(T) Dictionaries" to download Chinese dictionaries.

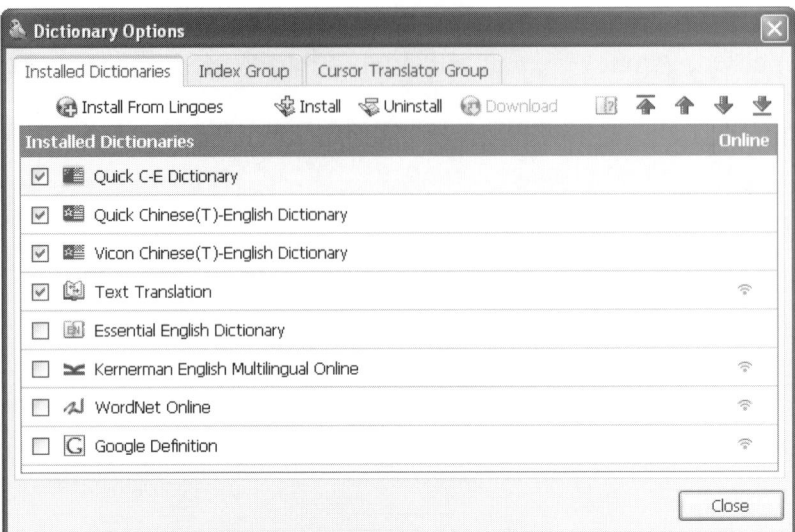

Figure 5.29 Lingoes—**Dictionary Options** dialog window

Listed below are dictionaries I have found to be useful for our purposes. The previous version of Lingoes assigned a unique ID for each dictionary. This is a good idea because some dictionaries may have similar names, which can cause confusion. Unfortunately they have stopped using that in the new version, so I have to list them just by name.

Quick C-E Dictionary
This is a simplified Chinese to English dictionary. It contains 273,640 words. My recommendation is to place it in the first or second order for words lookup.

Quick Chinese(T)-English Dictionary
This is a traditional Chinese to English dictionary. It contains 273,332 words. My recommendation is to place it in the first or second order for words lookup.

Vicon Chinese(S)-English Dictionary
This is a simplified Chinese to English dictionary with words, phrases, abbreviations and acronyms. It contains a total of 48,001 words. You can use this for complementary purposes.

Vicon Chinese(T)-English Dictionary
This is a traditional Chinese to English dictionary with words, phrases, abbreviations and acronyms. It contains a total of 48,631 words. You can use this for complementary purposes.

Langdao C-E Dictionary

This is a simplified Chinese to English dictionary. It contains a huge collection of 405,718 words. It covers special words in various categories such like engineering, medical, mechanics, architecture, chemical, law, computer, etc.

C-E Medicine Dictionary

This is a simplified Chinese to English dictionary. It contains 172,605 words in the medical category.

Advanced Chinese Dictionary

This is a simplified Chinese to English and simplified Chinese to simplified Chinese dictionary. It contains 8,757 index characters. (Each index character contains words that begin with the character, so the actual word count is much larger than this number.)

C-E Chinese Traditional Medicine Dictionary

This is a simplified Chinese to English dictionary. It contains 56,906 words in the medical category.

C-E Drug Name Dictionary

This is a simplified Chinese to English dictionary. It contains 7,137 entries of drug names.

C-E Jurisprudence Dictionary

This is a simplified Chinese to English dictionary. It contains 61,826 entries of words in the jurisprudence category.

Dict.CN Online

This is an on-line dictionary. It contains definitions of words both from simplified Chinese to English and English to simplified Chinese.

Yodao Web Definition

This is an on-line dictionary. It contains definitions of words both from simplified Chinese to English and English to simplified Chinese.

ICIBA Online

This is an on-line dictionary. It contains definitions of words from simplified Chinese to English and English to simplified Chinese. It also has traditional Chinese entries, but those definitions only refer to the equivalent simplified characters with no explanation in English, which are not very useful.

Dr.eye Online
This is an on-line dictionary. It contains definitions of words from traditional/ simplified Chinese to English and English to simplified Chinese. For looking up words in traditional characters, it converts the characters into simplified characters and then looks for definitions in English.

To download a dictionary, navigate to the dictionary information page and click any link listed in the **Download** section. Select the **Open** button from the **Download** dialog window to download and install the dictionary automatically, or click the **Save** button to save the dictionary to a local file and then install from there. At the time of installing, you will be asked to select two options: "Add to Index Group" and "Add to Cursor Translation Group." These options tell Lingoes if it should assign the dictionary to the specified usage groups. Only dictionaries that are added in the usage groups will be used in Index lookup or for the Cursor Translation. Just check both boxes to add the dictionary to both groups for now. If you don't need to use a dictionary in a group, you can unselect the checkbox later.

Click the **Install** button from the **Installed Dictionaries** tab on the **Dictionary Options** dialog to manually install a dictionary that was saved but not yet installed. Click the **Index Group** tab or the **Cursor Translation Group** tab to manage the installed dictionaries in that group. You can add or remove any installed dictionary and to enable or disable a dictionary from the group list. Use the move up and move down buttons to arrange the order of dictionaries in the group.

5.9.5 Text Translation

Text Translation is the function for performing the primary task in our Chinese reading process—the full text translation. You need to be online to use this feature. Behind the scenes, Lingoes takes the specified block of text, submits it to the selected translation service through the Internet, and gets the results back to display.

To start full text translation, click the **Translation** button located on the right most side of the toolbar on top of the **Results Pane**. This brings the Text Translation section to the **Results Pane** (Figure 5.30).

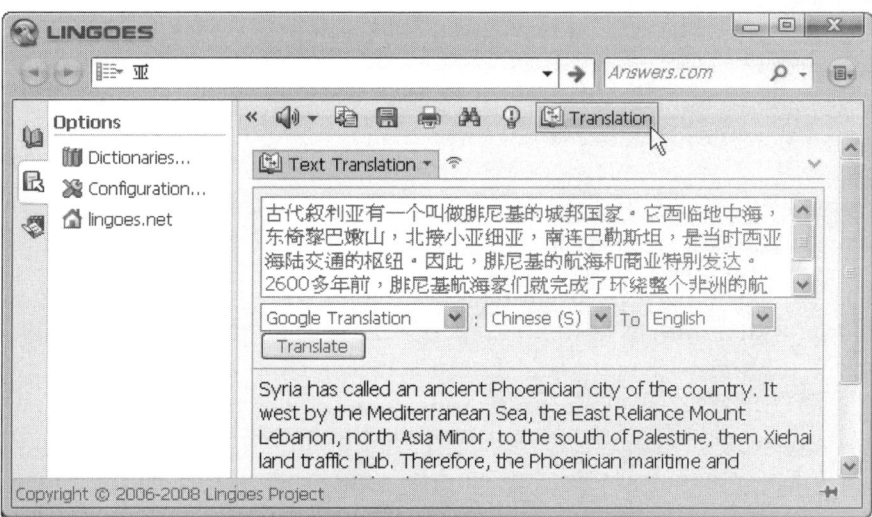

Figure 5.30 Lingoes—Text Translation

Choose the source of the translation service and then select the source and target languages from the dropdown boxes. Paste the block of text into the **Text Translation** text box and hit the **Translate** button to initiate the translation.

Not all the services listed in the dropdown box support translation from Chinese to English. Those that have the Chinese to English feature are: Google Translation, Yahoo Translation, Yahoo Babel Fish, AltaVista, SYSTRAN, KODENSHA, Huajian Translation, and LEC Translation. Among these I like Huajian Translation best because it gives the highest quality of results. One inconvenience about Huajian is that they only allow input of simplified Chinese. Technically, this is not a big issue because translation from traditional Chinese to simplified Chinese is a unique one-to-one mapping, which is easy to do. When you need to translate traditional Chinese using Huajian, you can use the Chinese (T) to Chinese (S) service from Google or Yahoo to get the simplified Chinese text first, and then translate into English. The real issue behind Huajian is that it is limited to the language used in mainland China. In additional to Huajian, SYSTRAN and Goggle are also very good choices.

5.9.6 Text-to-Speech

Like Babylon, Lingoes has a text-to-speech function. When you click the speaker-shaped icon, it will speak the word that comes in the **Term Box**. Again, this feature only works with English. In fact the program uses the exact same

Microsoft TTS (text-to-speech) engine as used in Babylon, so even the speech sounds the same.

5.9.7 Conclusion

Like Babylon, Lingoes has powerful dictionary products, which can be used to complement full text translators to help you read Chinese. The program provides convenient hookups to many different translation services from a single place. The user interface for the translator is a bit primitive, and there is no option you can set for using these translators. However, if you are planning to use web-based software as the primary translation tool, this will be your best choice. My experience with Lingoes is it that works similarly and sometimes a little better than Babylon for most of the functions we need.

5.10 Other Translation Software

华建集团 (Huajian Group Co., Ltd) consists of a group of five companies that make translation-related software products. The headquarters are in Beijing, and it has a close relationship with the China Science Institute. Because 华建 is a popular name in Chinese, and there are also names of different characters that are homophones of 华建, a search of the web for the name "Huajian" is likely to yield lots of unrelated entries.

The website of the Huajian Group that makes the translation software is located at:

http://www.hjtek.com/

I used their on-line translator and was impressed with the quality of the results. Unfortunately, I can not find any of their end-user products for international users. Their products do not have an English user interface and do not run on US Windows systems. At this time, there is really no way for us to use their products, other than to select the Huajian Translation from the Lingoes program and retrieve translated results from there.

Some software vendors develop translation products but unfortunately do not make them available to general consumers. An end user probably has no way of using these so I am not going to spend much time on them. I would just like to briefly mention them so you know that such products exist.

There is a company called Language Weaver, and their website is at:

http://www.languageweaver.com

Their primary product is the Statistical Machine Translation Software (SMTS). According to the description, their translation engine does not use traditional linguistic rule-based methodologies, which incorporate grammar and syntax rules to analyze the source and map it to a target. Instead, they use statistical techniques to train the translator with results obtained from human translations. It lists all the possible combinations for translating a sentence, and uses statistical formulas to calculate the most appropriate combination of words and ways to describe it in the target language.

Their website provides a few sample sentences showing the results of their Chinese to English translator, and the results looked promising. Unfortunately, from the website I was not able to find any place for me to actually test out how good it is. There is a place on their site to request an evaluation, but there is a special note saying: "Language Weaver's translation software is an enterprise solution that is typically deployed on a large scale. Pricing for this software starts at $5,000 and most installations require a system integration effort and IT knowledge. Currently, we do not have a consumer product available."

As an engineer for twenty plus years, I have made a habit of testing things out myself. As such, I filled out the form from there requesting an evaluation. I was honest with them, saying that I was not a big company looking to buy their product, but was only interested in trying the software to see how good it is. To my surprise they responded the next day, and set me up with an account for a 30 day free access to their server. With this account, I was able to run some tests and share the results with our readers. Please refer to our supporting website at http://www.georgekung.com/translators.html for more information on the evaluation results.

Another company you may have heard of is IBM. I believe they also have a Chinese to English translator, but the information I can acquire about it is minimal. All I know is that they have developed a product called AlphaWorks a few years ago, but now I can no longer find information about it. From my personal experience, I would not be surprised if they have already developed a prototype ten years ago that can beat the top of the line products we can find in the market today. They seem to have this habit of spending money developing something, testing it out, and then putting it to sleep.

5.11 Comparison of Translation Programs

In an effort to help you to compare different translation programs to each other, I have conducted some very simple tests. Since the amount of test data is really small, these tests give very rudimentary comparisons. All the results should be viewed as indicative only.

The results of the tests are posted in our supporting website at:

http://www.georgekung.com/translators.html

6. Viewing Translated Results

Machine translated results may contain broken sentences, words composed of phonemic spelling, unintelligible words, etc. Occasionally the results may even contain Chinese characters or other strange symbols. In this chapter let's look at some issues we will face when viewing machine-translated text. These problems may originate from source texts, software settings, limits of the translator programs, nature of the languages, or some combinations from the above. You will learn how to identify, resolve or avoid such problems.

Reading English text translated from Chinese by a machine can be quite different from reading text from human writers. A lot of common grammatical rules no longer apply in these translated sentences. We are going to look at some practical examples of machine translation and compare them to human translation.

6.1 Partially Translated Sentences

Sometimes, Chinese characters or box symbols may be mixed with English words in the translated outputs. When you see partially translated sentences like these, you should check the source language selection of the translation software. It is likely that the setting for the simplified or traditional Chinese has not been made correctly. What happens is that the software is expecting characters from simplified Chinese but is getting characters from traditional Chinese, or vice versa. Since many characters are identical in both sets, the software is still able to translate common characters and words. When seeing characters that are not in the correct set, it renders the non-recognized characters to the output directly. Instead of yielding the Chinese characters, some programs may also put out box symbols, as shown in Figure 6.1.

Some translators, like those from Google and SYSTRAN, are capable of automatically identifying characters from different sets. For others, be careful in specifying the source language. I do hope that software design can be improved to at least give a warning in situations like these. For now, you just have to pay attention to this pitfall.

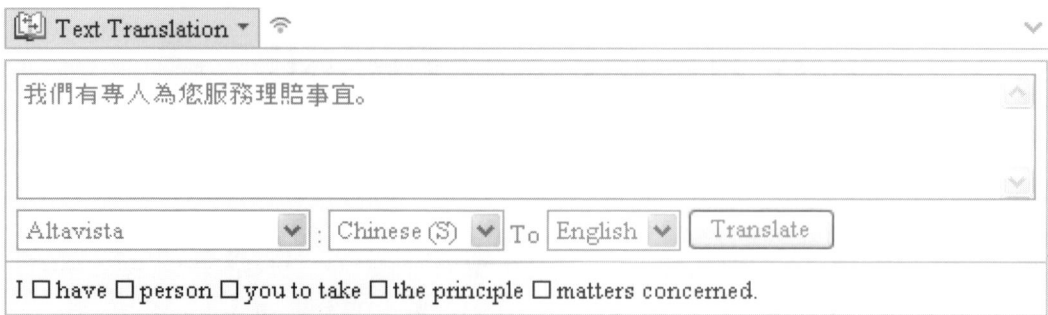

Figure 6.1 Box symbols in the translated text

6.2 Reading Machinglish

With the current technologies, we should probably not expect machine-translated results to be anything close to the writing from a human. Once in a while, the software may give you good translations, but usually, be prepared to read some funny sentences. You can probably say the root cause of this is the linguistic differences between the two languages. What actually happens is that the translation program has failed to properly construct the output sentence using the grammatical rules, or even worse, unable to properly analyze the source text.

Sometimes it seems like the program had just substituted words and concatenated them together. There are also times when the software had decided to spice up a word with something that should not be there, like an extra "the." It may also decide to use the infinitive form of a verb when it should use the real verb. Often the program may use literally translated Chinese words that are not suitable in English. For example, in Chinese texts, people do not "play" baseball or soccer, but they "hit" baseball and "kick" soccer. When those words are translated directly, they may appear funny.

I like to think of the machine translated results from Chinese words as not real English, but something called "Machinglish," which stands for "**Ma**chine & **Chin**ese style En**glish.**" Let us look at a few examples to see some differences between English and Machinglish:

1. A verb in Machinglish may not be the correct verb of that sentence. An infinitive (or adjective) form may be the actual verb in the sentence. A sentence may have none or multiple verbs.

经常进行体能活动有益身心。
Exercising regularly benefits body and soul. (The proper translation)
Regular physical activity wholesome.
Carries on the physical ability activity beneficial body and mind frequently.

盖房子最要紧是把基础打好。
Laying a good foundation is the most important thing when building a house.
(The proper translation)
Builds the house most to be important is hits the foundation.

为了争取好成绩请大家多加努力。
Please put in extra effort to strive for good results. (The proper translation)
In order to strive for the result to ask everybody to add diligently.
For fighting for the good result to invite everyone to more work hard.

2. The order of the words in Machinglish may be different from normal English
usage.

这场球赛他表现得比上回好多了。
He performed much better than last time in this game. (The proper translation)
The match his performance much better than on the back.
This sports match he displayed other day compares was much better.

今天天气很冷。
It is very cold today. (The proper translation)
Today the weather very is cold.
Today, cold weather.

商务部数据显示肉类价格两个月以来首次下跌。
Data from the Commerce department show that the price of meat has fallen
for the first time in two months. (The proper translation)
The department of commercial affairs data display meats price two months have fallen
for the first time.

3. For each Chinese word there may be multiple choices of English words to use
for translation. The software may not pick the proper word to use.

愈来愈多人开始每天运动。
More and more people start to exercise everyday. (The proper translation)
More and more people start to make the movement every day.

这次演唱会办得很成功。

This concert has been a great success. (The proper translation)
This concert manages very much successfully.

多年来，我们培养出无数优秀人才。

Over the years, we have fostered numerous outstanding talents. (The proper translation)
Over the years, we develop numerous talents.
For many years, we have trained countless outstanding talents.

4. The subject in a Chinese sentence is sometimes omitted when there is no ambiguity. The machine may not be able to properly identify the subject and translate accordingly.

技术太差，搞了很久还没好。

Because of my poor skill, I have not finished it despite trying for a long time. (The proper translation)
The technology was too bad, has done very for a long time also not good.
Technology bad, not good engage in a long time.
Technology is too poor, it is not good yet to do for a long time.

北京工地挖出一具清朝完好男尸。

A well preserved man's corpse from the Qing dynasty was unearthed from a work site in Beijing. (The proper translation)
The Beijing work site digs out a Qing Dynasty fine-looking man corpse.
Beijing site dug up a dead Qing dynasty intact.

5. Some words are used differently in Chinese and English. Sometimes the program translates such words literally. The results can look strange or even incomprehensible.

他小提琴拉得很好。

He plays violin very well. (The proper translation)
His violin pulls very much well.

6. Some common usage Chinese phrases get translated literally. These can make the results incomprehensible.

他只知其一，不知其二。

He knows only one aspect (does not know the whole truth) of this thing. (The proper translation)
He only knows its one, does not know its two.

These examples are taken from the actual outputs of translation programs. It will take you some time to get familiar with reading these machine generated sentences. Usually you will see uncommon words being used or words not in their right order, but the sentence is still comprehensible as a whole. Once in a while, poorly translated sentences can be ambiguous or totally senseless. Later in this chapter we will look at how to deal with meaningless outputs from translators. In the next few sections let us focus on a few other topics related specifically to translating Chinese.

6.3 Proper Nouns

When proper names in Chinese are identified and translated into English, the resulting words may appear in Pinyin or other Romanized spelling of the characters. For names of famous persons, places, companies, organizations, etc., translators may be able to pick their commonly known English names. Among all the translators I have used, the Google translator does the best job in translating well-known names.

Here are some examples with translated proper nouns:

新加坡前总统李光耀，13 号到医院探视苏哈托。
Former President of Singapore Lee Kuan Yew, on the 13th to the hospital to visit Suharto.

Both Lee Kuan Yew and Suharto are well known persons. In this example, the translator has successfully identified the two persons and picked the proper English names to use.

郑少秋至玛丽医院，探望前妻沈殿霞。
Zheng Shaoqiu to the Mary hospital, visits ex-wife Shen Dianxia.

The translator has correctly identified the names of the two persons, and translated them using Pinyin in here. Both persons mentioned here are movie stars who are famous in Hong Kong and Taiwan. Their English names are "Adam Cheng" and "Lydia Shum" respectively, but people usually know them by their Chinese names only, so the use of Pinyin is actually more appropriate. The name "Mary hospital" is the proper translation of 玛丽医院. The formal name of the hospital is actually the "Queen Mary Hospital (QMH)," but the source text does not contain this information.

《西线无战事》的作者是雷马克。
"West line Does not have War" the author is Remarque.

The name Remarque has been properly translated. The book name "All Quiet on the Western Front" should have been used in this translation, since it is well known.

湖南卫视为何突然在宁波消失?
1. Hunan Satellite TV in Ningbo why suddenly disappear?
2. Why does Hunan health regard vanishes suddenly in Ningbo?

The name "Hunan Satellite TV" in sentence #1 is the proper translation. The MT in sentence #2 gave a character-by-character interpretation of the characters 卫 and 视, which was incorrect. It also failed to pick the proper interpretation for both characters and produced these words "health regard," which were meaningless and confusing. The correct translation of this sentence should be: "Why has the Hunan Satellite TV suddenly vanished from Ningbo?"

任天堂社长岩田聪召开了记者招待会，介绍了该公司游戏业务的计划。
1. Iwata, president of Nintendo held a press conference to introduce the company's game plan.
2. Was appointed the heaven organization head crag field acute hearing to hold the press conference, introduced this company played the service plan.
3. Ren Tiantang the organization head Iwata acute hearing held the press conference, introduced this company plays the service plan.

Both the company name 任天堂 (*Nintendo*) and the name of its president 岩田聪 (*Iwata Satoru*) were translated correctly in sentence #1. In sentence #2, the company name "the heaven" was translated based on the Chinese word 天堂. The name "crag field acute hearing" is also a character-by-character interpretation of the person's name. In sentence #3, "Ren Tiantang" is the Pinyin of the company's name. This is not ideal, but is better than using "the heaven." Even if you can't relate the similarity between "Ren Tiantang" and "Nintendo", at least you know that it is a name. Mr. Iwata's family name 岩田 was correctly translated into "Iwata," but the name "acute hearing" is a direct interpretation of his given name character 聪. Note that in Chinese, Japanese and Korean, a person's family name is written before the given name.

One difficulty in reading or translating Chinese is identifying the proper nouns in the sentence. Unlike English, where you can count on the first letter of a proper noun to be capitalized, there is no such mechanism in Chinese. Unless the proper name punctuation mark is used, names of persons or places just appear together with other characters in Chinese writing. It is the responsibility of readers to identify these words by themselves. This is really not a very convenient situation come to think of it. Strangely enough, it does not seem to bother most native readers, or at least not to raise major concerns among them, otherwise people would have enforced the usage of punctuation. In reality, proper name marks are rarely used in modern publications or websites. When they are used, it is either in old publications or in textbooks. In school, we are taught to use the punctuation mark, but unfortunately this is ignored in real life.

Theoretically, it is sometimes impossible to identify proper nouns in Chinese by merely looking at the contents. For instance, you can say something like 大树在后院 (*Big tree is in the backyard*) while the word "big tree" can actually be someone's name. There are also cases when a character can be either viewed as part of a person's name, or as belonging to another word. When that happens, all you can do is to look further down the text to see if there are any other places that mention the person's name again. I started to pay attention to this a while ago as I read articles in magazines and have noticed that the ambiguity does not happen as often as I first thought, but it does occur once in a while. I suppose the writers should be responsible of preventing any ambiguity that may occur.

A person's full name in Chinese is normally two to four (usually three) characters long, and consists of the family name followed by the given name. Most family names have only one character, and a few have two characters. Given names usually contain two characters, but single-character given names are commonly seen as well. A few months ago, I read a story about how given names of three characters have recently gained popularity in mainland China.

Figure 6.2 lists the twenty most popular family names in China based on the 2006 study published by the Chinese Academy of Science, institute of Genetics and Developmental Biology.

李	王	張 张	劉 刘	陳 陈	楊 杨	黃 黄	趙 赵	周	吳 吴
Li	Wang	Zhang	Liu	Chen	Yang	Huang	Zhao	Zhou	Wu
徐	孫 孙	朱	馬 马	胡	郭	林	何	高	梁
Xu	Sun	Zhu	Ma	Hu	Guo	Lin	He	Gao	Liang

Figure 6.2 Popular Chinese family names

Since many family-name-characters are also used for other purposes, we cannot simply assume that it is a family name whenever a family-name-character appears in writing. As you read and hear more about people's names you start to have a feel about which characters are commonly used for first and last names. It is not easy to summarize rules to identify Chinese names and I have not heard of any such rules.

Chinese like to address people by their family name, but a family name is rarely used alone in a sentence. Usually they put the person's title after the family name to show respect, or to address people whom they are not very close to. Examples are Chen president, Wu manager, Li director, Wang owner, Zhang teacher, Hu General, Lin Sir, Lu Miss, and so on. When talking about a person in an article, such as in a newspaper or magazine, the first time a person's name appears in the article, it will usually be the full title followed by the full name of that person. For example, it may say "China President Hu Jin Tow…" or "Hunan Gourmet (restaurant) owner Lin Deng Yu…" In all subsequent places in the article, it will then use the surname followed by the title: "Hu President" or "Lee owner."

For closer friends or persons, Chinese like to use 老 (old), or 小 (little) in front of the surname to address that person, for example, "old Fang" or "little Tseng." The word "little" is usually used for people that are young, but the "old" does not mean old in age. For male friends, people also like to use the word 兄 (brother) after the surname, for example, "Lin brother" etc. Even though these words are more commonly used in spoken language, sometimes you see them in writing as well. In Taiwan and some southern regions of China, 阿 (Ah) is commonly used together with one character from the first name to address that person. The character 阿 has no special meaning; it is just used ahead of a first name character to become a nickname of that person. For example, Chen Shui-bian (the former president of ROC) may be referred to as 阿扁 (Ah bian) by his friends.

For the names of places, sometimes the words 省 (province), 市 (city), 县 (county) are used after the names, for example, 北京市 (Beijing city). This makes the identification of names easier. However, such words are usually used in formal documents only. They are usually omitted in regular dialogs or writings.

People unfamiliar with Chinese have to rely mainly on the translation software to identify proper nouns in the text. To my surprise, I found that most translation software handled this quite well. They usually don't have much trouble with names of well known places or people.

6.4 The Number System in Chinese

In English, a large number is presented by the grouping of three digits, using the words thousand, million, billion, and trillion. In Chinese, the grouping is made in four digits. The Chinese character 万 (*myriad*) represents 10,000 and the character 亿 represents 100,000,000. The number 123,000 is written as "twelve myriads three thousands" instead of "one hundred twenty three thousands."

Luckily, the translator automatically handles the conversion of numbers. The translated output will either describe numbers using the familiar thousands and millions, or just use numeric values. I have tried feeding Chinese text with various numbers in either pure Chinese characters or numeric symbols. Most of the translator software converted and translated them properly.

6.5 Spotting Problems in Translated Sentences

There are times when you may find the translated text ambiguous or not intelligible. One possible way to resolve this issue is just to try a different translator.

The Text Translation function in Lingoes (see Chapter 5.9.5) allows you to translate a block of writing using services from different providers. There are eight choices for Chinese to English translation: Google Translation, Yahoo Translation, Yahoo Babel Fish, AltaVista, SYSTRAN, KODENSHA, Huajian Translation, and LEC Translation. The translation engines from these products have different designs and use their own dictionaries. Sometimes the translated results they produce can be very different. When you can't get intelligent results from one product, it may be helpful to try others.

Among them I find that the Huajian translator usually stands out. I suggest trying the Huajian translator first when you need to get a second opinion. However, one problem with Huajian translator is that it does not perform translations of new words well, especially words that are used outside of mainland China.

For the other seven translators, I found that SYSTRAN and Google translators produce very good results as well. SYSTRAN works best for simple, regular text. It is stable and consistently performs well. On the other hand, Google is more of a genius type. It may produce exceptionally good results when other translators fail, but then it can totally miss the boat with some simple ones. The large collection of well-known names in Google's dictionary is very impressive, but the algorithm in identifying the names becomes too aggressive sometimes. Once in a while, it mistakenly takes a regular character that is not part of a name as a name, and produces some strange translations. It also has a habit of omitting some words it has trouble with from the source sentence. This strategy may work well occasionally, but sometimes it can make problems worse.

One other thing I like about SYSTRAN and Google is that they allow the mixed use of traditional and simplified characters. This should really become a standard feature for the next generation of Chinese OCR and translation software.

For other translators, the results from Yahoo, Yahoo Babel Fish and AltaVista are usually similar to SYSTRAN's output. Yahoo and AltaVista usually produce exactly the same outputs most of the time. I suppose these four translators use the same translation engine, but from different versions, and with slightly different dictionaries. Once in a while, LEC gives good results while all others fail. As for KODENSHA, a lot of the time I can't understand what it says.

If using different programs still fails to give a satisfactory translation, you need to resort to the use of dictionaries. A dictionary shows you a list of all the possible explanations of a word. Instead of relying on the software to pick the translation of individual words in a sentence, you can manually interpret them yourself. Often, machines fail to correctly translate text simply because they misinterpret some key words in the sentence. Looking for alternative explanations of words manually works very well in such a situation. With the help of dictionary programs like Lingoes or Babylon, doing word-by-word translation is not as painful as it sounds.

Take the following sentence for example:

什么食物可以润喉?
What types of food soothe the throat? (The proper translation)
1. What food can be throat?
2. What food can wet one's whistle?

The word 润喉 means to moisten or soothe one's throat. The first MT program fails to translate the character 润 completely. The second MT program interprets the word 润喉 as "wet one's whistle" (to have a drink), which is also incorrect. Now let's try to use the dictionaries to look up for definitions manually. The first three words, 什么 (*what*), 食物 (*food*) and 可以 (*can; may*) are very simple. You should not have any trouble finding the proper definitions from any dictionaries. For the last word 润喉, you will find "wet one's whistle" from one dictionary and "moisten one's throat" from another. Apparently, the latter makes more sense. If it happens that there is no dictionary that gives the proper translation of the word 润喉, you will end up with a character-by-character looking up of the word. As you do that, the first character 润 is identified as "lubricate," "moist," "smooth," "profit" and "sleek," and the second character 喉 can be "larynx," "throat" or "throttle." It is not hard to conclude that the word should mean "moisten the throat."

One area that the translation software may have trouble in is translating the title blocks in the news or advertisements. Non-essential characters may have been omitted in the title in exchange for a larger font to draw attention. I guess sometimes they make them ambiguous on purpose so people will read on. This is also a place where using word-by-word manual translation may be productive.

6.6 When the Source Contains Wrong Characters

When you type the word "Scotish" in the search box on Yahoo! or Google, they come back with a warning message:

Did you mean: *Scottish*

Similarly, when you send text out for translation, the source may have errors as well, even though the situation may be slightly different from English. First of all, the Chinese language does not have an alphabet, so incorrect spelling as such is impossible. When something goes wrong in Chinese, it occurs at the character level. For instance, when text is produced from an OCR program, it is possible that some characters are confused with other similar-looking ones. We have discussed this in the previous chapter when talking about OCR. There are many characters in Chinese that look alike, for example, 己 and 已, 鳥 and 烏, just to give a couple. This sort of confusion can still happen even when you are not using OCR to recognize things. One possibility is that the text you read from the websites or other resources may be the output of OCR software. People usually proofread after doing OCR, but some characters can still be missed. The other interesting situation is that a wrong character can actually be typed using the keyboard. When entering Chinese characters into the computer, in the last step, people usually need to pick one from a list of characters that sound alike or look alike. It is not unusual for people to get confused and pick the wrong character.

In the previous chapter, I mentioned an interesting case in which the word 新聞 was mistakenly recognized as 新閒 by the OCR, and that in turn caused problems in the translation. Out of curiosity, I entered the incorrect word 新閒 in the Yahoo! and Google search engines to see what would happen. Since I did not expect them to catch Chinese "spelling" problems, I was not surprised to see that they didn't give me the "Did you mean: 新聞" warning message. What amazed me was that I actually got quite a lot of hits. Initially, I thought this must be a new word people used for describing "a new generation of idling people." As I looked further into the detailed descriptions in each instance, I found that all except one of them are meant to say 新聞, but had mistakenly typed the character 聞 as 閒.

Similarities in the shape of characters are not the only reason for such a problem. A more common mistake is when two characters sound the same. Similar to how people sometimes confuse *affect* and *effect*, characters with same pronunciation can confuse native Chinese users. For example, a lot of times people say 不恥 (not ashamed of) but what they really want to say is 不齒 (despise). What makes the situation more complex is that there are actually places where you should be using 不恥, so you can't just flag the 不恥 as an error either.

When the source text contains an incorrect character, you will usually see some strange words coming out of the translation programs. One way to deal with this is just to ignore the strange words and read around them. If the mistake is not in a key word, then usually you can still understand the sentence. I will show you some examples of reading text containing incorrect characters in Chapter 8. Other than that, there is basically no way to cope with such problems. None of the translation software I know of is able to check for errors in the source text. Maybe this is a good place where software vendors can bring their products to the next level.

6.7 Getting Related Information from the Internet

When you are stuck with a word of a phrase, it can be useful to search for it from Chinese-based websites such as Yahoo! China, Yahoo! Taiwan, or even the regular Yahoo or Goggle sites. These can lead you to pages with more information related to the words. Even though these pages might be written entirely in Chinese, they will give you some clues or even the full explanation about the word you are looking for. You can then use the web translator to translate the web page again to get the information you want. The good thing about using search engines is that even if the word you entered contains extra characters, it will still yield some valid results.

I recently came upon the word 还瞳子 as I was reading an article from a magazine. The contents are related to traditional Chinese medicines, and that word is a nick name for cassia seed. When I entered the paragraph in different translators, I got results such as "returns the pupil," "also Tongzi," etc., which make little sense. I also looked it up from the dictionaries in Lingoes and Babylon, and couldn't find anything in there either. After I tried searching the word from the Yahoo! Taiwan website, I got lots of results with all the information I needed right away.

6.8 Conclusion

In this chapter, I described issues relating to machine translation and ways to deal with them. You read real sentences produced by translation programs, and saw that they can be quite different from regular English. We discussed how proper names are handled by the translators and how they can be misinterpreted. When the output from one translator is not intelligible, you now know to switch to another program. You learned that you can use a dictionary program to do a word-by-word lookup when all translators failed to give reasonable results. You also saw that how problems can be caused by wrong characters in the source document.

Don't worry if you are still not very clear on some of these topics. In Chapter 8, I am going to show you a lot of real-life examples of reading Chinese text. You will see exactly how these techniques actually get used to solve problems. After finishing Chapter 8, you shall become very familiar with reading Chinese with the help of a computer.

7. Advanced Topics

In this chapter, we are going to look at a few advanced topics related to Chinese translation. These are special but practical situations that the translation software will face. The results from different translators under these circumstances can vary a lot, depending on the quality of the software. In most cases the dominant factor is actually the dictionaries the software uses and not the translation engine itself. Although the real resolution of these problems needs to come from the translation programs, knowing the root causes can help you pinpoint the trouble spots easier and earlier. You can either look for help from alternative translators, or be aware of the patterns of bad results and avoid or ignore them. In addition, these problematic areas are also good candidates for benchmarking different products and for vendors to make improvements. In the last section, I am going to briefly talk about getting help from human translators on the Internet.

For those readers who can't wait to begin reading Chinese, you can skip this chapter now and come back at a later time.

7.1 Translate Transliterated Words

Nowadays, it is very common to see foreign translated words in Chinese writing. Persons, places, companies, books, movies, etc. can all have translated names in Chinese. When the names of persons or places get transliterated into Chinese, the selected words are usually meaningless on their own, but the sound of these words closely matches the pronunciation of the original names.

Some commonly used English persons' names have their standard transliteration because they have been well known for a very long time, for example:

John (約翰), Mary (玛丽), David (大卫), Tom (汤姆), George (乔治), Judy (茱蒂), Henry (亨利), Anna (安娜)

Since each Chinese character can represent only one syllable in pronunciation, most English words are transliterated into two or three Chinese characters. To show people's full name in the transliteration, the proper representation should be the first name, followed by a dot sign, and then the last name. The dot sign is a special punctuation mark to help separate a foreigner's first name from the last name, since there is no such provision in the original Chinese language. The dot sign looks like a period in English, except it appears at the center of a character instead of at the bottom. The Chinese period symbol, on the other hand, looks like a circle, which is different from that in English. If a middle name also appears in the transliteration, a similar mechanism is used. The name will be written as the first name, dot, middle name, dot, and then last name. For example, the name "George Walker Bush" is represented by:

乔治·沃克·布什

The other use of the dot sign in Chinese is for separating things in a hierarchy, such as the name of a place, represented by province, county, town, etc. When you see a dot in the text, it gives you a hint that the words around the dot are names for persons or places. Unfortunately, just like the proper noun mark, the dot marks are sometimes omitted. When this happens, the full name is written as the first and last names lumped together, for example: 乔治布什 (*George Bush*)

There is one interesting difference between the use of a Chinese family name and a transliterated family name in Chinese. It is very common in Chinese writing to address foreigners in their transliterated family name directly, but this rarely occurs with a Chinese family name. In Chinese writing, a Chinese family name will not be used alone to address people. You may see 布什访问日本 (*Bush visits Japan*), but you won't see 胡访问日本 (*Hu visits Japan*).

One challenge with a translated name is that there may be different versions for the same name. For a common name like "George," which has probably been well known since President Washington's era, its transliteration 乔治 is used in both Taiwan and China. In contrast, there are many different versions of the name Bush. The word is officially translated into 布希 in Taiwan, 布什 in China, and 布殊 in Hong Kong. I do not know whether this should be categorized as the lack of a standard or just too many standards.

We need to rely mainly on the translator to identify transliterated names in the sentence. If an English name has been transliterated into a less commonly known word, then the translator software may not be able to identify or translate it properly. A better result in such a situation is that the software still knows that it is a name, and gives you the Pinyin or Romanized spelling of it. Although it may not be exactly the same as the original English word, at least you know that it is a name and hopefully the pronunciation sounds close to the original word. For example, here are the Pinyin words of three versions of the transliterated name "Bush":

布希 (*Buxi*)   布什(*Bushi*)   布殊 (*Bushu*)

The worst case scenario will be a blind character-to-character translation, based on the meaning of individual characters. This is not only useless, but can also cause confusion. For example, I have noticed that the word 布殊, the least commonly known transliterated version of the name "Bush," gets translated back to "cloth extremely" by some translators.

Place names are mostly translated to Chinese in a similar way—based on their pronunciations in the original language. For countries and big cities that were already well known before the communist party took over China, the same transliterated names are usually used in both Taiwan and China. For newly established countries, the transliterated name may have two different versions. For even smaller geographic areas, they may have many different transliterated names. Some of the names may be given just randomly by the author of the article. In such cases, they sometimes put the names from the original language after the transliterated Chinese names, enclosed by parentheses, such as:

大宝丘山 (Mt. Tapochau) 位于塞班岛中央。
(*Mount Tapochau is located at the center of Saipan.*)

Technically, translating transliterated Chinese words back to English should not be a problem for translation software. Even though an English word may have two or three different versions of transliterated words in Chinese, they can all be entered into the dictionaries and used together. The whole thing basically comes down to the effort of creating these dictionaries to be used in the programs.

7.2 Neologisms

Like all other natural languages, Chinese is "alive." As over one billion people use it every day, new words are invented quickly. This is especially true among the younger generation and Internet users. Besides, the Chinese language itself is intrinsically more liberal in allowing for the creation of new words. When a new word is needed, people just find the least number of characters that can put together to describe the thing or concept. If the invention is a good one, it will quickly become popular.

Sometimes people get carried away further and intend to invent new characters, as if the existing 30,000 characters are too limited for their brilliant ideas. This intent usually occurs when people try to write something that only exists in a dialect or spoken language. Such a practice has not become popular, because there is basically no way to enter a non-existent character into a computer. Nevertheless, this technical difficulty hasn't stopped the enthusiasm of some hardcore dialect language promoters. Instead of creating a new character, people will try to find an existing character with a similar pronunciation and give it a new meaning. When there is no suitable character available, they will use phonetic (e.g., Zhuyin) symbols in their writing to represent it.

A few months ago, I read about a couple in China who had tried to use the symbol "@" for naming their newborn child. I don't know how the story ended, but I am afraid to think just how much it is going to cost society to accommodate such strange requirements. On the other hand, it feels good to know that young people these days have become more creative than the previous generation. At least they dare to do things differently and are not afraid to act like a true "revolutionary." To be honest, I am getting tired of seeing so many people of my generation from mainland China using the character 紅 (*red*) in their given names.

Anyway, let's get back to our topic. Here are a few scenarios that I can think of where new words can be invented:

Scenario 1: A word is needed to describe a thing or concept that does not exist or has rarely been seen previously. With the opening up and rapid growth in economy and personal wealth, we now see the word 新貴 (*an upstart, a parvenu*) used almost everywhere. Another example is the word 卡奴 (*card slave*) for describing people who work hard to pay for the high credit card interests every month. The "blog," a special style of website, is given the name 博客 in China, and 部落格 in Taiwan. 珍珠奶茶 (*bubble tea; BOBA*) is a drink with sweetened tea, milk, and gummy balls made of tapioca or yam starch.

Scenario 2: A new word can be given for concepts that are already named. The reason for the new name may be because it is easier to use, more closely resembles a foreign word both in sound and meaning, or is just simply "cool (酷)." For example, cell phone was originally known as 行動電話 (*Movement Telephone*), but the four-character word is long and clumsy. The new name 手機 (*Hand Machine*) is much easier to use, so it became popular. The word 血拼 ("*Xiepin*" in Pinyin) is now used to mean "shopping," even though there were many existing words for that purpose. Other than the similarity in the pronunciations to "shopping," the character 血 means "blood," and 拼 means "go all out," which very much resembles the way shoppers act. The word "lottery" has a new name 樂透 ("*Letou*" in Pinyin) in Chinese, where 樂 means "happy," and 透 means "fully." The colloquial word "cool" has an analogy in Chinese 酷 ("*Ku*" in Pinyin). The original meaning of the character is "cruel" or "extreme."

Scenario 3: A character can be given a meaning that it did not have before. This is popular especially among users of Instant Messaging (IM), newsgroups or blogs. In Chinese, there is no equivalent to using words like BRB (*Be right back*) or GR8 (*Great*), but they have other ways to mess with the language. One example is to use the character 偶 to replace 我. The character 偶 originally had nothing to do with 我. It just so happens that when people pronounce 我 with a Taiwanese accent, it ends up sounding like 偶. Another good example is the use of 糗. The Chinese character 糗 originally meant "cooked or dry food." Because it sounds the same as a spoken word with no written form that means "embarrassing," now the character 糗 is used for that instead. The funny thing is that "cooked or dry food" is the only meaning found in dictionaries, but in reality nobody knows or uses it for that. When you see this character used, it almost always means "embarrassing." Some other examples of using a character for a new meaning include the use of 虧 to mean "teasing," the word 扁 for "to beat up (someone)," and 係 for "is."

I ran some tests with these new words in translators. The words from scenario 1 are usually handled correctly. For scenario 2, I got mixed results. Some were translated correctly but others weren't. Words from scenario 3 were mostly not recognized.

7.3 Regional Characters and Words

Many dialects are spoken by Chinese language users in different geographic regions. It is not unusual for some words from these dialects to enter written Chinese. One major dialect is Cantonese, which is widely used in Canton, Hong Kong and many overseas Chinese communities. The unique thing about Cantonese is that not only does it have its own words, but it also developed its own set of characters containing more than 3,000 entries. Text written in this dialect contains the mix of traditional Chinese and the Cantonese characters. These characters are used only by people speaking the dialect, and not by other Chinese speaking populations. Some of the OCR products we have examined can be set up to recognize this special set of characters. None of the translation software I have used is able to handle Cantonese characters. When you feed

Cantonese text to the translators, you are likely to get results similar to those described in Chapter 6.1, where you get a mix of English words and Cantonese characters or box symbols. Luckily, the use of Cantonese characters is limited to very small amounts of materials that appear in local papers and publications only. Most of the writing used in Hong Kong is still in pure traditional Chinese characters.

Because of the influence from Britain, Hong Kong uses quite a few Chinese words that are transliterated directly from English. Don't think that you are able to take advantage of such situation because of your English background. Without knowing the pronunciation of characters, you will not be able to read them. In fact, even knowing the sound won't help because the pronunciation is based on Cantonese, which is very different from Mandarin. Here are some examples of these transliterated words with their Pinyin representations. You can see that they may not sound close to English.

曲奇 (*cookie*), "*Quqi*" in Pinyin
貼士 (*tips*), "*Tieshi*" in Pinyin
的士 (*taxi*), "*Dishi*" in Pinyin
士多 (*store*), "*Shiduo*" in Pinyin
波士 (*boss*), "*Boshi*" in Pinyin

Many popular colloquial words have entered written Chinese from other Chinese speaking areas as well. Some examples of popular slang words used in mainland China include:

打車 (*take the taxi*)
大款 (*big shot; rich person*)
下岗 (*unemployed*)
倒爷 (*profiteer*)

Shanghai is the biggest city in China, and it is one of the earliest places that opened up to foreign countries in modern Chinese history. It has been greatly influenced by foreigners ever since the early nineteenth century. A lot of words used by local Shanghai people are also directly transliterated from English. The pronunciations of these words are close to the sound from the Shanghai dialect. Some of these words have also become popular in the whole country. For example:

水门汀 (*cement*) "*Shuimenting*" in Pinyin
发烧友 (*fancier*) "*Fashaoyou*" in Pinyin
开司米 (*Kashmir*) "*Kaisimi*" in Pinyin
罗宋 (*Russian*) "*Luosong*" in Pinyin

The Taiwanese dialect originates from the southern part of Fujian province in China. Since Taiwan had been ruled by Japan for 50 years, some words in the Taiwanese dialect originated from Japanese. Unlike the Cantonese or Shanghai dialects, most Taiwanese words entered mainland China only recently. As more people from Taiwan started doing business and investing in mainland China over the past decade, the use of Taiwanese colloquial words became popular.

Some examples of slang words originated from Taiwan include:

便當 (*lunch box*)
運將 (*taxi driver*)
夭壽 (*A cursing word, similar to "damn"*)
馬殺雞 (*massage*) "*Masaji*" in Pinyin

The handling of colloquial words and transliterated words in the translation software relies mainly on the dictionaries. If a word does not exist in the dictionaries, then the translation will be meaningless. Colloquial words that are not transliterated from foreign words are somewhat in a better situation. A direct translation may remotely provide some hints to the word. For example, a character-by-character interpretation of the word 打車 (*take the taxi*) can yield the result of "hit; beat" and "car." Looking up for the word 下岗 (*unemployed*) is likely to come back with the translation: "down," "off" and "duty," "post."

Sometimes one concept can have different names known by people from different Chinese speaking regions, usually between Taiwan and China. This is similar to the use of words "autumn" and "fall," or "elevator" and "lift" in English.

Refrigerator: 冰箱 (Taiwan)   雪柜 (mainland China)
LASER: 雷射 (Taiwan)   激光 (mainland China)

7.4 Getting Help from Human Translators

There may be times when you are really stuck and wish to get help from human translators. Many translation services are listed on the Internet. They can provide very fine quality translations. However, such services are usually used for the purpose of producing professional documents. They are costly and also take time to set up initially. These services are not suitable for our needs to occasionally understand the meaning of a phrase or short paragraph.

When searching the Internet, I found a few websites that network between people seeking a translation, and volunteer translators. Some sites provide a forum-type environment for users to post and reply to messages. You can post the source text and wait for messages from other users with translated results. Another website uses e-mail for communication. It formats a source text entered by requesters into e-mail messages and sends them to one of the selected translators registered with the site. You need to give your e-mail address to receive the translated results in your e-mail. Since these services are offered solely by volunteers, you cannot count on getting your questions answered within a certain time, or at all. In addition, you should be aware that there is no guarantee of the accuracy of the translated results. In a forum, since the messages are viewable by everyone, it is easier to get second opinions about the translation.

There aren't many such resources on the Internet, and I do not know if the situation will improve. Most of these websites are in the professional translation service business, and they offer the free environment as a way to entice traffic.

Listed below are all such resources I know that have Chinese to English support with reasonable activity. I will keep this list updated on our supporting website.

Freelang.net
http://www.freelang.net/

Free-translator.com
http://www.free-translator.com/forum

ProZ.com
http://www.proz.com/

8. Real-Life Examples

In this chapter, let me show you some real-life examples of reading Chinese. You will see how text images from different sources are captured, fixed as needed, recognized, translated and read. You will face with real problems caused by misrecognition of the OCR and unintelligible outputs from the translators, and learn how to deal with them. You will read a lot of sentences in Machinglish and find ways to understand them. You will have to choose between traditional and simplified character sets, and learn what to do when the choice is incorrect. You will see the practical use of many techniques described earlier in this book.

Previously, when discussing the use of various products, I described many different ways of doing things, some of them quite complex and advanced. In real life, you will see that the most basic, simplest and fastest method is usually all we need. To keep the process simple, I scan the document directly from the OCR program whenever possible, avoiding the trouble of saving and opening image files. I also run the translator program together with the OCR. This allows me to move the recognized text from the OCR to the translator directly through Windows Clipboard.

8.1 Reading a Magazine Article

In the first example, I picked a document with a simple layout, with no mixing of graphics and text. You will most likely see things like this in a book or magazine. It is an article from a Chinese magazine *Tzu Chi Medical Monthly*, published by Tzu Chi Foundation. This is a charity organization that originated in Taiwan more than forty years ago, providing social and humanitarian services. At first they were limited to Taiwan, and now work around the world.

Step 1: Evaluate the material
Figure 8.1 shows a picture of the material. The layout of this page is very simple. There is no complex color background or mixing of graphics within the text area. An image editor will not be needed in such a case, so I decided to scan from the OCR program directly. The printing quality is good, and the text is printed in a regular-sized font. This calls for using of the most common 300 dpi resolution, B/W scanning.

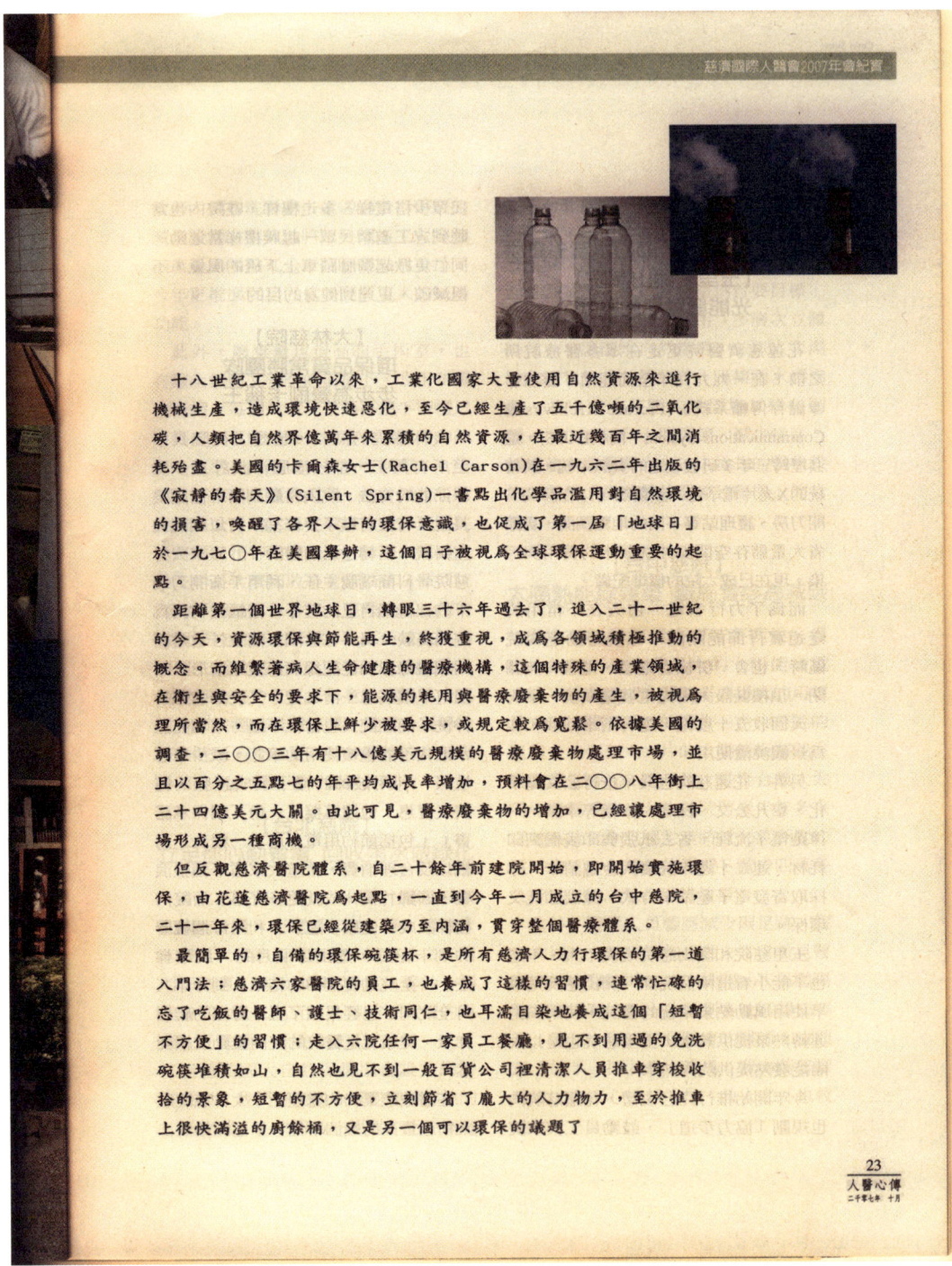

Figure 8.1 The magazine article

© 2007-2008 BUDDHIST COMPASSION RELIEF TZU CHI FOUNDATION All rights reserved.
Author: 吳宛霖

When using OCR, one thing I need to worry about is whether the text uses traditional or simplified Chinese characters. From the layout of the text, I could easily see that they go horizontally. This didn't provide me any clue about the character set. Looking around, I found that the address of the publisher (in English) is in Taiwan. The website URL of the organization listed in the back of the magazine, with the ".tw" country code top-level domain name, also indicates that it is from Taiwan. These gave me hints that the material was printed in traditional Chinese. I also applied the technique described in Chapter 2.12. By looking at the first few characters, I noticed that the radical of the 4th character 紀 is written in the traditional way and not using the simplified way 纪. Anyway, for the sake of demonstration, let me assume that I did not know which character set it used and had made a wrong guess.

Step 2: Scan the material from the OCR

I used MaxReader 5 for my OCR task. After starting the program, I clicked **Acquire** from the **File** menu. This brought me the TWAIN dialog window provided by my Canon scanner (Figure 8.2).

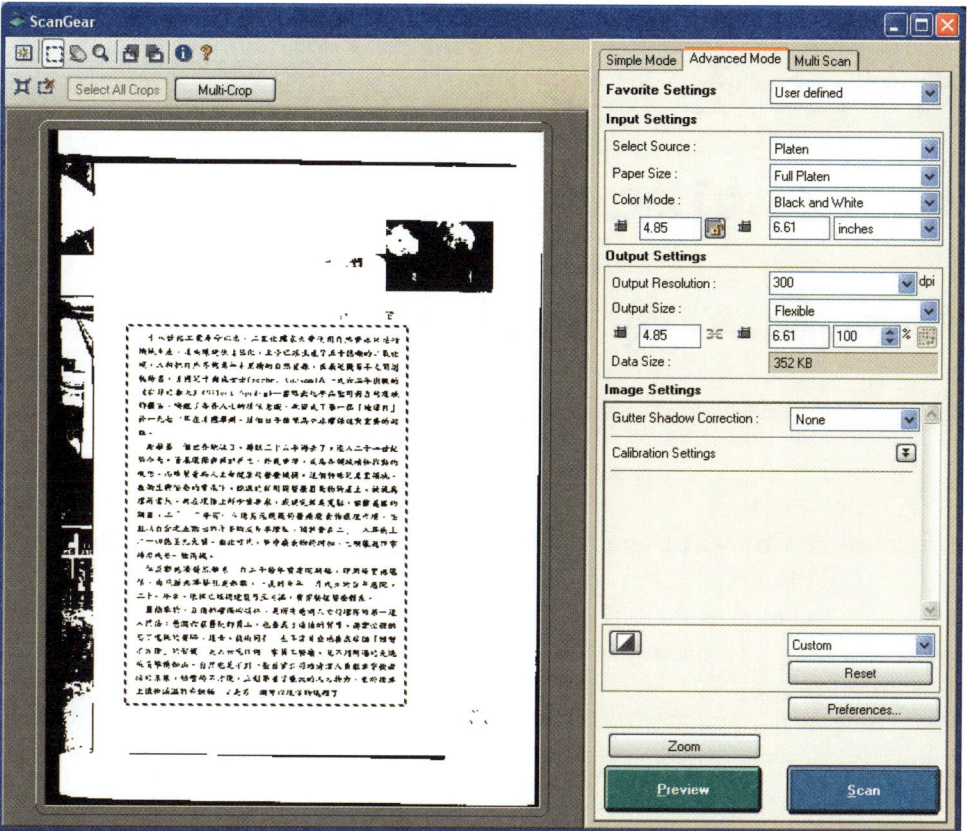

Figure 8.2 Select scanning area and parameters from the TWAIN dialog window

I selected the **Advanced Mode** tab on the right-hand side of the dialog window. This allows me to make detailed adjustment of the parameters to change the B/W intensity. I dragged a rectangular region to mark the area to scan. I excluded the two small pictures at the right top corner as well as the subtitle at the right bottom corner because they seemed irrelevant. I chose Black and White mode, 300 dpi resolution, and also adjusted the intensity level for the text to show up properly. I pressed the **Scan** button and waited for the scanning to complete. After the scanning, the TWAIN dialog went away and the result appeared in the OCR window. I zoomed in the view to 200% to examine the scanning results and the image looked very good (Figure 8.3).

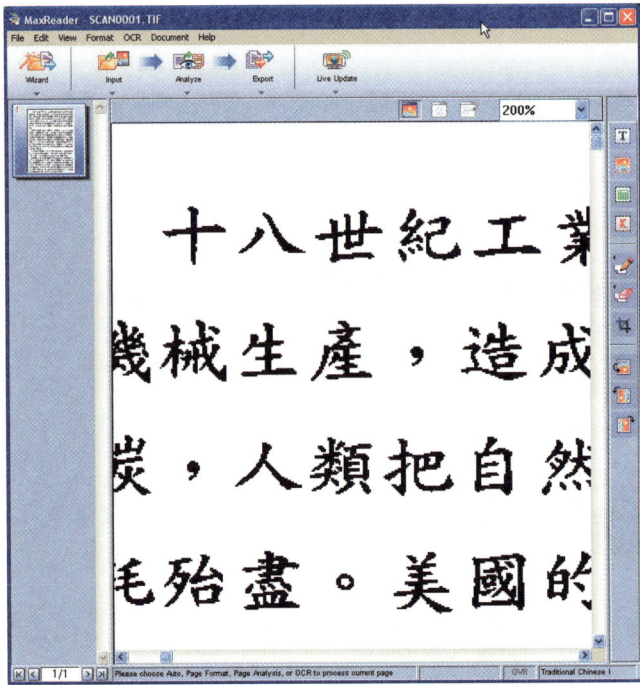

Figure 8.3 View scanned result in MaxReader

Step 3: Recognize the text
I clicked **Recognize Current Page** from the **OCR** menu to recognize the text. When it finished, I clicked the **Proof Mode** icon at the top right corner of the program window to check the OCR result (Figure 8.4). I noticed right away something was wrong because there were too many uncertain characters, which were shown in blue. As I have mentioned in Chapter 4.1.6, we should normally see less than 10% of the characters marked as suspicious. If this ratio is too high, it means there is a problem with either the character set setting or the image quality. In here, we were seeing good image quality, yet almost half the characters were shown in blue. This was apparently incorrect.

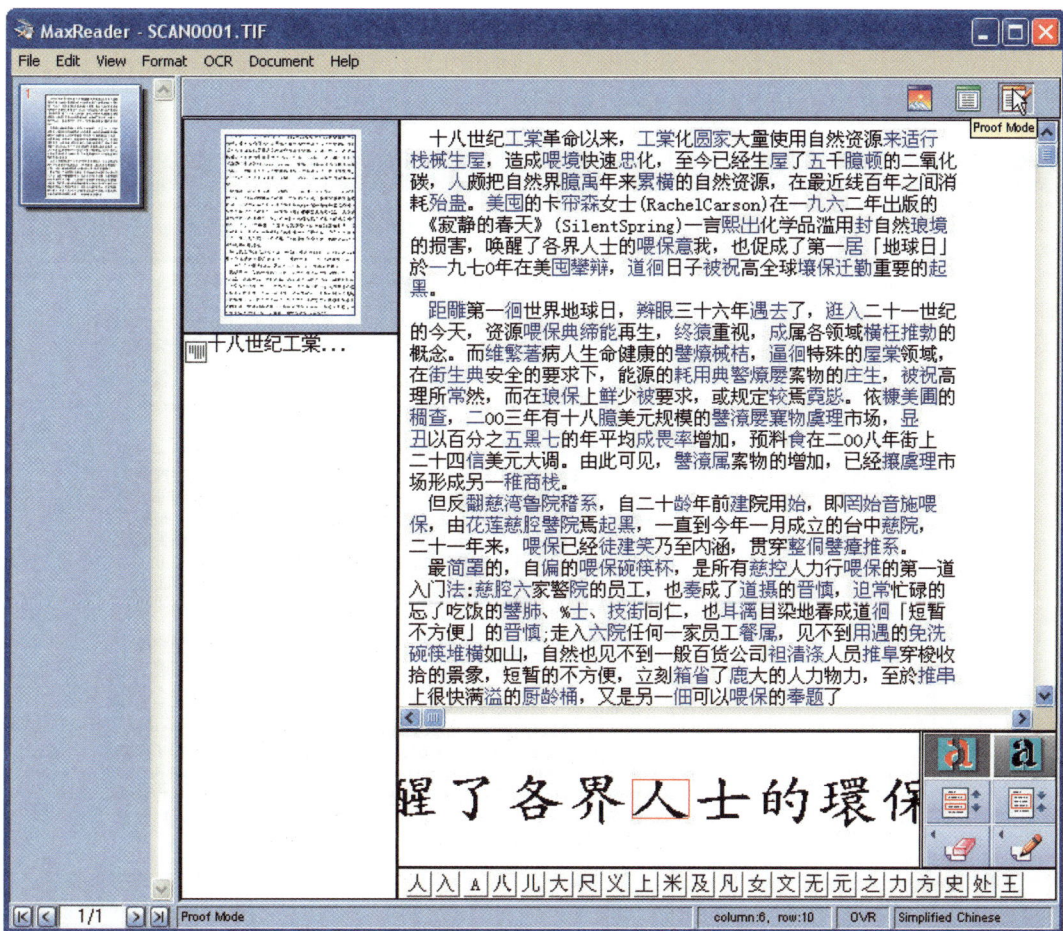

Figure 8.4 OCR results with uncertain characters shown in blue—incorrect character set

I clicked the **Format** menu, selected **Set Character Set**, and noticed the setting is in **Simplified Chinese**. I suspected this setting was incorrect and decided to change it. Before doing so, I had to delete the OCR results first. I clicked the **Discard OCR Result of Current Page** from the **OCR** menu. After that, I went back to change the character set to **Traditional Chinese I**. This selection is suitable for traditional Chinese used in regular text, as oppose to **Traditional Chinese II**, which is more suitable with documents composed of ancient words. I followed the same steps to recognize the page, and clicked the **Proof Mode** icon after the recognition. The OCR result looked much better this time (Figure 8.5). I found only a few characters that were marked in blue, but they looked like regular Chinese characters to me.

The next step should really be proofreading, but this task would not be easy for people that don't read Chinese, so I skipped it and went directly to translation.

While in Proof Mode, I clicked **<Ctrl>** C to copy the recognized result into Windows Clipboard. I started Windows WordPad and pasted the text into a new document there. Figure 8.6 shows the OCR output of the text.

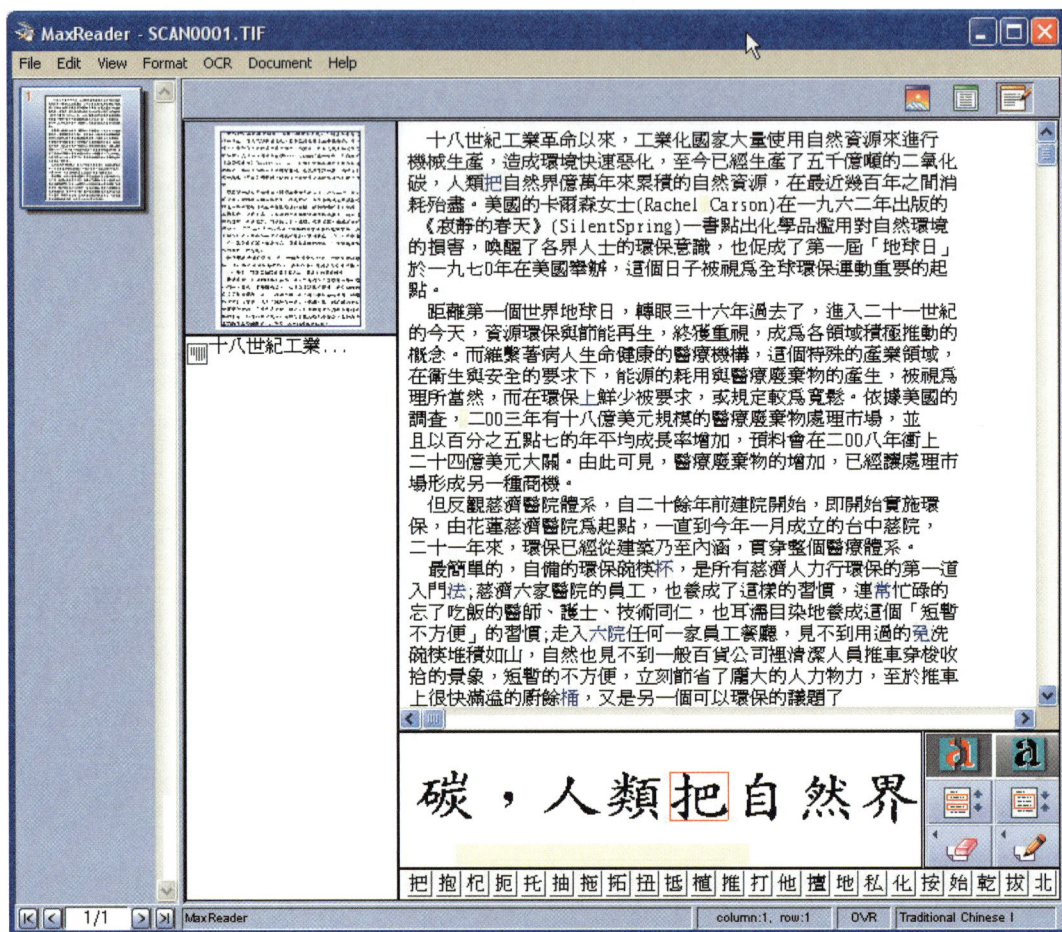

Figure 8.5 OCR results with uncertain characters highlighted—correct character set

　十八世紀工業革命以來，工業化國家大量使用自然資源來進行
機械生產，造成環境快速惡化，至今已經生產了五千億噸的二氧化
碳，人類把自然界億萬年來累積的自然資源，在最近幾百年之間消
耗殆盡。美國的卡爾森女士(RachelCarson)在一九六二年出版的
《寂靜的春天》(SilentSpring)一書點出化學品濫用對自然環境
的損害，喚醒了各界人士的環保意識，也促成了第一屆「地球日」
於一九七０年在美國舉辦，這個日子被視為全球環保運動重要的起
點。
　距離第一個世界地球日，轉眼三十六年過去了，進入二十一世紀
的今天，資源環保與節能再生，終獲重視，成為各領域積極推動的
概念。而維繫著病人生命健康的醫療機構，這個特殊的產業領域，

在衛生與安全的要求下，能源的耗用與醫療廢棄物的產生，被視爲
理所當然，而在環保上鮮少被要求，或規定較爲寬鬆。依據美國的
調查，二00三年有十八億美元規模的醫療廢棄物處理市場，並
且以百分之五點七的年平均成長率增加。預料會在二00八年衝上
二十四億美元大關。由此可見，醫療廢棄物的增加，已經讓處理市
場形成另一種商機。

但反觀慈濟醫院體系，自二十餘年前建院開始。即開始實施環
保，由花蓮慈濟醫院爲起點，一直到今年一月成立的台中慈院，
二十一年來，環保已經從建築乃至內涵，貫穿整個醫療體系。

最簡單的，自備的環保碗筷杯，是所有慈濟人力行環保的第一道
入門法;慈濟六家醫院的員工，也養成了這樣的習慣，連常忙碌的
忘了吃飯的醫師、護士、技術同仁，也耳濡目染地養成這個「短暫
不方便」的習慣;走入六院任何一家員工餐廳。見不到用過的免洗
碗筷堆積如山，自然也見不到一般百貨公司裡清潔人員推車穿梭收
拾的景象，短暫的不方便，立刻節省了龐大的人力物力，至於推車
上很快滿溢的廚餘桶，又是另一個可以環保的議題了

Figure 8.6 Text output from the OCR program

Step 4: Translate and read the text
I started Lingoes and clicked the **Translation** icon to bring up the Text
Translation portal. I selected SYSTRAN as the translator and selected Chinese
and English as the source and target languages respectively. I pressed **<Ctrl> V** to
paste text from the Clipboard into the text box and clicked the **Translate** button to
get the whole page translated (Figure 8.7).

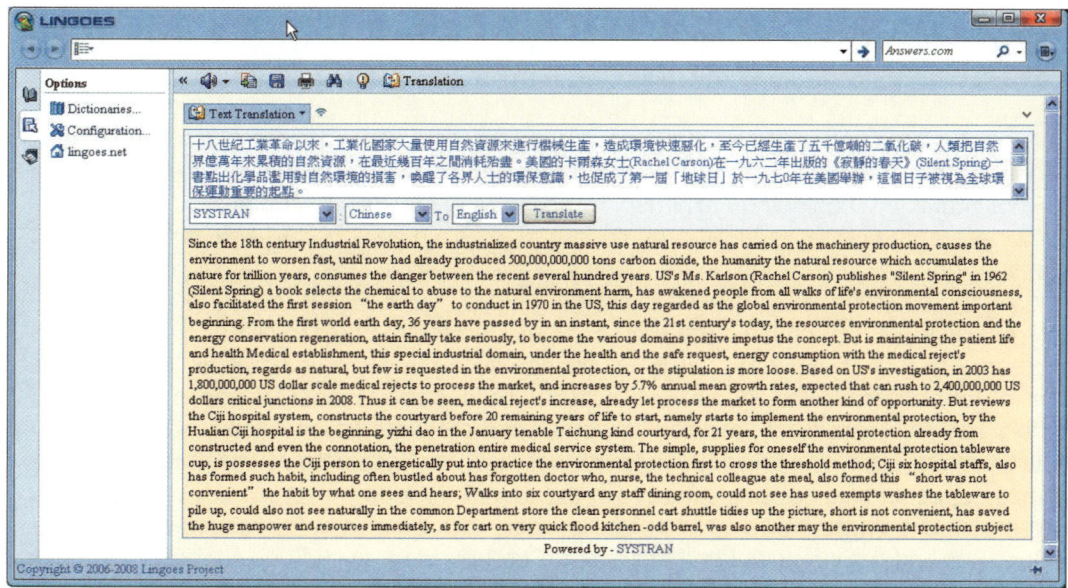

Figure 8.7 Use SYSTRAN in Lingoes Text Translation portal

I noticed the translated result had no separation between the three paragraphs. I added some new-line (carriage return) characters at the end of each paragraph in the source and redid the translation, but the result came back the same. Finally, I had to translate one paragraph at a time and pasted the result from each round of translation to the WordPad document.

The SYSTRAN produced the following translation:

Since the 18th century Industrial Revolution, the industrialized country massive use natural resource has carried on the machinery production, causes the environment to worsen fast, until now had already produced 500,000,000,000 tons carbon dioxide, the humanity the natural resource which accumulates the nature for trillion years, consumes the danger between the recent several hundred years. US's Ms. Karlson (Rachel Carson) publishes "Silent Spring" in 1962 (Silent Spring) a book selects the chemical to abuse to the natural environment harm, has awakened people from all walks of life's environmental consciousness, also facilitated the first session "the earth day" to conduct in 1970 in the US, this day regarded as the global environmental protection movement important beginning.

From the first world earth day, 36 years have passed by in an instant, since the 21st century's today, the resources environmental protection and the energy conservation regeneration, attain finally take seriously, to become the various domains positive impetus the concept. But is maintaining the patient life and health Medical establishment, this special industrial domain, under the health and the safe request, energy consumption with the medical reject's production, regards as natural, but few is requested in the environmental protection, or the stipulation is more loose. Based on US's investigation, in 2003 has 1,800,000,000 US dollar scale medical rejects to process the market, and increases by 5.7% annual mean growth rates, expected that can rush to 2,400,000,000 US dollars critical junctions in 2008. Thus it can be seen, medical reject's increase, already let process the market to form another kind of opportunity.

But reviews the Ciji hospital system, constructs the courtyard before 20 remaining years of life to start, namely starts to implement the environmental protection, by the Hualian Ciji hospital is the beginning, yizhi dao in the January tenable Taichung kind courtyard, for 21 years, the environmental protection already from constructed and even the connotation, the penetration entire medical service system. The simple, supplies for oneself the environmental protection tableware cup, is possesses the Ciji person to energetically put into practice the environmental protection first to cross the threshold method; Ciji six hospital staffs, also has formed such habit, including often bustled about has forgotten doctor who, nurse, the technical colleague ate meal, also formed this "short was not convenient" the habit by what one sees and hears, walks into six courtyard any staff dining room, could not see has used exempts washes the tableware to pile up, could also not see naturally in the common Department store the clean personnel cart shuttle tidies up the picture, short is not convenient, has saved the huge manpower and resources immediately, as for cart on very quick flood kitchen -odd barrel, was also another may the environmental protection subject

I started reading the text. For the first two paragraphs, most of the sentences were comprehensible, even though some were a little hard to read. I have included the proper (human) translations at the end of this section for your reference.

At the time of reading, I was confused with the term "medical reject." It appeared twice in the second paragraph. One in the middle of the 6th line, and the other was in the last sentence of the paragraph. I decided to see what Google translator would say about that, but I didn't want to read the whole paragraph again because it was only that phrase I needed clarification on. I decided to locate the last sentence of the second paragraph in the source and translated only that in Google. We learned from Chapter 2.6 that most punctuation symbols used in Chinese are the same as in English, but the period symbol in Chinese punctuation looks like a circle (" 。 "). In the source text from my WordPad document, I looked back from the end of the second paragraph for a circle that ended the previous sentence, and that helped me to locate the last sentence. I copied that to Lingoes Text Translation window and selected Google Translation to have the sentence translated (Figure 8.8).

Figure 8.8 Using Google Translator in Lingoes Text Translation portal

The original Chinese text:

由此可見，醫療廢棄物的增加，已經讓處理市場形成另一種商機。

Google translated that into:

Evidently, the increase in medical waste has been formed to deal with another kind of market opportunities.

With the help from Google translator, I understood that the term "medical reject" actually meant "medical waste." The words in the translation were in the wrong order to make sense. The problem can be fixed by rearranging the order of words into: "Evidently, another kind of market opportunities has been formed to deal with the increase in medical waste."

I continued with the last paragraph. The first sentence was very long, and I also had a hard time understanding the translation:

But reviews the Ciji hospital system, constructs the courtyard before 20 remaining years of life to start, namely starts to implement the environmental protection, by the Hualian Ciji hospital is the beginning, yizhi dao in the January tenable Taichung kind courtyard, for 21 years, the environmental protection already from constructed and even the connotation, the penetration entire medical service system.

From the translated text, I vaguely knew that it talked about the Ciji hospital system, the Hualian Ciji hospital, and something about the environment protection has already constructed and penetrated the entire medical service system. I decided to consult Google again. I located the first sentence in the third paragraph and translated that using the Google translator (Figure 8.9).

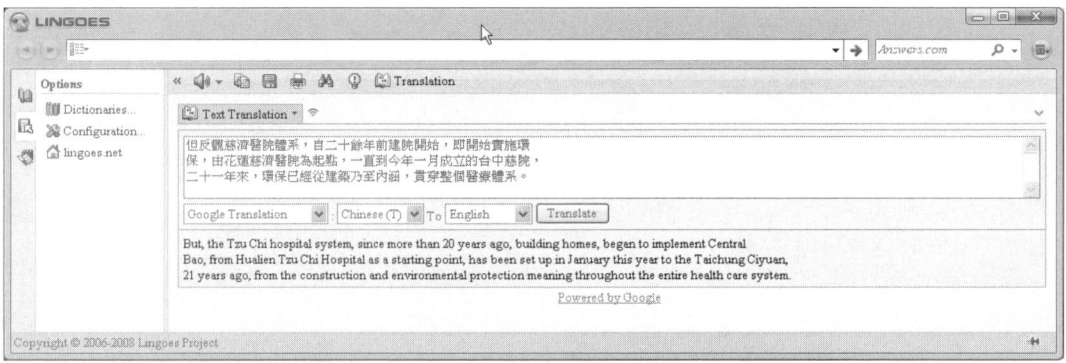

Figure 8.9 Google Translator—extra carriage returns in the source

但反觀慈濟醫院體系，自二十餘年前建院開始，即開始實施環
保，由花蓮慈濟醫院為起點，一直到今年一月成立的台中慈院，
二十一年來，環保已經從建築乃至內涵，貫穿整個醫療體系。

But, the Tzu Chi hospital system, since more than 20 years ago, building homes, began to implement Central
Bao, from Hualien Tzu Chi Hospital as a starting point, has been set up in January this year to the Taichung Ciyuan,
21 years ago, from the construction and environmental protection meaning throughout the entire health care system.

The translated results from Google read funny. The first line of text ended abruptly at the word "Central," and the second line started with "Bao." I looked closely to the Lingoes Text Translation window (Figure 8.9) and then realized what happened. The OCR program had added a new line (carriage return) character to each line automatically, based on the original layout in the magazine. The Google Translator had taken these extra characters seriously. It treated each new line character as the end of a sentence and translated them accordingly. Knowing that, I went to the end of the line and hit the **<Delete>** key to remove all the new line characters. After that I hit the **Translate** button to translate the sentence again. This time the translated results made more sense.

但反觀慈濟醫院體系，自二十餘年前建院開始，即開始實施環保，由花蓮慈濟醫院為起點，一直到今年一月成立的台中慈院，二十一年來，環保已經從建築乃至內涵，貫穿整個醫療體系。

But, the Tzu Chi hospital system, since more than 20 years ago, building homes, started the implementation of environmental protection, from Hualien Tzu Chi Hospital as a starting point, has been set up in January this year to the Taichung Ciyuan, 21 years ago, from the construction of environmental protection and the content, throughout the entire health care system.

It still read a little awkward, but at least I was able to understand the overall meaning. I found that I could improve the sense by rearranging the order of these words and fixing some punctuation:

"But, the Tzu Chi hospital system, building homes since more than 20 years ago, started the implementation of environmental protection. From Hualien Tzu Chi Hospital as a starting point, to the Taichung Ciyuan set up in January this year, has been 21 years ago, the environmental protection, from construction and of the content, throughout the entire health care system."

The next sentence went all the way to the end of the paragraph. It seemed to be even longer than the previous one. Luckily I noticed there were two semicolons in there, which allowed me to separate it into three small sentences to easily review the translation. The first part said:

最簡單的，自備的環保碗筷杯，是所有慈濟人力行環保的第一道
入門法;

The simple, supplies for oneself the environmental protection tableware cup, is possesses the Ciji person to energetically put into practice the environmental protection first to cross the threshold method;

At the time of reading, my understanding of the above translation was: "Simply supplying oneself with environmental-friendly tableware and cup is what Ciji person energetically put into practice, and that is the first environmental protection method." I did not know what the phrase "cross the threshold" meant, so I had to ignore it.

The next part:

慈濟六家醫院的員工，也養成了這樣的習慣，連常忙碌的
忘了吃飯的醫師、護士、技術同仁，也耳濡目染地養成這個「短暫
不方便」的習慣；

Ciji six hospital staffs, also has formed such habit, including often bustled about has forgotten doctor who, nurse, the technical colleague ate meal, also formed this "short was not convenient" the habit by what one sees and hears;

Now that's a little challenging. I believed the order of the words in the translation were very wrong. The words "often bustled about has forgotten doctor who, nurse, the technical colleague ate meal" should really say: "the doctors, nurses, and technicians are often too busy to eat meal." However, I still could not figure out what it meant by "short was not convenient" and "the habit by what one sees and hears." I decided to ask Google for help again. I remembered to remove the extra newline characters before using Google this time. Google gave me back the following result, which was much clearer:

6 Tzu Chi Hospital staff, but also develop the habit of this, even often forgot to eat busy physicians, nurses, technicians colleagues, and so to develop this "temporary inconvenience" the habit;

By using Google translator, I finally understood that "short was not convenient" actually meant "temporary inconvenience." I guessed what it really tried to say is that to bring in one's own tableware and cup (instead of using disposable ones) has caused temporary inconvenience, but all the employees, including doctors, nurses, and technicians, got used to it.

The last part:

走入六院任何一家員工餐廳，見不到用過的免洗
碗筷堆積如山，自然也見不到一般百貨公司裡清潔人員推車穿梭收
拾的景象，短暫的不方便，立刻節省了龐大的人力物力，至於推車
上很快滿溢的廚餘桶，又是另一個可以環保的議題了

Walks into six courtyard any staff dining room, could not see has used exempts washes the tableware to pile up, could also not see naturally in the common Department store the clean personnel cart shuttle tidies up the picture, short is not convenient, has saved the huge manpower and resources immediately, as for cart on very quick flood kitchen - odd barrel, was also another may the environmental protection subject

From the previous contexts, I figured that the "exempts washes tableware" meant "disposable tableware." The words "short is not convenient" had shown up again, and I knew what that meant this time. I realized it was trying to say: "a temporary inconvenience has saved huge manpower and resources immediately."
I could not figure out the meaning of the last sentence: "as for cart on very quick flood kitchen -odd barrel, was also another may the environmental protection subject."

I looked this up in Google translator, and it gave me this output:

As soon overflowing cart in the kitchen barrels, is another can be the theme of environmental protection

The translation from Google seemed to be equally mysterious. When putting all the common words from the two translators together, I knew they said something about "quick (soon) flood (overflow) of the kitchen barrels on the cart may be another environmental protection subject (theme)." I did not know what "kitchen barrels" meant. I was also not sure why that can become an environmental protection topic. The translation from SYSTRAN said "kitchen-odd barrel," which was even odder.

I decided to use the dictionaries in Lingoes to translate it myself. Each Chinese character or word may have more than one interpretation. The problem with translation programs is that they don't always pick the most appropriate one. By using a dictionary, you get a list of all the terms and you can do your own judgments.

I already had all my Chinese dictionaries installed in Lingoes, and I had also got the Quick Chinese(T)-English Dictionary in the first order, as I had recommended in the book. (Refer to Chapter 5.9.4 for details on setting up and using dictionaries in Lingoes.) I placed my mouse cursor over each word in the text (Figure 8.10) and got the word-by-word translation results.

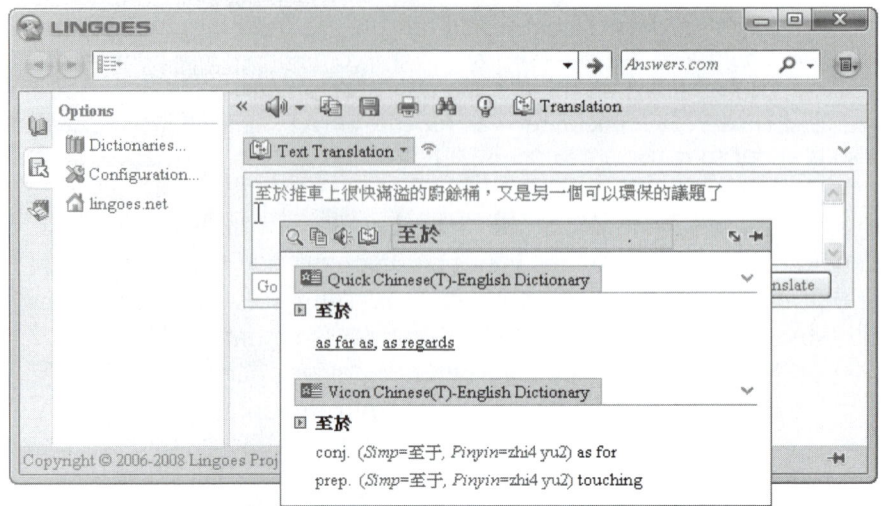

Figure 8.10 Word-by-word looking up from Lingoes

A word-by-word looking up of the text:

至於推車上很快滿溢的廚餘桶，又是另一個可以環保的議題了

至於	as far as, as regards
推車	go-cart
上	ascending, go to, go up, previous, submit, superior, upper
很快	soon
滿	full, completely, expire, fill, complacent, impletion
溢	excessive, overflow, spill, spillover
的	of, target
廚	hutch, kitchen
餘	extra, surplus, spare, odd
桶	barrel, bucket, cask, pail, runlet, tub
，	
又	again, and, as well as, both
是	am, are, be, being, correct, is, right, that, this, yes
另一個	the other one
可以	can, may, not bad, Ok
環	annulus, hem in, link, loop, ring, surround
保	defend, keep, protect
的	of, target
議題	topic of discussion
了	end, finish, know clearly, oversee, settle, understand

A word-by-word look up of the sentence solved the mystery of the "kitchen-odd barrel." What it meant in the source should be the "kitchen surplus barrel," (scrap barrel or compost barrel), a container for dumping left-over food.

Looking back at this afterwards, I guess what the source is trying to say is that even though the workers have been practicing environmental protection by bringing in their own tableware, still, there were too much left-over food people had wasted, and that can become an environmental protection topic to discuss at another time. I said "I guess" because this is not completely clear to me even from looking at the Chinese text. In addition, the 廚餘桶 is not a commonly-used word, and unfortunately, SYSTRAN had picked the least proper meaning, "odd," to use in here.

The following is the proper translation of the entire document. You may notice there are more periods in the translated text than the original source. I have found a few places in the source where they should have been separated sentences, but commas had been used. I have changed them in the translation.

Since the industrial revolution in the 18th century, industrialized countries have used massive natural resources for machinery production, causing rapid environmental deterioration, and have produced 500 billion tons of carbon dioxide so far. The human being has consumed in the past few hundred years the resources which took nature a few billion years to accumulate. American author Ms. Carson (Rachel Carson) pointed out in her book "Silent Spring" (Silent Spring) published in 1962, that the abuse of chemicals has caused damage to the natural environment, awoke the environmental protection awareness of people from the world, which also in turn facilitated the first "Earth Day" activity in 1970 in the USA. This date marked an important starting point of the global environment protection movement.

Since the first Earth Day, thirty-six years have passed at a glimpse. Today in the 21st century, the concepts of conservation, environment protection and reuse of resources have finally been taken seriously and been actively promoted in all industry domains. However, for the health care and medical industry concerning human life and well being, in this special industry domain, because of the sanitary and safety requirement considerations, the use of resources and generation of medical wastes have been taken for granted. There are very few environmental protection requirements, or the regulation is loose. Based on US research data, the market size for processing medical wastes was one 1.8 billion dollars in 2003, with an average annual increasing rate of 5.7%. It is estimated to reach 2.4 billion dollars in the year

2008. Evidently, the increase of medical wastes has created another business opportunity for the market.

On the other hand, the Tzu Chi medical service group has already practiced environment protection since its first establishment 20 years ago. Starting from the Tzu Chi Hualian hospital all the way to the Tzu Chi TaiChung hospital established January this year, for twenty-one years, the environment protection concept has been established throughout the entire medical service system, from the outside physical building to inside of people's hearts. Taking the simplest example, everyone brings their own bowl, cup and chopsticks. This is the most basic rule for all Tzu Chi workers for practicing environment protection, which has also become the habit of the employees from all six Tzu Chi hospitals. Even the doctors, nurses, and technicians, who sometimes are too busy to eat, have been influenced because of seeing and hearing it regularly, and are getting used to this "little inconvenience." When walking to the employee cafeteria in anyone of the six hospitals, you will not see a pile up of disposable bowls and chopsticks, or cleaners busily walking around with clean-up carts as we seen in the department stores. A little inconvenience saves huge amount of efforts and resources right away. As for the left-over food that quickly filled up the scrap barrels in the carts, it may become another environmental protection topic that we can discuss.

8.2 Reading a Newspaper

In this section, let us look at an example of reading a newspaper. This is a page of weekly news digest on April 4, 2008, from *The SinoAmerican Times*, a weekly Chinese newspaper published in North America. The page contains texts in multiple columns, of various fonts, going in different directions, and mixing with graphics. Using an OCR and a translation program to read a document of such complex layout is quite challenging. However, I figured an example like this is necessary to convince people that the idea of reading Chinese without knowing it is feasible.

Step 1: Evaluate the material
Figure 8.11 shows a picture of the material. There is no color background, but the layout looked quite complex. An image editor may be needed because there are pictures and a few of them are mingled with the text. I decided not to use an image editor yet, but to scan and recognize the page from the OCR and see how that works first. The finest text is printed in a regular sized font.

一周要聞集萃

98%美國人隱私不保

【本報訊】《華盛頓郵報》4 月 2 日報道稱，美國各州的情報中心能夠獲取數百萬美國人的個人資料信息。《華盛頓郵報》還報道稱，賓夕法尼亞州購買美國人的信用報告，羅德島州的分析師們還能夠獲取人們的汽車租賃數據。馬里蘭當局利用被稱爲 Entersect 的數據經紀人獲取美國人的個人信息。該 Entersect 號稱擁有近 98%的美國人的 120 億份紀錄。

布什：將出席奧運開幕式

【本報4月2日綜合報道】西藏騷亂事件導致國會和白宮在如何應對這一事件上出現意見分歧。不過，白宮表示，布什總統仍計劃出席北京奧運會開幕式。

國會議員4月1日在參議院發起一項議案，禁止包括布什總統在內的所有聯邦政府官員和雇員出席北京奧運會開幕式，以表達抗議。此外，來自民主和共和兩黨的15名議員也要求布什總統放棄出席奧運會的決定。

伯南克：經濟前景不樂觀

【本報記者吳越華盛頓報道】聯儲會主席伯南克4月2日在國會作證時首次承認，美國經濟有可能陷入衰退，不過他同時指出，隨著降息和其他經濟刺激措施逐漸步入正軌，美國經濟有可能在今年下半年重拾活力。

自去年9月以來，美聯儲已將基本利率調至2.25%，降幅近3個百分點，希望藉此拯救飽受房市和信貸市場拖累的疲軟的美國經濟。伯南克表示，降低利率的措施及其他經濟措施刺激隨著時間的推移將有助於經濟的增長。

限槍遊行

爲紀念本學年本在槍擊案中的遇難者，呼籲強加槍支管理，數百名芝加哥公立學校的學生 4 月 1 日參加到了警察、校方官員以及教會負責人聯合發起的遊行。
美聯社

2800 萬人靠食券生活

【本報訊】在美國，食品券一直是貧困的象徵，是由政府發放給低收入者用於換取食物的憑證。4 月 1 日，有英國媒體以《美國 2008：經濟大蕭條》爲題披露了一個驚人的事實：根據美國國會公佈的最新數字，從今年 10 月開始，有 2800 萬美國人將不得不依賴食品券維持生活，這一數字將打破食品券福利計劃實行 40 多年來的最高紀錄。英國媒體稱，這是世界上最富有的國家面臨經濟危機的明確迹象。

鮑爾森提交改革方案

【本報訊】3 月 31 日，財政部長亨利·鮑爾森向國會提交了一份長達 128 頁的金融改革方案，準備對美國金融市場監管體系動一次大手術，包括精簡一些監管機構，並給予聯邦儲備委員會新的權力，使之成爲金融監管核心。

鮑爾森在公佈其改革藍圖時強調，這一系列金融監管體系改革並不是對當前金融市場動蕩的一種回應，因此不應

教堂大火

威斯康星州的一個教堂4月2日發生爆炸，兩所房屋被毀，傷及7人，其中包括3名消防隊員。
美聯社

該在金融動蕩解決之前實施。這一大刀闊斧的結構性改革將是 1920 年代末至 1930 年代初經濟大蕭條以來最大的一次金融監管體制改革。

龍捲風過後

3 月 31 日：一場龍捲風突襲密蘇里州的 Buffalo。圖爲龍捲風過後，當地警官克里莎·史密斯（Krissa Smith）在一家被嚴重毀壞的便利店門口值勤。
美聯社

美緊急召回疑受污香瓜

【本報訊】美國幾家食品公司正緊急召回一批從洪都拉斯進口的香瓜，這批香瓜疑遭沙門氏菌污染，已造成數十人染病。

據 FDAM 網站消息，這批香瓜是由洪都拉斯 Agropecuaria Montelibano 公司生產、包裝並運輸到美國的，美國食品和藥物管理局懷疑它們被沙門氏菌污染，並造成美國至少 50 人染病，加拿大至少 9 人染病。

美國人花錢越來越小氣

【本報訊】2 月份，美國經通貨膨脹因素調整的實際消費者支出幾無增長，表現之疲弱爲 17 個月來所僅見，進一步增加了人們對美國經濟陷入衰退的擔憂。

商務部公佈的報告顯示，上個月，消費者支出僅增長了 0.1%，爲 2006 年 9 月以來的最低增幅；剔除通貨膨脹因素後，實際消費者支出與 1 月份持平。至此，消費者需求已經連續 3 個月處於十分疲軟的狀態。

由於經濟不景氣，美國消費者花錢越來越小氣。
美聯社

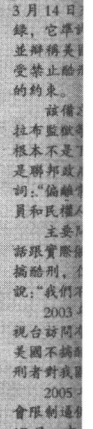

"我們

4 月 2
3 月 14
並稱美
要禁止他
的約束。

置業餐館電腦
617-773-8833
28 B Billings Rd. N. Quincy, MA 02171

專營餐館電腦，誠摯服務紐英倫
堂食、外賣、酒吧、自助餐、中餐、日餐、
特價：熱敏紙(Thermal) $45/箱；白紙(Bond) $30/箱

Figure 8.11 Newspaper page (Courtesy of *The SinoAmerican Times*)

The printing quality is not as good as the magazine, but is okay. I decided to stick with 300 DPI, B/W scanning first, and change it to 400 DPI if that didn't work.

Since I was going to use the OCR, I had to choose between the traditional and simplified character set. You have seen from our previous example that it is not a big deal to correct a wrong character set setting, but let us just try to see if we can tell. Using the techniques described in Chapter 2.12, I noticed the fourth character in the newspaper header (and also in the big title underneath it) is 聞. The radical of this character is 門 (*door; gate*). In traditional Chinese, a door is drawn like a swinging gate seen in western movies, while in simplified Chinese, it is written as 门. Because 聞 looks like that instead of like 闻, I knew this must be in traditional Chinese.

Step 2: Scan the material from the OCR

I used MaxReader 5 for my OCR task. After starting the program, I clicked **Acquire** from the **File** menu. This brought me the TWAIN dialog window provided by my Canon scanner. I selected the **Advance Mode** tab on the right-hand side of the dialog window to make detailed adjustments of the parameters. I dragged a rectangular region to mark the region that I wished to scan (Figure 8.12), which included the three columns of text in the page.

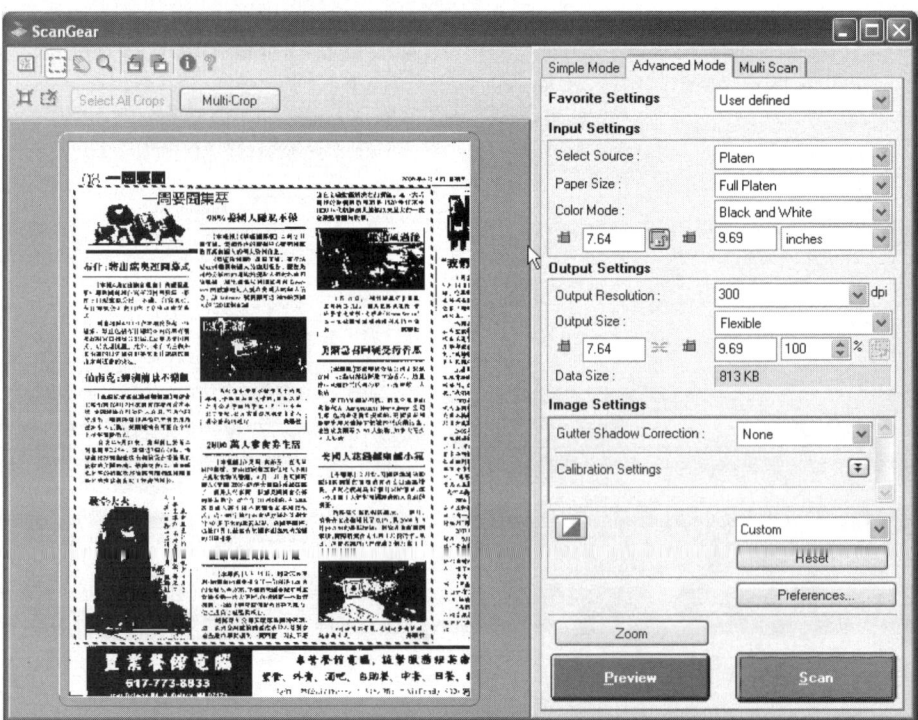

Figure 8.12 Mark the region for scanning

I chose Black and White mode, 300 DPI, and adjusted the intensity level for the text to show up properly. Following that, I pressed the **Scan** button and waited for the scanning to complete. After the scanning, the TWAIN dialog went away and the result appeared in the OCR window. I zoomed in the result view to 100%. Instead of seeing crisp strokes, I saw characters with dark areas smudged together (Figure 8.13a). Apparently, the scanning was too dark. I clicked **File**, followed by **Delete Page** to remove the scanned page. After that, I did the scanning again and adjusted the intensity to a lighter value. This time the scanning showed up just right (Figure 8.13b).

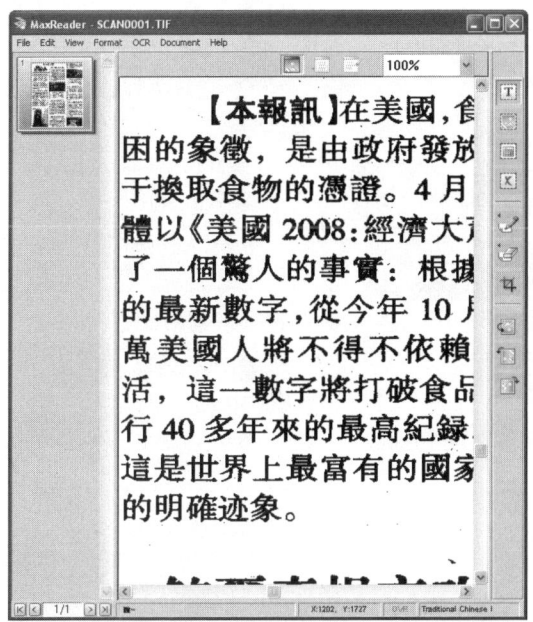
Figure 8.13a Scanning result—too dark

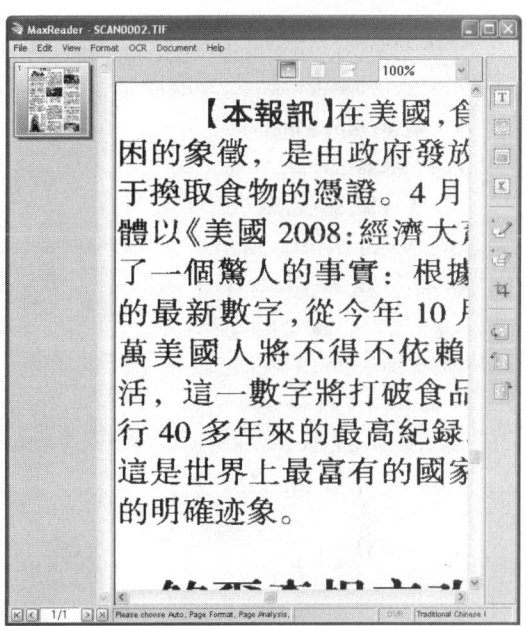
Figure 8.13b Scanning result—just right

Step 3: Recognize the page
I clicked **Set Character Set** from the **Format** menu and verified that **Traditional Chinese I** is selected. I clicked **Recognize Current Page** from the **OCR** menu to recognize the text. This kicked off the analysis and recognition process. When that finished, the result looked like Figure 8.14. The OCR had identified 17 text blocks and 6 image blocks.

There were a few problems with the blocks automatically identified by the OCR. Block A and F were identified as image blocks but contained texts that I needed to extract. Block B contained text of different sized fonts and there was also a (faint) line between the title and the contents. Even though the program is able to handle text of different fonts within a block, the extra line might be recognized as some garbage and cause problems. Block T was identified as an image block by mistake. Besides, there were just too many blocks in there on the page. I could easily get confused by them.

Figure 8.14 OCR automatically-identified blocks (Letters at the corner of blocks are added as descriptive labels. They do not appear on the program screen.)

Step 4: Manually identify blocks in the first column for recognition

There were too many blocks in the page and I had a hard time telling which was which. Since I can only read one block at a time anyway, I decided to change my approach. Instead of identifying the entire page all at once, I separated the recognition into batches. I also wanted to manually mark the blocks in each batch and recognize the blocks in that batch. I would read a block at a time, and move forward to the next batch after all the blocks in the batch were completed.

I pressed the **<F11>** key to discard the current OCR result. After that, I started to mark the blocks I wishes to read in the first batch, as shown in Figure 8.15.

Figure 8.15 Mark blocks from the first column manually (Letters at the corner of blocks are added as descriptive labels. They do not appear on the program screen.)

I dragged my mouse cursor around blocks to mark the big title and all the blocks in the first column. For block B and C as well as block D and E, I put titles and contents into separate blocks to avoid those lines between the title and the contents. I have marked seven blocks in total.

I clicked the **Recognize Current Page** from the **OCR** menu to recognize the text. When that completed, I clicked the **Verify Text Tool** to review the confidence level (Figure 8.16). There was a small percentage of characters marked as suspicious, which seemed normal. I also noticed that the OCR had separated my block C into two blocks because it contains two paragraphs.

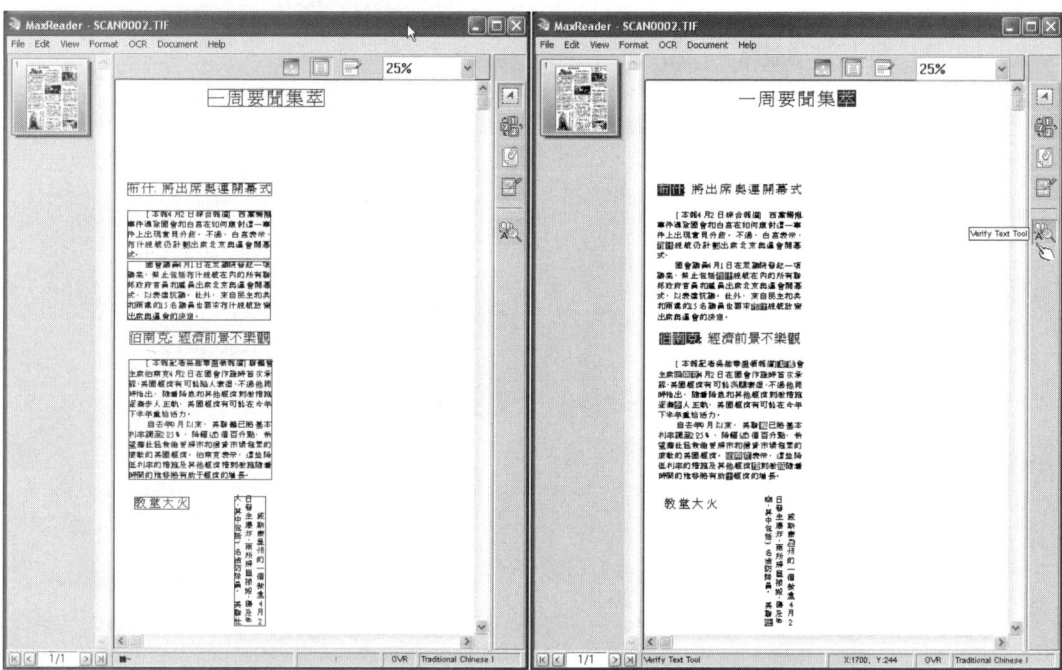

Figure 8.16 Viewing OCR result (left) and using **Verify Text Tool** (right)

Step 5: Translate and read the recognized text

The next step should really be proofreading, but this task would not be easy for people who don't read Chinese, so I skipped it and went directly to translation. I opened Lingoes, clicked the **Translation** icon, selected SYSTRAN and chose Chinese and English as the source and target languages respectively. From MaxReader, I clicked the **Proof Mode** icon so that I could copy the text into Windows Clipboard. In **Proof Mode**, the Working area is divided into four quadrants (Figure 8.17). A thumbnail view of the page appeared on the top left quadrant, and I could see a tiny blue rectangle enclosing the first block—the big title of the page.

Figure 8.17 Enter **Proof Mode** to copy results to Windows Clipboard

From the left bottom quadrant there were eight blocks listed there. I clicked the first block, and pressed the **<Ctrl> C** key to copy the contents of it (Block A) into the Clipboard. In Lingoes, I clicked the **Translation** icon, highlighted the **Text Translation** text box and pressed **<Ctrl> V** to paste the text in there.

一周要聞集萃   一周要聞集萃

Source image and OCR result (Block A)

I hit the **Translate** button and got the result back. It said: "One week important news collection," which made sense. At first, I was a little worried because this newspaper title is printed in a special, arty-looking font. However, it appeared that the OCR program had recognized all the characters correctly without any issue.

I clicked the next block (Block B) on the list from the left bottom quadrant of the Working area in MaxReader, and watched the blue highlight advance to the second block in the left bottom quadrant. I copied and pasted the text into Lingoes the same way as I did previously.

布什：將出席奧運開幕式   布什：將出席奧運開幕式

Source image and OCR result (Block B)

I hit the **Translate** button and the result said: "Bush: Will attend the Olympic opening ceremony," which also sounded right.

I repeated my process on the third block (Block C1).

【本報4月2日綜合報道】西藏騷亂事件導致國會和白宮在如何應對這一事件上出現意見分歧。不過，白宮表示，布什總統仍計劃出席北京奧運會開幕式。

[本報4月2日綜合報道]西藏騷亂事件導致國會和白宮在如何應對這一事件上出現意見分歧。不過，白宮表示，布什總統仍計劃出席北京奧運會開幕式。

Source image and OCR result (Block C1)

The translation of Bock C1 said:

[the newspaper on April 2 report] Tibet chaotic incident causes Congress and the White House how, to deal with at this event to present the difference of opinion. However, the White House indicated that President Bush still planned attends Beijing Olympic Games opening ceremony.

This output looked very good for a translation made by a machine. There is an extra comma between the word "how" and "to," but overall it is comprehensible.

I continued with the fourth block (Block C2).

國會議員4月1日在眾議院發起一項議案，禁止包括布什總統在內的所有聯邦政府官員和雇員出席北京奧運會開幕式，以表達抗議。此外，來自民主和共和兩黨的15名議員也要求布什總統放棄出席奧運會的決定。

國會議員4月1日在眾議院發起一項議案，禁止包括布什總統在內的所有聯邦政府官員和雇員出席北京奧運會開幕式，以表達抗議。此外，來自民主和共和兩黨的15名議員也要求布什總統放棄出席奧運會的決定。

Source image and OCR result (Block C2)

The translation of Block C2 said:

Member of national assembly on April 1 initiates a bill in House of Representatives, forbids all Federal state officials and the employee attends Beijing Olympic Games opening ceremony including President Bush, expresses the protest. In addition, also requests President Bush from democratic and republican two party's 15 congressmen to give up attending Olympic Games' decision.

This translation was also not bad. The order of words in the second sentence is incorrect and hard to read. The proper translation should be: "In addition, 15 congressmen from both Democratic and Republican parties also request President Bush to give up the decision to attend the Olympic Games."

When reviewing the translated result, I found that SYSTRAN is at fault here, because the source text is written in the regular way. It was the SYSTRAN translator which actually reversed the order of the subject and the object, and I can't see the reason for doing that.

Moving on to Block D:

伯南克:經濟前景不樂觀   伯南克:經濟前景不樂觀

Source image and OCR result (Block D)

The translation of Block D said:

Bonake: The economic prospect is not optimistic

The translation was fine except that I was not certain who "Bonake" was. I decided to ask the Google Translator, which is usually good at names of persons and places.

I selected Google Translation from Lingoes and hit the **Translate** button. Google gave me a better translation:

Bernanke: Economic outlook is not optimistic

I switched back to SYSTRAN after that.

The next block (Block E) also contains two paragraphs. For some reason, the OCR program did not separate it into two blocks, as it did to Block C.

【本報記者吳越華盛頓報道】聯儲會
主席伯南克4月2日在國會作證時首次承
認，美國經濟有可能陷入衰退，不過他同
時指出，隨着降息和其他經濟刺激措施
逐漸步入正軌，美國經濟有可能在今年
下半年重拾活力。
　　自去年9月以來，美聯儲已將基本
利率調至2.25%，降幅近3個百分點，希
望藉此拯救飽受房市和信貸市場拖累的
疲軟的美國經濟。伯南克表示，這些降
低利率的措施及其他經濟措刺激施隨着
時間的推移將有助于經濟的增長。

[本報記者吳越華盛頓報道]聯儲會
主席伯南克4月2日在國會作證時首次承
認，美國經濟有可能陷人衰退，不過他同
時指出，隨看降息和其他經濟刺激措施
逐漸步人正軌，美國經濟有可能在今年
下半年重拾活力。
　　自去年9月以來，美聯儲已將基本
利率調至2．25%，降幅近3個百分點，希
望藉此拯救飽受房市和信貸市場拖累的
疲軟的美國經濟。伯南克表示，這些降
低利率的措施及其他經濟措刺激施隨看
時間的推移將有助于經濟的增長。

Source image and OCR result (Block E)

[newspaper reporter the Wu and Yue kingdoms Washington reported that] unites Chu Hui President Bonake on April 2 to acknowledge for the first time during the congressional hearing, the American economy has the possibility falling person to decline, but he also pointed out that along with looked the reducing the interest rate and other economic stimulus measure the step person stock rail, the American economy has the possibility to ascend the vigor again gradually in the second half of this year. Since last September, the Federal Reserve transferred to the primary rate 2.25%, the range of fall nearly 3 percentage points, hoped that took advantage of this saves fully suffers the worn out American economy which the housing market and the credit market implicated. Bonake indicated that these cut the interest rate the measure and other economies handle stimulate Shi Sui to look the time the passage will be helpful to the economical growth.

I understood most of the translation in this paragraph, but noticed quite a few problems. Two places in the first line looked strange to me. One said "the Wu and Yue kingdoms" and the other said "unites Chu Hui." I switched to Google translator, and it translated the beginning of the paragraph into the following:

"[Wuyue this reporter in Washington] Fed Chairman Bernanke on April 2 when testifying in Congress for the first time…"

For some unknown reason, SYSTRAN had incorrectly translated the name of the reporter as well as the word "Fed (Federal Reserve)." The result from Google looked much better. One comment I need to make is that the word "this reporter" means "our newspaper's reporter."

In the middle of the third line of the translated text, the words "has the possibility falling person to decline" sounded strange. I figured it meant "has the possibility of falling" or "has the possibility to decline" at the time of reading. Later on I found that the problem in here was actually caused by misrecognition of the OCR program. The 10th character (not counting the punctuations) in the 3rd row was incorrect. The actual character should be 入 (*in*), but got recognized incorrectly as 人 (*human; person*) because of similarity. In the translated sentence, the place that said "falling **person** to decline" was meant to be "falling **in**to decline." The exact same problem also occurred at the 4th character in the 5th row. That mistake caused a translation problem in the middle of the fifth line of the translated text. The place that said "step **person** stock rail" should really be "step **into** rail." 步入 正軌 is an idiom that means "to step into the right track."

The 5th character in the 4th row and the last character in the 11th row were also misrecognized. The original characters should be 着, but they were misrecognized as 看 (*see; look*). The word 隨着 means "along with" in Chinese. Because of the mistake of the OCR, the sentence in the fourth line became "along with **looked** the reducing the interest rate…" This is okay as long as you don't take that extra word "looked" too seriously. For the second occurrence of the problem, the consequence was intensified by a mistake in the newspaper itself. The text near the end of the 11th line meant to say 經濟刺激措施, but was misprinted as 經濟措 刺激施. The translator program was totally confused by this, and gave me these words "Shi Sui to look," which appeared at the beginning of the last line.

Luckily, all these mistakes happened in non-critical places. If you ignore the funny places and read "around" them, you are still able to make out what all those sentences mean.

Moving on to the next block (Block F):

教堂大火   教堂大火

Source image and OCR result (Block F)

The translation result "Church fire" from SYSTRAN looked fine, although the proper translation should be "Big church fire."

The next block (Block G) contained vertical text. I followed the exact same process to copy and paste the text, and it showed up correctly in Lingoes without any issue.

The translated text from SYSTRAN said: "A Wisconsin's church on April 2 has the detonation, two houses are destroyed, wound and i@ person, including 3 firemen. Associated Press Du"

威斯康星州的一個教堂4月2
日發生爆炸，兩所房屋被毀，傷及i@
人，其中包括3名消防隊員。 美聯社

（威斯康星州的一個教堂4月2日發生爆炸，兩所房屋被毀，傷及7人，其中包括3名消防隊員。美聯社）

Source image and OCR result (Block G)

The numeric character "7" was mistakenly recognized as "i@." This kind of problem can occur when Chinese characters are mingled with alphanumeric characters. In this example, it was easy for me to see the correct character when I compared the OCR result with the original document.

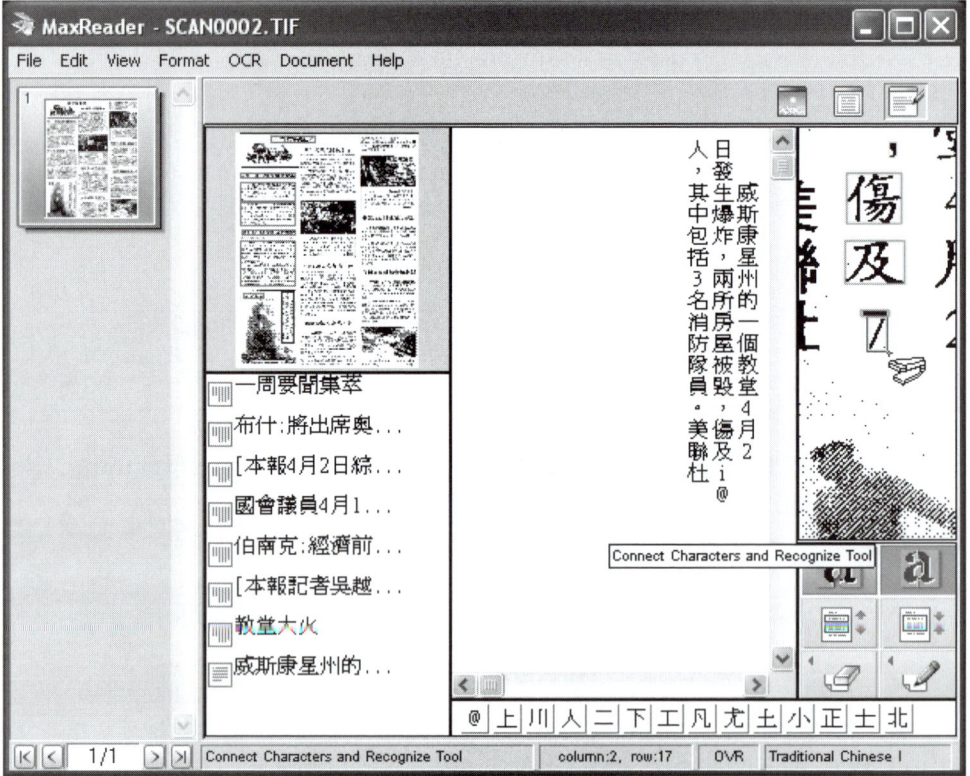

Figure 8.18 Correcting OCR error using **Connect Characters and Recognition** Tool

Because of the vertical-going text, instead of having quadrants, the right half of the Working area was divided into two vertical columns (Figure 8.18). The column on the left displayed the translated result, and the one on the right displayed the source image.

To properly fix this problem, I clicked the place that showed "@" in the column on the left. In the column on the right, I saw that the character "7" was recognized as two pieces. The red rectangle which highlighted the location in the image enclosed only half of the character "7." I clicked the "**Connect Characters and Recognize Tool**" button and enclosed the whole character "7" in the image. As soon as I did that, the OCR recognized the character again and showed the correct OCR result, a character "7."

One other problem with this paragraph is that the last character 社 was mistakenly recognized as a similar character 杜. The word 美聯社 means "Associated Press." Without the last character, the program was still smart enough to know that the first two characters mean the "Associated Press." Because the misrecognized character 杜 happens to be a Chinese surname, the program translated that into the surname "Du,' thinking that to be the name of the reporter.

Step 6: Repeat the process to recognize and read the rest of the document
After reading the first batch, I was more comfortable with the process. I figured that if I marked blocks manually, the OCR would list the blocks in the correct order I wanted. For the next batch, I was going to follow the same procedures, but to read the rest of the page (two columns) in one batch.

I clicked the **Image Mode** icon on the **Display Toolbox** to switch back to Image mode and clicked **<F11>**, which is a shortcut key to discard the current OCR result. After that I marked the rest of the text in separate blocks and started the recognition (Figure 8.19).

When that finished, I got the fourteen blocks (Block H to U) of text that I wanted. I noticed that the OCR did not break some of the blocks, such as Block I or N, into two blocks like it did to Block C previously.

Figure 8.19 Text blocks for second batch of reading (Letters at the corner of blocks are added as descriptive labels. They do not appear on the program screen.)

The first block in the second batch is Block H:

98%美國人隱私不保   98%美國人隱私不保

Source image and OCR result (Block H)

Using SYSTRAN, Block H was translated into:

98% American privacy do not guarantee

These translated words were comprehensible but somewhat obscure. However, the ambiguity actually originated from the source text itself. These words can be interpreted as: "private information has been lost," "privacy has been violated," or "private information is at risk." You really need to consider the broader context to know what this news title actually means.

Moving on to the next block (Block I)

【本報訊】《華盛頓郵報》4 月 2 日報道稱，美國各州的情報中心能夠獲取數百萬美國人的個人資料信息。 　《華盛頓郵報》還報道稱，賓夕法尼亞州購買美國人的信用報告，羅德島州的分析師們還能夠獲取人們的汽車租賃數據。馬里蘭當局利用被稱爲 Enter-sect 的數據經紀人獲取美國人的個人信息。該 Entersect 號稱擁有近 98%的美國人的 120 億份記錄。	[本報訊]《華盛頓郵報》4月2日報道稱，美國各州的情報中心能夠獲取數百萬美國人的個人資料信息。 　《華盛頓郵報》還報道稱，賓夕法尼亞州購買美國人的信用報告，羅德島州的分析師們還能夠獲取人們的汽車租賃數據。馬里蘭當局利用被稱為Enter-sect的數據經紀人獲取美國人的個人信息。該EnterseCt號稱擁有近98%的美國人的120億份記錄。

Source image and OCR result (Block I)

[the newspaper news] Washington Post on April 2 reports said that the American various states' information center can 夠 gain several million American's individual material information. Washington Post also reports said that Pennsylvania purchases American's credit report, the Luo Dedao state analysts can also 夠 gain people's automobile lease data. The Maryland authority use the data manager who is called Enter- sect is gained American's individual information. This EnterseCt is known as has the nearly 98% American's 12,000,000,000 records.

This paragraph was basically understandable. There were two Chinese characters that appeared in the translated result. At the time of reading, I had to take the same approach to read around and ignore them. That seemed to work well. There were also these words "Luo Dedao state" in the 4th line, which looked like a Pinyin translation. By reading other contexts, my guess was that it's the name of a state, but I just didn't know which one it was.

As you may have guessed, I decided to ask for help from Google again because it is usually good with names. From the lesson I learned previously, I knew that I need to remove all the new line characters that the OCR program added prior to using Google translator. The translation of the block from Google came back like this:

[-] "Washington Post" reported on April 2, states that the information center of millions of Americans access to the personal information.

"Washington Post" also reported that the purchase of Pennsylvania, Americans credit report, Rhode Island, analysts also access to people's car rental data. Maryland authorities use sect known as Enter-Americans access to the data brokers of personal information. The so-called EnterseCt has nearly 98 percent of Americans 12 billion records.

Even though the result from Google translator didn't help me much in other places, I could see that the words "Luo Dedao state" are meant to be "Rhode Island State."

The two Chinese characters 夠 in the translated output were caused by the problem in the SYSTRAN program.

Moving forward to the next block (Block J):

爲紀念本學年在槍擊案中的遇難者,呼籲強加槍支管理,數百名芝加哥公立學校的學生 4 月 1 日參加到了警察、校方官員以及教會負責人聯合發起的遊行。　　美聯社	爲紀念本學年在槍擊案中的遇難者,呼籲強加槍吏管理,數百名芝加哥公立學校的學生4月1日參加到了警察、校方官員以及教會負責人聯合發起的遊行。　　美聯杜

Source image and OCR result (Block J)

In order to commemorate this school year in armed assault case's victim, appealed that imposes the gun government official to manage, several hundred Chicago "Public school's student on April 1 attended the parade which police, the school authorities officials as well as the church person in charge initiated jointly. Associated Press Du

This section was also mostly understandable. Again, there was a problem with the result from the OCR. The 8th character in the 2nd row 支 was misrecognized as 吏 (*government official*). The word 槍支 means "guns" in Chinese. Fortunately the key word in here is 槍 (*guns*), while the character 支 is not that important. The translated result said "imposes the gun government official to manage," but the source text actually says: "imposes gun control." The phrase "government official" was an addition caused by the misrecognized character. While reading the text, you would most likely think it meant "…appealed that the government officials to impose gun management…"

Again, I was seeing this "Associated Press Du" problem that we discussed earlier.

The next block (Block K):

2800 萬人靠食券生活	2800萬人靠食券生活

Source image and OCR result (Block K)

28,000,000 people depending on food ticket life

This sounded weird but I thought I understood what it meant. The translation from Google was clearer:

28 million people live on food vouchers

The next block (Block L):

【本報訊】在美國,食品券一直是貧困的象徵,是由政府發放給低收入者用于換取食物的憑證。4月1日,有英國媒體以《美國2008:經濟大蕭條》爲題披露了一個驚人的事實:根據美國國會公佈的最新數字,從今年10月開始,有2800萬美國人將不得不依賴食品券維持生活,這一數字將打破食品券福利計劃實行40多年來的最高紀錄。英國媒體稱,這是世界上最富有的國家面臨經濟危機的明確迹象。	[本報訊]在美國, 食品券一直是貧困的象徵, 是由政府發放給低收入者用于換取食物的憑證。4月1日, 有英國媒體以《美國2008經濟大蕭條》 為題披露了一個驚人的事實:根據美國國會公佈的最新數字, 從今年10月開始, 有2800萬美國人將不得不依賴食品券維持生活, 這一數字將打破食品券福利計劃實行40多年來的最高紀錄。英國媒體稱,這是世界上最富有的國家面臨經濟危機的明確迎象。

Source image and OCR result (Block L)

[the newspaper news] in the US, food ticket has been the impoverished symbol, is provides for buys a girl child lowly uses in receiving in exchange for food by the government the certificate. On April 1, has the British media by "the US 2008: Economical the great depression" has disclosed an astonishing fact for the topic: Newest digit which announces according to the United States Congress, starts from October, some 2800 ten thousand Americans will be able not but to rely on food ticket maintenance life, this digit will break food ticket welfare plan to implement for more than 40 years highest records. The British media said that this is in the world the richest country is clear about jia the elephant faced with the economic crisis.

Again there were a couple of problems caused by misrecognition. The 14th character in the 2nd row 入 (*in*) was misrecognized as 人 (*human; person*) once again. This made the word 低收入 (*low income*) translated into "a girl child lowly," which seems unexpected even if I look at the misrecognized characters. Luckily, without looking too much into these senseless words, the sentence itself was still understandable as a whole. The other problem appeared near the end of the sentence. The 4th character on the last row 迹 was misrecognized as 迦. As such, the original word 迹象 (*sign; indication*) was translated into "jia the elephant," which was meaningless. Other than these two problematic areas caused by the OCR, the other parts of the translation were quite good.

The next block (Block M) is a title:

鮑爾森提交改革方案   鮑爾森提交改革方案

Source image and OCR result (Block M)

Bauer woods submission reform plan

"Bauer woods" seemed to be a person's name here. I used Google for help on that again. It gave me:

Paulson to the reform programme

Google had successfully translated the name of the Treasury Secretary, but incorrectly omitted the word "submit." The proper translation of this title should be "Paulson submits reform plan."

The next block (Block N and O):

【本報訊】3 月 31 日，財政部長亨利·鮑爾森向國會提交了一份長達 128 頁的金融改革方案，準備對美國金融市場監管體系動一次大手術，包括精簡一些監管機構，並給予聯邦儲備委員會新的權力，使之成爲金融監管核心。
　　鮑爾森在公佈其改革藍圖時強調，這一系列金融監管體系改革並不是對當前金融市場動蕩的一種回應，因此不應該在金融動蕩解決之前實施。這一大刀闊斧的結構性改革將是 1920 年代末至 1930 年代初經濟大蕭條以來最大的一次金融監管體制改革。

[本報訊]3月31日，財政部長亨利·鮑爾森向國會提交了一份長達128頁的金融改革方案，準備對美國金融市場監管體系動一次大手術，包括精簡一些監管機構，並給予聯邦儲備委員會新的權力，使之成爲金融監管核心。
　　鮑爾森在公佈其改革藍圖時強調，這一系列金融監管體系改革並不是對當前金融市場動蕩的一種回應，因此不應該在金融動蕩解決之前實施。這一大刀闊斧的結構性改革將是1920年代末至1930年代初經濟大蕭條以來最大的一次金融監管體制改革。

Source image and OCR result (Block N and O)

This paragraph was cut into two pieces during the recognition. I pasted the second block after the first to form a single block and sent that to Lingoes for translation.

[newspaper news] on March 31, Minister Henry. The Bauer woods have submitted one to Congress are 128 page of financial reform plan, prepares to move one time to the US money market supervision system the major surgery, including simplifies some supervision organization, and gives the federal reserve committee new authority, causes it to become the financial supervision core. The Bauer woods when announce its reform blueprint stressed that this a series of financial supervision system reform is not to the current money market turbulent one kind of response, therefore should not before the monetary disturbance solution implements. Since this resolute constitutive reform will be 1920 end to 1930 at the beginning of economical the great depression a biggest financial supervision organizational reform.

I found that most of the sentences were understandable but required some reordering. For example, when I rearranged the words "is not to the current money market turbulent one kind of response" into "is not one kind of response to the current money market turbulent," they became easier to understand. By the same token, "should not before the monetary disturbance solution implements" can be rearranged into "should not implements before the monetary disturbance solution." After some practice, you could become good at this, and may even find the game addictive. Let's try this on the last sentence. My solution is: "This resolute, constitutive reform will be a biggest financial supervision organizational reform since the great depression at 1920 end to the beginning of 1930."

The next block (Block P):

3月31日，一場龍捲風突襲密蘇里州的 Buffalo。圖爲龍捲風過後，當地警官克里莎·史密斯（Krissa Smith）在一家被嚴重毀壞的便利店門口值勤。　　　　　　　美聯社	3月31日；一場龍捲風突襲密蘇里州的Bu田o。圖為龍捲風過後，當地警官克里莎．史密斯(KIisSaSmilh)在一家被嚴重毀壞的便利店門口值勤。　　　　　　　美聯杜

Source image and OCR result (Block P)

On March 31; Tornado attacks Missouri Bu field o. Picture shows the tornado from now on, local police officer Kerry sha. Smith (KIisSaSmilh) the convenience store entrance which destroys seriously is been in charge of quarters in one. Associated Press Du

The English word "Buffalo" was misrecognized, which caused the translator program to stutter and produced "Bu field o." Such problems can be identified by comparing the OCR result with the original source. The phrase "the tornado from now on" was an interesting translation, which actually meant "after the tornado." The military term "in charge of quarters" had been used at the end of the sentence to mean to be on duty. I was able to figure out the meaning of this after some thinking and rearranging the words into:

"Picture shows tornado from now on, local police officer Krissa Smith is been in charge of quarters in one the convenience store entrance which destroys seriously."

The next block (Block Q) is a title:

美緊急召回疑受污香瓜   美緊急召回疑受污香瓜

Source image and OCR result (Block Q)

US recalls urgently doubts the dirty muskmelon

This looked okay except for some word usages. The proper translation should be: "U.S. urgently recalls possibly-contaminated cantaloupes."

The next block (Block R):

【本報訊】美國幾家食品公司正緊急召回一批從洪都拉斯進口的香瓜，這批香瓜疑遭沙門氏菌污染，已造成數十人染病。
據 FDAM 網站消息，這批香瓜是由洪都拉斯 Agropecuaria Montelibano 公司生產、包裝並運輸到美國的，美國食品和藥物管理局懷疑它們被沙門氏菌污染，並造成美國至少 50 人染病，加拿大至少 9 人染病。

[本報訊]美國幾家食品公司正緊急召回一批從洪都拉斯進口的香瓜，這批香瓜疑遭沙門氏菌污染，已造成數十人染病。
據FDAM網站消息，這批香瓜是由洪都拉斯A肛OpeCu茄，MAntelibmO公司生產、包裝並運輸到美國的，美國食品和藥物管理局懷疑它們被沙門氏菌污染，並造成美國至少50人染病，加拿大至少9人染病。

Source image and OCR result (Block R)

[the newspaper news] the US several Food companies recall one batch urgently the muskmelon which imports from Honduras, this batch of muskmelons doubt suffer the salmonella bacillus pollution, has caused dozens of people to catch an illness. According to the FDAM website news, this batch of muskmelons are from Honduran The anus OpeCu eggplant, MAntelibmO Corporation produce, the packing and transport to the US, American food and the medicine administrative bureau suspected that they by the salmonella bacillus pollution, and create the American 50 people to catch an illness at least, the Canadian 9 people catch an illness at least.

I had to say this translation was not bad at all. There was an OCR problem again when recognizing Latin-letter words "Agropecuaria Montelibano." This should not be a big problem if you have another look at the original source.

The next block (Block S) is a title:

美國人花錢越來越小氣   美國人花錢越來越小氣

Source image and OCR result (Block S)

The American spends is getting more and more mean-spirited

I was confused with this word "mean-spirited," especially when it appeared in a short title like that. I asked Goggle translator, and it said:

Americans spend more stingy

That cleared my confusion.

Moving on to the next block (Block T):

【本報訊】2 月份，美國經過通貨膨脹因素調整的實際消費者支出毫無增長，表現之疲弱爲 17 個月來所僅見,進一步增加了人們對美國經濟陷入衰退的擔憂。
　　商務部公佈的報告顯示，上個月，消費者支出僅增長了 0.1%,爲 2006 年 9 月份以來的最低增幅；剔除通貨膨脹因素後,實際消費者支出與 1 月份持平。至此，消費者需求已經連續 3 個月處于十分疲軟的狀態。

[本報訊]2 月份，H國經過通貨膨脹因素調整的實際消費者支出毫無增長，表現之疲弱為17個月來所僅見，進一步增加了人們對美國經濟陷人衰退的擔憂。
　　商務部公佈的報告顯示，上個月，消費者支出僅增長了0.1%，為2006年9月份以來的最低增幅；剔除通貨膨脹因素後，實際消費者支出與1月份持平。至此，消費者需求已經連續3個月處于十分疲軟的狀態。

Source image and OCR result (Block T)

[the newspaper news] in February, the H country disburses after the inflationfactor adjustment's actual consumer does not grow, the performance weak is 17 month institutes only sees, further increased the people worrying which declines to the American economy falling person. The department of commercial affairs announces the report showed that the previous month, the consumer disbursed only grew 0.1%, since has been September's, 2006 lowest increased range; After rejection inflationfactor, the actual consumer disburses and in January is impartial. Hence, the consumer demand was already continual for 3 months to be at the very worn out condition.

When reading the "the H country" at the beginning of the first line, I noticed immediately that something was not right. By comparing the result from the OCR with the source, I can see that an English letter "H" appeared at the location where it was supposed to have a Chinese character. Even though identifying this problem was easy, it was difficult to resolve because I had to know what the original Chinese character was. In addition, unlike other misrecognized characters that can be ignored in some situations, this is actually a critical word.

Up until now I had no absolute need of using the proofreading tool, but I had to use it here to find out what that "H country" was. I clicked the recognized character "H" from the top right quadrant part of the Working area and watched the red rectangle box highlighting the source image of the character on the bottom right quadrant (Figure 8.20).

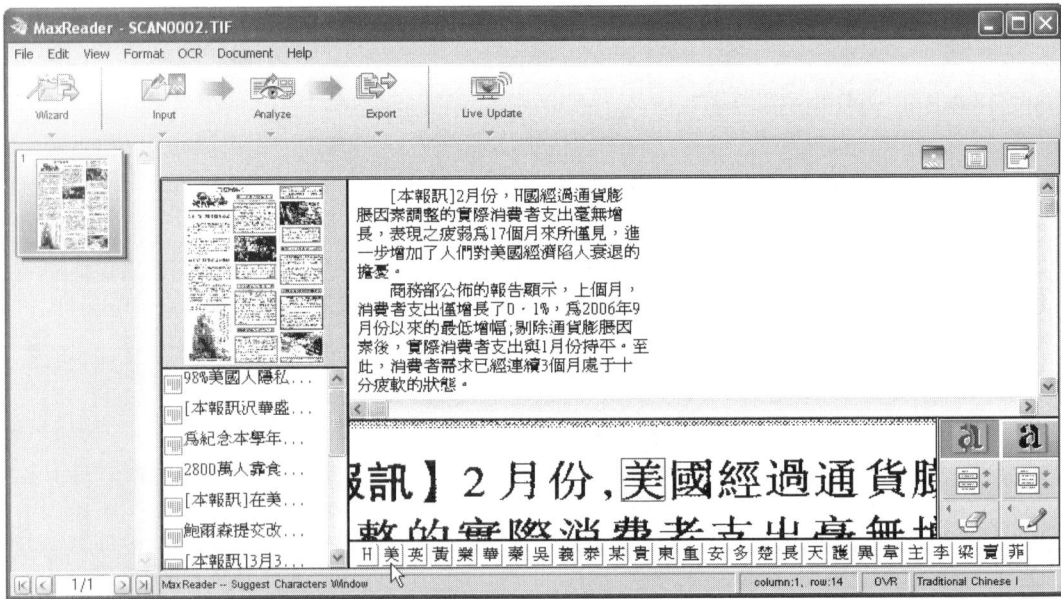

Figure 8.20 Use Proofreading tool to fix misrecognized characters

I looked for the character from the **Suggest Characters Window** on the bottom of the Working area to match up with the image enclosed in the red rectangle. The first item in the list showed the "H," which was the original recognized character, so I looked further down. The second selection 美 looked like the character shown in the red rectangle, so I clicked that and the OCR replaced it for me.

After that, I copied and pasted the result to Lingoes to translate it again. The result became "[the newspaper news] in February, US disburses after the inflationfactor…," and that solved my problem. Well, I guess proofreading Chinese may not be as difficult as it sounded after all. The only remaining thing that still puzzled me is why the 美 got misrecognized as "H" in the first place. These two characters look really very different to me.

The other parts of the first sentence were mostly comprehensible, except for the last two words "falling person." At the time of reading I could only ignore the last word "person." This turned out to be the infamous OCR problem of recognizing 入 (*in*) as 人 (*person; human*) again. The word "institutes" at the beginning of the 3rd line was a mistranslation, and that can be ignored too.

The last block (Block U):

由於經濟不景氣，美國消費者花錢 越來越小氣。　　　　　美聯社	由於經濟不景氣，　美國消費者花錢 越來越小氣。　　　　　美聯杜

Source image and OCR result (Block U)

Because the economy is not booming, the American consumers spend are getting more and more mean-spirited. Associated Press Du

Since I already knew that "mean-spirited" meant "stingy," I could understand this without much trouble.

Now let me show you the proper translation of all the blocks below.

Block A:
One week's important news digests

Block B:
Bush: Will attend Olympic opening ceremony

Block C1:
[General report by our reporter on April 2nd] Turmoil in Tibet has caused the Congress and White house to have a difference of opinion on how to respond to it. However, the White House acknowledged that President Bush is still planning on attending the opening ceremony of the Beijing Olympics.

Block C2:
Members from the House of Representatives introduced a bill on April 1st seeking to prohibit Federal government officials and employees, including President Bush, from attending the opening ceremony of the Beijing Olympics, for protest. In addition, fifteen House members from both the Democrat and Republican parties urged President Bush to renounce his decision to attend the Olympics.

Block D:
Bernanke: Economic outlook not optimistic

Block E:
[Report by our staff Wu Yue from Washington] When testifying before Congress on April 2nd, Federal Reserve bank Chairman Bernanke acknowledged for the first time that the US economy could reel into recession. Nevertheless, he also pointed out that due to the lowering of interest rate and other stimulant measures, the US economy has moved into the right track, and it could regain its activity starting the next half year.

Since September of last year, US Fed has adjusted the key rate down by almost 3 percents to 2.25%, in the hope that it can save the weak US economy burdened by the housing and mortgage markets. Bernanke indicated that as time goes by, the lowering of interest rates and other stimulus measures will help the growth of economy.

Block F:
Big church fire

Block G:
A church in Wisconsin exploded on April 2nd, destroying two houses and injuring seven persons, including three firefighters. AP

Block H:
98% Americans' personal information tapped into

Block I:
[News from our paper] The Washington Post reported on April 2nd that intelligence centers run by States across the country have access to personal information about millions of Americans.

The Washington Post also reported that the state of Pennsylvania buys credit report data, while analysts in Rhode Island have access to car-rental databases. In Maryland, authorities rely on a data broker called Entersect to grab personal information about Americans. Entersect claims to maintain 12 billion records about 98 percent of Americans.

Block J:
Several hundred Chicago Public School students, joined by police, school officials and church leaders, rally on April 1st, to remember classmates killed by gun violence this school year and call for stiffer gun control measures. AP

Block K:
28 million people live on food stamps

Block L:
[News from our paper] Food stamps, certificates issued by the government for low income people to exchange for food, are symbols of poverty in the US. On April 1st, British media disclosed an astonishing fact using the title: "USA 2008: The Great Depression," stating that based on the newest numbers from US Congressional office, starting from October of this year, 28 million people in the US will have to rely on food stamps for essential needs, breaking the all time record of the food assistance program in over 40 years. British media says this is a clear indication that the world's wealthiest country is now facing an economic crisis.

Block M:
Paulson submits reform plan

Block N & O:
[News from our paper] On March 31st, Treasury Secretary Henry Paulson submitted a 128-page-long financial reform proposal to Congress, getting ready to have a major overhaul to the US financial market regulatory structure, including simplification of certain regulatory organizations as well as giving new powers to the Federal Reserve committee to make it become the core of the financial regulatory system.

At the time he unveiled the reform blue print, Paulson emphasized that these series of financial structure reforms should not be viewed as a response to the current financial market turmoil. As such, they should not be implemented until after the present financial turmoil is past. This constitutive reform will be the biggest reform to the financial regulatory system since the Great Depression happened at the end of 20's to the beginning of 30's.

Block P:
A tornado abruptly hit Buffalo, Missouri on March 31st. The picture shows that local officer Krissa Smith stands guard outside a heavily damaged convenience store after the tornado.

Block Q:
U.S. urgently recalls possibly-contaminated cantaloupes

Block R:
[News from our paper] A few US food companies are urgently recalling a batch of cantaloupes imported from Honduras. This batch of cantaloupes may have Salmonella, and has caused illness in dozens of people.

According to information from the FDAM website, this batch of cantaloupes was imported from a Honduras company Agropecuaria Montelibano, which produced, packaged, and shipped to the US. The FDA suspected that it has been contaminated with Salmonella, and has caused the illness of at least 50 people in US and of at least 9 people in Canada.

Block S:
Americans have become stingier in spending

Block T:
[News from our paper] Real consumer spending adjusted for inflation in February in the US has not increased, which is the weakest performance seen in the last 17 months; this has added to people's worries in the recession of the US economy.

Reports from the U.S. Commerce Department indicated that real consumer spending increased a scant 0.1% last month, the smallest increment since September 2006. Excluding adjustment for inflation and other factors, the real consumer spending stayed the same as January. At present, consumer demand has been extremely weak for three months in a roll.

Block U:
Because of the weakness in the economy, US consumer has become stingier in spending.

8.3 Reading Text Captured from a Camera

In Chapter 3, I talked about using cameras to capture text images from places that are inaccessible to scanners. Let us look at some examples of this process here. The materials I used are some pictures I took in Boston's Chinatown recently, using a Nikon Cool PIX 4300 digital camera. I have made them available on our supporting website at http://www.georgekung.com/examples.html, in case you are interested in experimenting with them yourself.

8.3.1 Camera Example 1 (Shop Sign)

Figure 8.21 shows a picture of a shop sign with some Chinese characters.

Figure 8.21 Camera Example 1 (Shop Sign)

The background color was simple and the contrast was good. I decided to open it from MaxReader OCR without using the image editor. The picture was saved as a JPEG (.jpg) file by the digital camera program. I opened the file directly from MaxReader by clicking **Open Image File** from the **File** menu. Since the picture was taken from an overseas Chinese region, I assumed that the text was in traditional Chinese characters. I clicked **Set Character Set** from the **Format** menu and verified that the setting was in **Traditional Chinese I**. After that, I dragged my mouse cursor to enclose the text in a rectangle and clicked the **Recognize Current Page** from the **OCR** menu to recognize the text (Figure 8.22).

Figure 8.22 Mark a text block in MaxReader for recognition

The OCR result did not look right at all (Figure 8.23). Only one text block should be in the output, but it ended up with six different blocks. Some characters were even treated as images and enclosed in red rectangles. One text block contained strange spots and another text block was almost blank. It appeared that the OCR was not able to handle this color picture.

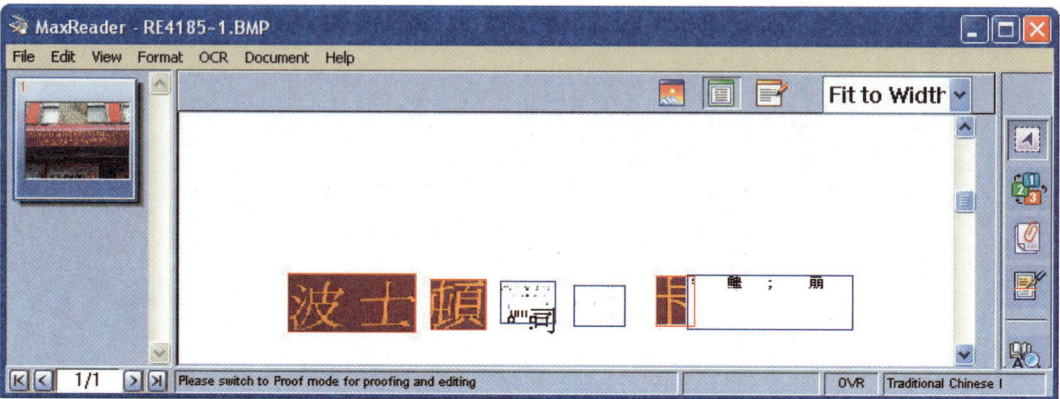

Figure 8.23 Incorrect OCR results—Text recognized as multiple text and image blocks

I started GIMP image editor and opened the picture file. I clicked the **Select rectangular regions** button located at the top left corner of the main window. I went to the **Image Window** and enclosed only the area containing the text. I pressed **<Ctrl> C** to copy the region to Windows Clipboard, and then clicked **Paste as New** from the **Edit** menu on the **Image Window**. By doing that, I got a clean image with only the text I wished to read (Figure 8.24).

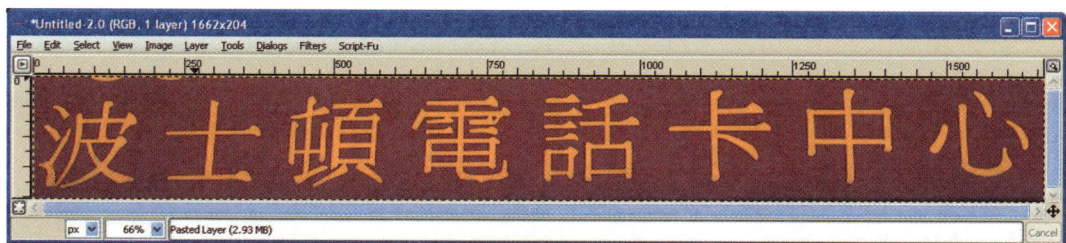

Figure 8.24 A clean image containing only the text to read

On the **Image Window**, I clicked **Layer**, **Colors**, and then **Threshold** to open the **Threshold** tool. I dragged the scroll bar in there until the picture showed a very nice image of white text on a black background (Figure 8.25).

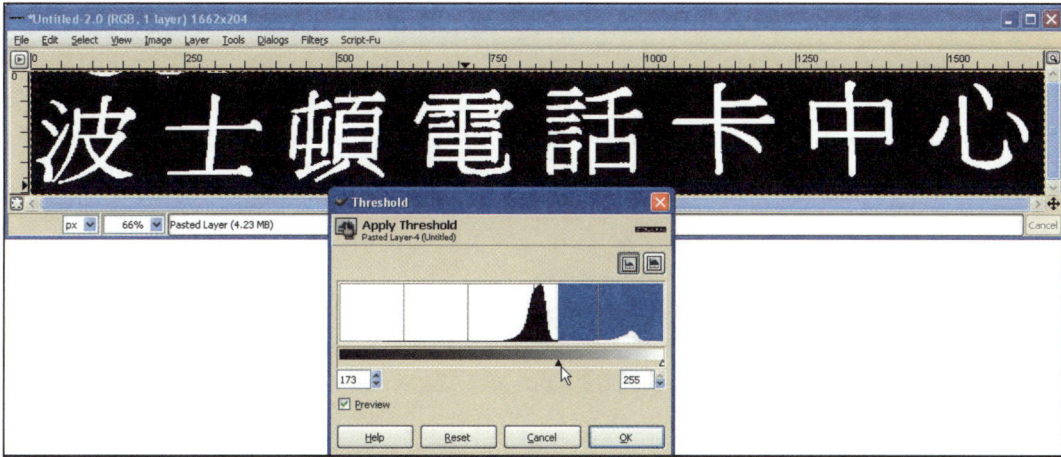

Figure 8.25 Use the **Threshold** Tool to convert a color image into B&W

At this time I suddenly realized why the recognition hadn't worked earlier. It was because the text was inverted (white on black), and MaxReader can not handle this. I clicked the **Layer**, **Colors**, and then **Invert** to change the text into black on white and saved the image file (Figure 8.26).

Figure 8.26 Inverted image after using the Invert Tool

I opened the new image file from MaxReader and did the recognition again. The result showed one Text (blue) block containing eight characters, which matched with what I had seen in the source (Figure 8.27). I clicked the **Verify Text Tool** button and saw no suspicious character there, which was perfect. I clicked the **Proof Mode** button and clicked **<Ctrl> C** to copy the text to Windows Clipboard.

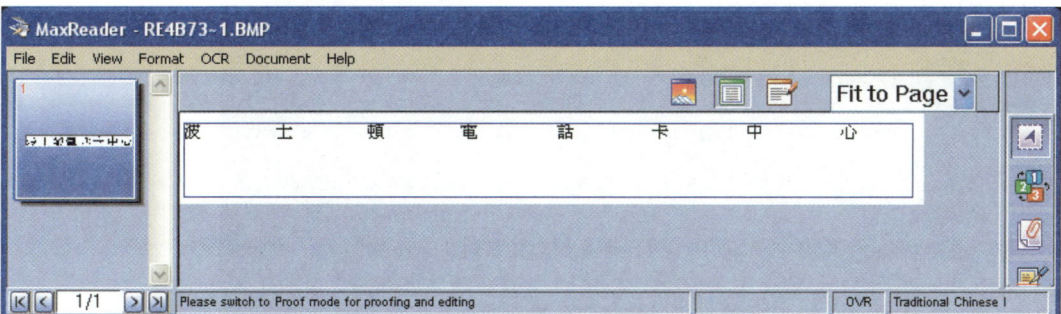

Figure 8.27 OCR result of Camera Example 1—Successful recognition showing eight characters in one text block

I started Lingoes and clicked the **Translation** icon to bring up the Translation portal. I selected SYSTRAN as the translator and selected Chinese and English as the source and target languages respectively. I pressed **<Ctrl> V** to paste the text from the Clipboard into the text box and clicked the **Translate** button to have it translated.

The Chinese text: 波士頓電話卡中心

The translated result from SYSTRAN: Boston calling card center

The translated result made perfect sense.

Reviewing my mistake in this example, I had failed to notice that the text was in reverse (light on dark) color until a very late stage. If I'd known this earlier, I could have used the **Invert Image** tool (selectable from the **Edit** menu) from the MaxReader program and saved me all the trouble of using the image editor.

8.3.2 Camera Example 2 (Sign Board)

The next example is a picture of a small sign in front of a building (Figure 8.28).

Figure 8.28 Camera Example 2 (Sign Board)

By looking at the numeric characters I knew the image needed to be rotated 90 degrees clockwise. The picture looked like a clean and simple color image and the color was not inverted, so I figured to open it directly from the OCR.

I did the same thing as the last example to open the file from MaxReader. I clicked the icon on the right bottom corner of the program to rotate the picture clockwise for 90 degrees, as shown in Figure 8.29.

Figure 8.29 Rotate the image clockwise by 90 degrees

I dragged the cursor to enclose the text that I wished to read in a rectangle (Figure 8.30).

I clicked **Recognize Current Page** from the **OCR** menu to recognize the text. The recognition ran very well and I noticed that the OCR had automatically separated the text into two different text blocks, which looked right. I could see there were six characters on the left and eight characters on the right (Figure 8.31), which matched with the source image. I clicked the **Verify Text Tool** icon and did not see any character marked as suspicious.

Figure 8.30 Mark the text for recognition

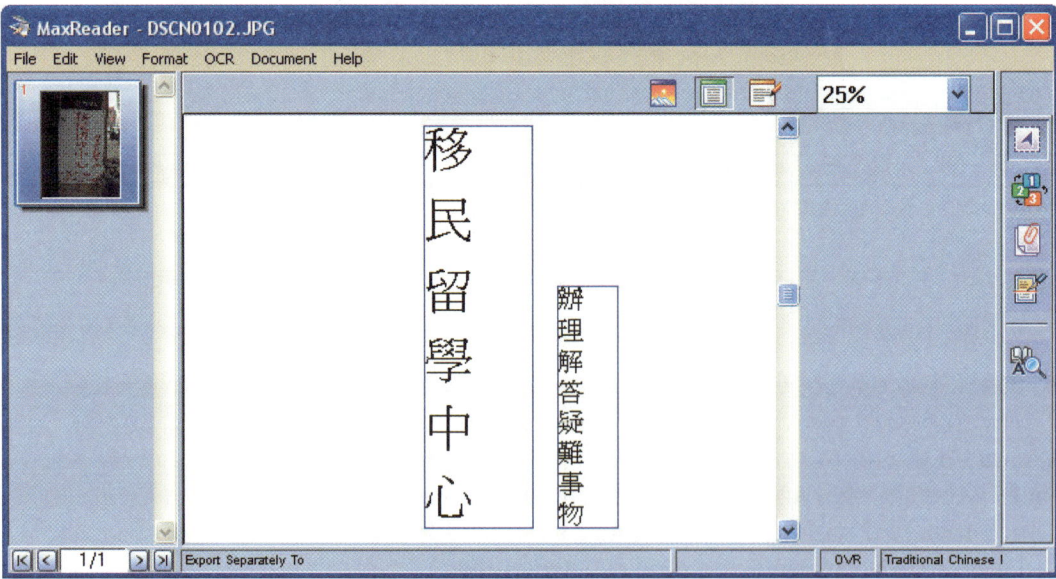

Figure 8.31 OCR result of Camera Example 2

I clicked the **Proof Mode** icon to switch to Proof Mode. There were two items listed in the bottom left quadrant. I clicked on the first item and pressed the **<Ctrl> C** key to copy the text to the Clipboard. I could see from the blue rectangle in the top left quadrant that I was viewing the smaller text on the right of the original image. I started Lingoes and clicked the **Translation** icon to bring up the Text Translation portal. I selected SYSTRAN as the translator and selected Chinese and English as the source and target languages respectively. I pressed the **<Ctrl> V** to paste the text from the Clipboard into the text box and clicked the **Translate** button to get it translated.

The Chinese text: 辦理解答疑難事物

The translated text: Handles the explanation difficult thing

Even though it's scarcely English, I had no trouble understanding it. I repeated the same steps to have the second item translated.

The Chinese text: 移民留學中心

The translated text: Immigration abroad study center

The wording in here was also understandable. When I referred back to the original Chinese text, I have to say that the translation is as accurate as it can be.

8.3.3 Camera Example 3 (Building Sign)

The next example is a sign hung in front of a building (Figure 8.32).

Figure 8.32 Camera Example 3 (Building Sign)

This picture contains six clear Chinese characters on a simple background and I figured it would be easy.

I followed the exact same steps as in the last example to open, rotate, select, and recognize the text. Unlike in the last example, this picture did not have any numeric characters to cue me which way to rotate. Fortunately, I always rotate my camera the same way (clockwise) when taking portrait pictures, so I knew I needed to rotate the pictures in the same way to get them back straight.

After the recognition, instead of seeing a column of text marked as a text block (i.e., in blue color), I saw part of the original image enclosed in a red rectangle (Figure 8.33). This meant that the OCR was unable to identify it but treated it as an image block.

Figure 8.33 Incorrect OCR results—Text recognized as an image block

I remembered from the example of Chapter 8.3.1 that MaxReader is not able to recognize light text on dark background, and I suspected that to be the problem.

I pressed the **<F11>** key to discard the current OCR result. I clicked **Invert Image** from the **Edit** menu to invert the color of the image (Figure 8.34).

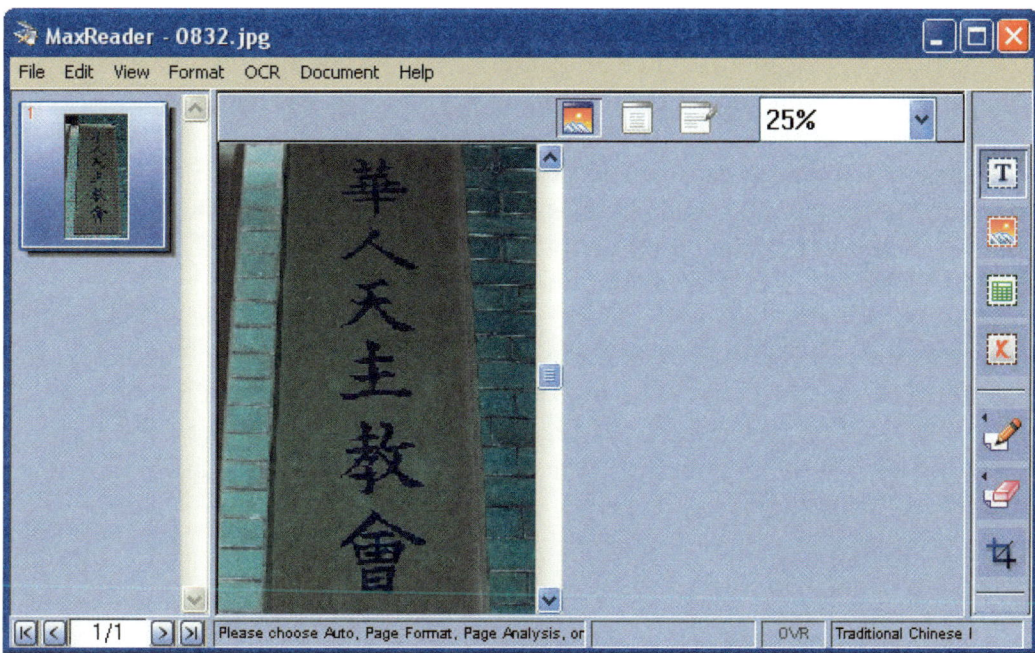

Figure 8.34 Inverting image color in MaxReader

I did the same things as before to recognize the text, and got a better result this time (Figure 8.35).

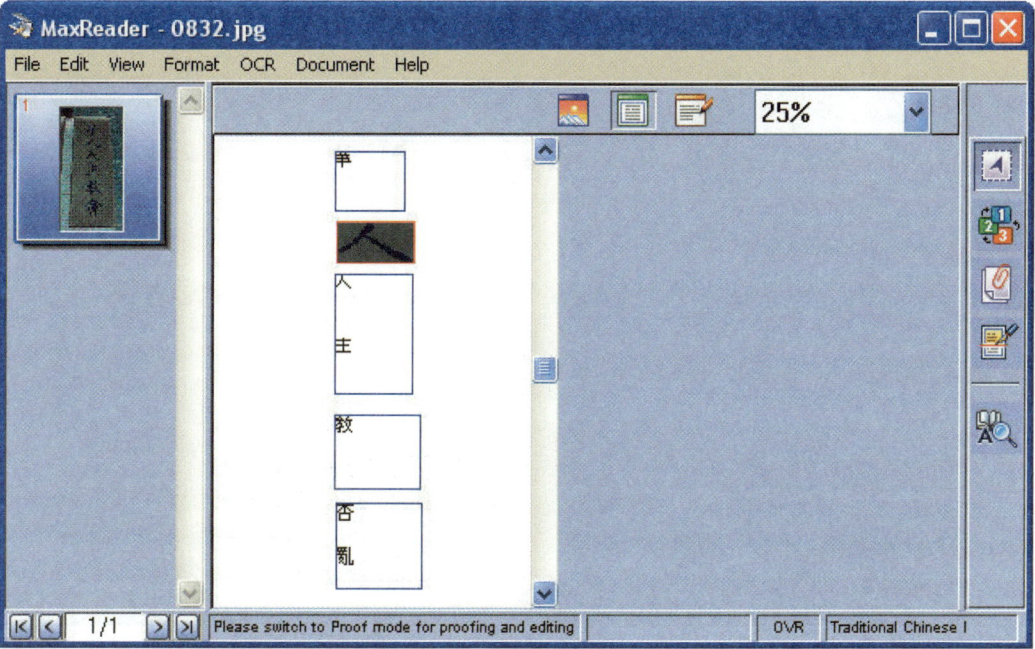

Figure 8.35 OCR results of Camera Example 3

I noticed something was still not right with this. I was expecting a clean column of six characters enclosed in a blue rectangle. Instead of seeing that, I saw four blue rectangles and one red rectangle (Figure 8.35) in the translated result.

This was obviously incorrect. I suspected the character set selection was wrong, so I decided to try the other character set. I pressed the **<F11>** key to discard the current OCR result. I clicked the **Format**, **Set Character Set** and then selected **Simplified Chinese**. I did the recognition again but I got a similar result.

The recognition failed in this example even though the quality of the image was fine, and the reversed color was fixed. The problem of this example is because these are hand-written characters. As I have mentioned earlier in the book, recognizing hand-written Chinese characters is still a challenging task with our current OCR technology.

8.3.4 Camera Example 4 (Store Sign)

In this example, I took the picture from a sign in front of a store (Figure 8.36).

Figure 8.36 Camera Example 4 (Store sign)

Unfortunately, the picture didn't seem to focus well on the horizontal text that I was really interested in reading. When I opened it directly from MaxReader and tried the recognition, it came back with a result that looked very strange (Figure 8.37). It had two text (blue) blocks with a mix of some characters and symbols, and also an image (red) block. Needless to say, this required some work using the image editor.

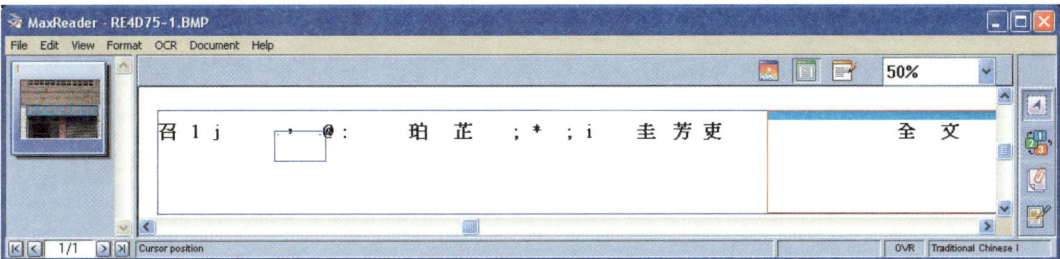

Figure 8.37 Incorrect OCR results—Text recognized as multiple text and image blocks

I opened the image from GIMP and did the same thing as in Chapter 8.3.1 to get a new image that contained only the area that I was interested in (Figure 8.38).

Figure 8.38 Select a rectangular region to contain only the text, and paste it to a new image

After that I used the **Threshold** tool to change the color image into black and white, only this time I couldn't find a suitable value to use. To make the characters black, I need to drag the scroll bar all the way to the right, but that would destroy most of the characters. While moving back and forth, I found that the best I could get was the outlines of the characters like the image shown in Figure 8.39. I hit the **OK** button to apply the change.

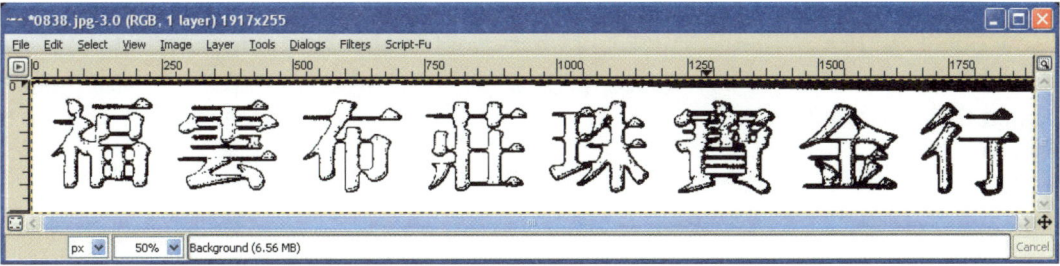

Figure 8.39 Using Threshold tool to convert the color image into B&W

I clicked the **Bucket Fill tool** icon and filled the hollow areas of all the characters (Figure 8.40).

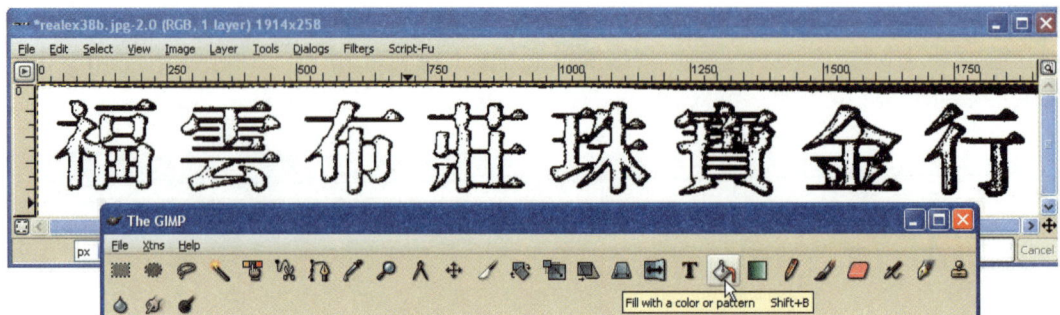

Figure 8.40 Use the Bucket Fill tool to fill the hollow area inside each character

The image after the bucket fill looked like Figure 8.41. I saved the result to a file and opened that from MaxReader.

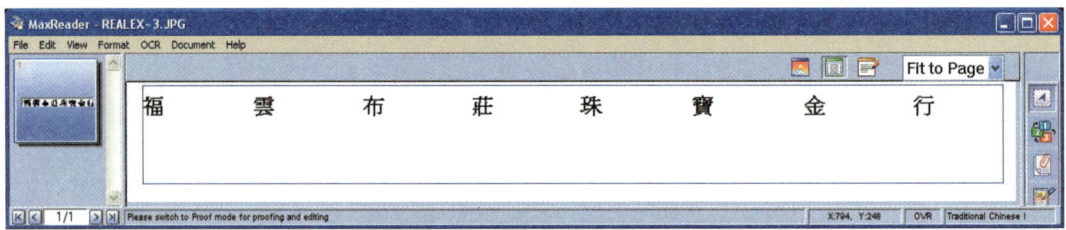

Figure 8.41 Results after the bucket fill

The recognition came back very good this time (Figure 8.42).

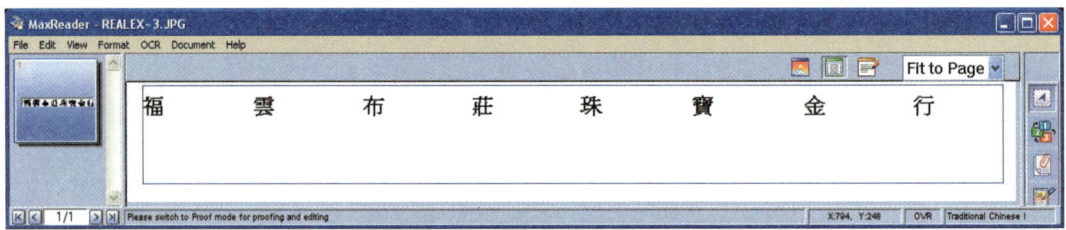

Figure 8.42 OCR result of Camera Example 4

I saw one Text (blue) block with eight characters in there, which matched with what I had in the source. Using similar steps I did in other examples, I copied and pasted the Chinese text to Lingoes Text Translation window and hit the **Translate** button.

Chinese text: 福雲布莊珠寶金行

The translated text from SYSTRAN: Lucky cloud cloth wholesaler jewelry Jin Xing

I did not understand what "Jin Xing" meant, so I switched to Google translator.

The output from Google translator: Fuyun cloth Zhuang jewellery shops to

That was actually more confusing, but it also confirmed that the text was related to a shop, which had something to do with cloth and jewelry.

Given that some of the words didn't make sense, I decided to take this matter into my own hand and used the dictionaries in Lingoes to translate it myself. Each Chinese character or word may have more than one interpretation in English. The problem with the translation programs is that they don't always know the most appropriate meaning. By using a dictionary, I will get a list of all the terms and I can do my own judgments.

I already had all my Chinese dictionaries installed in Lingoes, and had also set the Quick Chinese(T)-English Dictionary in the first order, as I have recommended in this book (Refer to Chapter 5.9.4 for details on setting up and using dictionaries in Lingoes). I placed my mouse cursor over each word in the text and got these word-by-word translation results:

福	blessing, good fortune
雲	cloud
布	cloth, fabric
莊	place of business, banker, manor, village, serious
珠寶	gem, jewel, jewelry
金	aurum, gold, golden, metals, money
行	all right, business firm, profession, capable, carry out, prevail, conduct, go, travel, range, row, soon

Even though the last character has many different meanings, I did not have much problem coming up with a proper translation for the text:

"Lucky Cloud fabric place (and) jewelry gold firm"

I came to the conclusion that the name of the store is "Lucky Cloud," and it sells fabric, jewelry, and gold.

8.3.5 Camera Example 5 (Poster)

This example is a poster printed on a piece of paper stuck outside a store (Figure 8.43).

Figure 8.43 Camera Example 5 (Poster)

I knew I might have problems with this one because of the hand-written text in the third row, but I decided to give it a try anyway. I was hoping at least to figure out what the poster was talking about.

The picture looked simple enough and the text was black on white, so I figured the MaxReader should be able to handle it directly. After opening the image I enclosed the two characters from the first row into one rectangle and enclosed the other three rows in another text block (Figure 8.44).

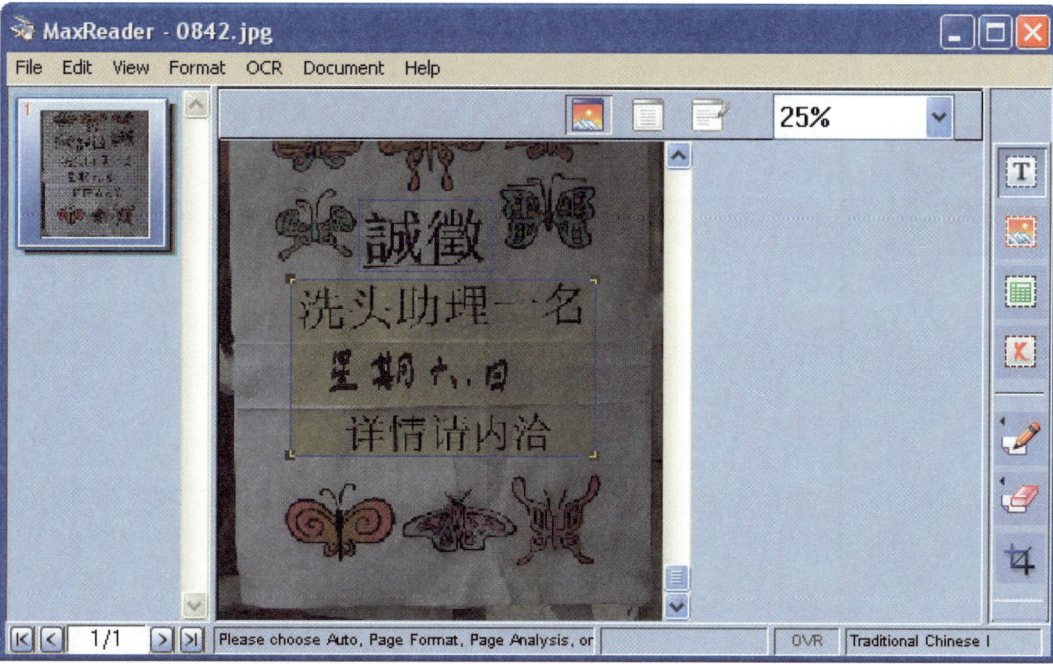

Figure 8.44 Mark text blocks for recognition

I used the traditional Chinese setting because I noticed the radical in the first character 誠 is written like that instead of the simplified way 诚 (Refer to Chapter 2.12 for descriptions about identifying Chinese character sets). I tried recognizing it like that, but the text on the first row got treated as an image block (enclosed in red) and not recognized. I noticed that the two characters in the first row were underlined characters and suspected that might be the issue.

I pressed **<F11>** to discard the incorrect OCR result. I marked the rectangular outlines of the two blocks once again. This time, I carefully exclude the line underneath the two characters in the first block. After that, I did the recognition again and the result of the first two rows looked fine (Figure 8.45).

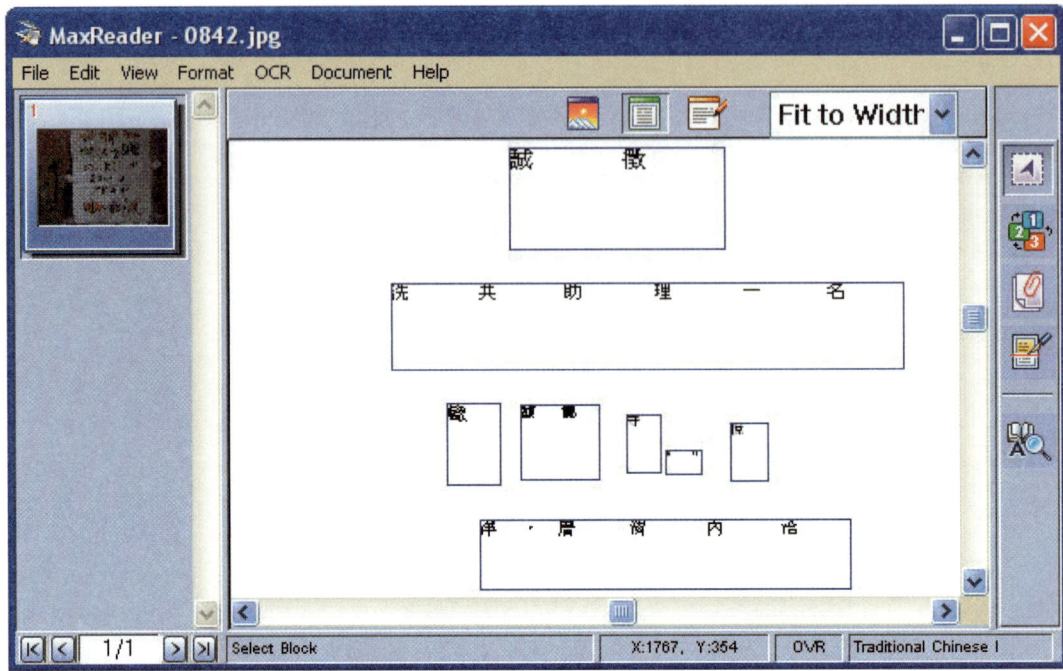

Figure 8.45 OCR result of Camera Example 5

I got two characters on the first row and six characters on the second row, which matched with the source image. The third row didn't look right at all, and I knew that must be the issue of hand-written characters. I noticed that the last row was also incorrect, because it contained five characters and an additional comma in between the first and second character. This suggested that either the first or the second character was recognized as a character with a comma, which was obviously incorrect.

I put the first row of text to the Lingoes Text Translation tool and translated it using SYSTRAN.

Chinese text: 誠徵

Translated result: Soliciting

This sounded correct.

Repeating this procedure with the second row of text, I got: "Washes altogether assistant one." This didn't make sense, so I switched to Google. It said: "A total wash assistant," which didn't sound right either. I tried using the dictionary, but even with that I couldn't find any reasonable translation.

With the clues I have, I figured this might be a "Help Wanted" advertisement, looking for a washing assistant of something, but that was all the information I could get. I had to conclude that my process had failed to understand the text in this case.

Let us review this example. If you look closely at the last row of text, you will notice that characters 详 and 请 are actually written with radicals in the simplified way, instead of the traditional way 詳 and 請. This is an example of a mixed use of traditional and simplified characters. The person who had made the poster must have got these characters from two different sources. This practice may not bother most Chinese readers, but it surely created a problem for us.

With more interactions between the people that use different character sets, I am starting to see more and more mixed use of traditional and simplified Chinese characters. Since the output of MaxReader OCR is in Unicode, it should really be made to recognize both character sets at the same time. Hopefully such a feature will become a standard for the next generation of OCR and translation software.

8.4 Conclusion

In this chapter, we looked at many examples of reading Chinese text from different types of materials. I demonstrated that it is feasible for people not knowing Chinese to read Chinese from printed text. Needless to say, if the material is already in electronic format, such as on websites or from e-mail, it will be even easier because there is no need to use OCR. There won't be any OCR mistakes either, which contributed to majority of problems in our examples.

As you can see from these examples, the actual process of reading from printed materials is not that complex. I have given very detailed instructions in the earlier chapters about using different tools, but a lot of those are really advanced techniques. In reality, in many cases we can do our job with the most basic tools and methods. In the first two sections and in some examples in the third section, we didn't need to use any image editor and could also operate the translator program directly off the output of the OCR program. Except in one case where a Chinese character was misrecognized as the English letter "H," we never had to use the proofreading tool. Even the troublesome identification of simplified vs. traditional character set that I have spent a lot of time discussing was not that a big issue. When you make the wrong choice, you can quickly identify and correct the problem. I also demonstrated that by using translator programs from

SYSTRAN and Google only, we can comprehend most of the text in our examples. We only used help from the dictionaries on a couple occasions.

You also see that most of the problems occur because OCR had misrecognized characters, due to similarities in characters, or when mingled with alphanumeric characters.

You learned a few techniques to help you read. The first is not much of a technique, but just to ignore the words that don't make sense and read around them. The second trick is to use a different translator to get complementary results. As I have mentioned previously, SYSTRAN does a good job with regular translations. Google Translator is usually very good with names. In our examples, which contain traditional Chinese text, we used these two to complement each other and that worked very well. If the contents were in simplified Chinese, I would have used Huajian together with Google. One other trick is that when all the words in the sentence seem to make sense but just hard to read, it will be helpful to rearrange the word orders. When reading from a newspaper, if the page layout is too complex, it is better to manually mark each block, and do the recognition in multiple rounds to avoid confusion.

9. Some Final Words

Most people who know me think of me as being quiet, but I always feel like saying something before a final good bye. I believe such a habit came from the composition classes I took in middle school. I was taught that an article should consist of three or four paragraphs. In the last paragraph, I need to give a conclusion to finish the article properly. Another thing I learned in composition class was the use of the proverb, so here it comes. This is a saying that I have learned at school when I was ten:

学如逆水行舟,不进则退。
(*Learning is like rowing upstream: struggle ahead or drift backward.*)

It wasn't until thirty years later when my elder son was learning Chinese that I really began to appreciate the wisdom behind this. My son started out learning characters when he was six. By the age of twelve he recognized about seven hundreds characters. My wife and I were hoping that by the end of his Chinese school years, he would be able to read Chinese newspapers. Unfortunately, his motivation for learning Chinese faded as he grew older. The seven hundred characters became the maximum he was able to remember. After that, he forgot old characters faster than he was able to learn new ones.

A few years later, I began working on this book and I felt that this task is much like my son's Chinese learning. Technology and software products move forward at a rapid pace. The information and materials that I describe are changed very frequently and I can't find a way to slow down. I started out with writing about Babylon 6 and Lingoes 1.53 a few months ago. By the time I was halfway through, Babylon came out with version 7, so I had to evaluate it over again and revise my materials and screen shots. Not long after I caught up with all the changes, Lingoes introduced version 2.1 and made a good amount of my writings obsolete again. In the meantime, new software emerged and existing products leapt forward. The most noticeable improvement I have seen is in the Google translator. There were quite a few problems I noted and wished to comment on as I started out, but a few months later when I wished to verify them again, I found a lot of them had already been fixed. There were times when I felt that I was never able to finish this book because of all these constant changes. It is really a relief to know that now that my writing finally comes close to the end.

I have put in a lot of effort to ensure the correctness of the materials. However, due to the nature of such information, it will not be possible to guarantee that it will be completely correct. Also, lots of the discussion is about software products, which can be changed frequently. Even though I have tried my best to update my descriptions, I would not be surprised to find out that some information has already been changed when this book is published. To provide up-to-date information to readers, I have set up a website to offer continuously revised information.

Even with the advanced information technologies we have today, I feel that people from western countries still know too little about China. I sincerely hope that this book can offer some help in bringing English speakers closer to reading Chinese. I am very excited at having the opportunity of playing such a role. At the same time, I am also worried that my English ability does not serve well enough for such a mission. I came to the US at age 27 and it wasn't until then that I really started to speak English. To be honest, I have never written anything in English other than technical documents and e-mail. For you to finish reading this book, I wish to say thank you very much for your patience and support. Now you are at these last words, hopefully I can assume that the book did not end up in your recycle bin because of my English writing skill. Any feedback or comments will certainly be appreciated, and any suggestions will be considered seriously. I hope you have enjoyed it and found it helpful, and I look forward to your comments.

To contact me, please visit the supporting website for this book at:

http://www.georgekung.com.

Appendix

A. Scanning Resolution Recommendations

Size (Characters Per Inch)	Samples	Usages	Recommended Resolutions (Dots Per Inch)
10 – 10.5	人各有体人各有体人各有体人各有体人各有体人各有体人各有体人各有体人各有体人各有体人各有体人各有体人各有体人各有体	Finest prints in magazines	600 – 1200
9 – 9.5	人各有体人各有体人各有体人各有体人各有体人各有体人各有体人各有体人各有体人各有体人各有体人各有体	Fine prints	400 – 600
7.5 – 8.5	人各有体人各有体人各有体人各有体人各有体人各有体人各有体人各有体人各有体人各有体	Newspapers	300 – 400
6.5 – 7	人各有体人各有体人各有体人各有体人各有人各有体人各有体人各有体人各有体人各有	Books, Magazines	200 – 300
4 – 6	人各有体人各有体人各有体人各	Large text	200
< 4	人各有体人各有体	Title	150

B. Installing Chinese Character Fonts

To display Chinese characters, you need Chinese character fonts installed on your Windows system. A few default fonts are installed for you automatically when you first set up Chinese language support. These include MingLiU, PMingLiU, SimSun, NSimSun, and SimHei. To help you proofread the recognized text from OCR software, you may wish to install additional fonts that closely resemble the typefaces used in the source printing. This makes the text of the output look similar to the text on the source images when they are placed side-by-side for comparison.

There are some places on the Internet where you can download free Chinese fonts. Most of the character fonts that are used in Windows system today are TrueType fonts. The TrueType font files have the filename extension of either ".ttf" or ".ttc." The ".ttf" file contains a single font and the ".ttc" (TrueType collection) file contains multiple TrueType fonts within a single file. Some websites may list each font file (.ttf or .ttc file) individually, while others may bundle multiple font files together with other information into zipped files. You should download and save the files to a folder on your system for installation. If the file is in the ".zip" format, you need to extract the ".ttf" or ".ttc" file(s) in the zip file using a zip utility. If you don't already have a zip program that you use regularly, you can find some tools on the Internet that can be used for free. The description of zip tools is beyond the scope of this book.

When downloading font files, you may find some with a "tar.gz" extension. This file type is more commonly seen in the Linux (Unix) system for bundling multiple files into single file for distribution. A "tar.gz" file is a bundle of files archived with the tar utility, and then compressed with the gzip utility. The zip utility that you normally used to zip or unzip files in your Windows system may be able to extract this type of file. Otherwise, you can use the gzip utility, which is available for free. Please visit the following website to find out more and download the gzip utility:

http://www.gzip.org/

To install a new font, go to Windows Control Panel and double click the **Fonts** icon to open the **Fonts** window (Figure 10.1) when the Control Panel is in Classic View. If the Control Panel is in Category View, click the **Appearance and Themes Category** first, and then click the **Fonts** in the **see Also** section located on the top left corner of the screen.

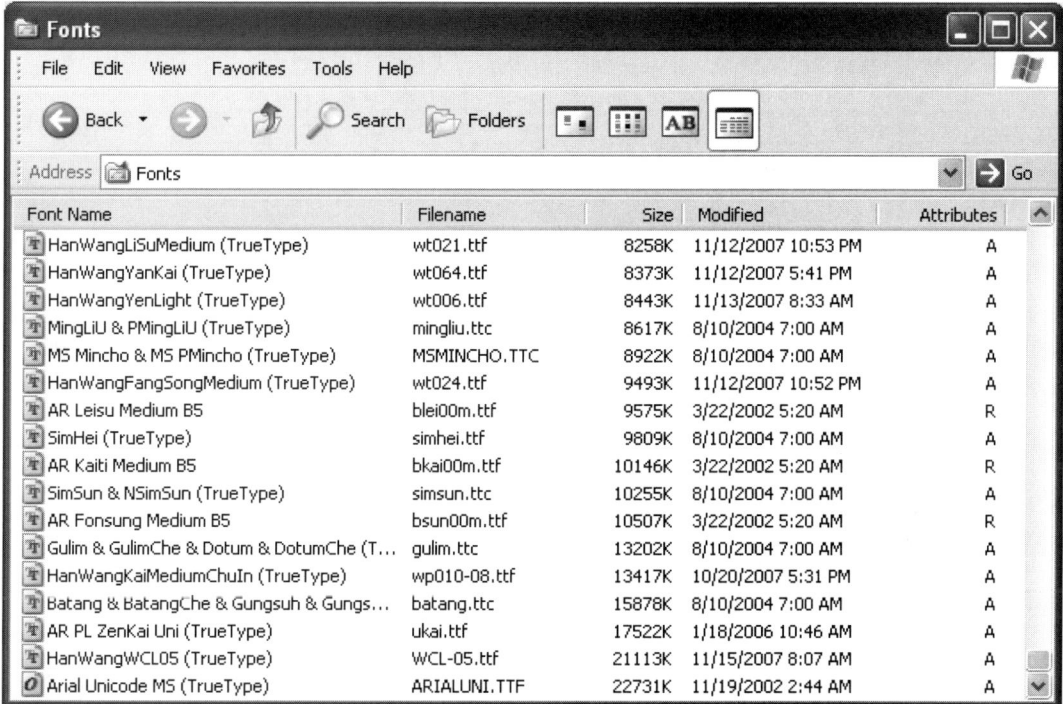

Figure 10.1 **Fonts** window

The **Fonts** window contains a list of all the fonts already installed on your system. To install additional fonts, select **Install New Font** from the **File** menu to navigate to the **Add Fonts** dialog window (Figure 10.2).

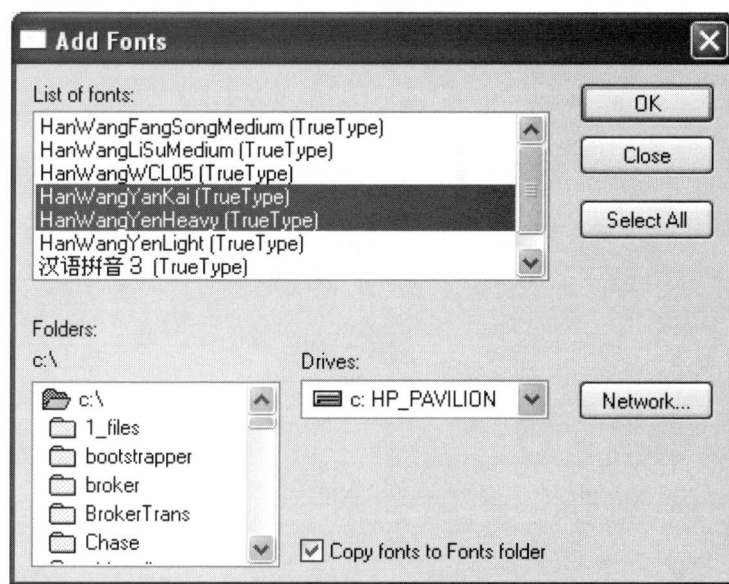

Figure 10.2 **Add Fonts** dialog window

Make sure the **Copy fonts to Fonts folder** checkbox is checked. From the **Folders** section of the **Add Fonts** dialog, navigate to the folder where you have your font files (".ttf" files) saved. You should see the font name of the fonts listed in the **List of fonts** listbox. Select the font(s) you wish to install and click the **OK** button. After that you will see the new fonts that you have just installed in the **Fonts** window.

When you wish to use a certain text font from your applications, you will need to specify the font by its font name or the typeface name, and not the filename (*.ttf) of the font. You can look up a font name based on its filename using the **Fonts** window. To do this, you should put the **Fonts** window in the "Details" view first, which can be done by selecting **View** and then clicking **Details**. After that you will see a list of all the fonts that are installed on your system. The list contains a **Font Name** column and **Filename** column. Click the **Filename** column header to sort the list by the filename and then you can find the corresponding font name from there. Double click the font name of a font to see more information about the font, including the typeface name of the font.

Listed below are some Chinese text fonts I have found on the Internet. To the best of my knowledge, these fonts are available to use for free. Your discretion is advised in downloading and using them on your system. Please also observe the copyright notice, and abide by the license agreements, if they are available.

Some traditional Chinese fonts I have found on the University of Heidelberg website are not made properly. The glyphs of these fonts are drawn as traditional Chinese characters but they are defined in the simplified character code spaces by mistake. Please remember not use these fonts, otherwise they will cause problems. These problematic font files include: hdzb_5.ttf, hdzb_6.ttf, hdzb_7.ttf, hdzb_9.ttf, hdzb_10.ttf, hdzb_24.ttf, hdzb_25.ttf, hdzb_27.ttf, hdzb_74.ttf, hdzb_86.ttf, and hdzb_96.ttf.

Font Name	MingLiU (细明体)			File Name	mingliu.ttc
Typeface	MingLiU (细明体)	Family	Song	Character Set	Trad./Simp.
Sources	Comes with Windows East Asian language setup				
Samples	國這來個說国这来个说				

Font Name	PMingLiU (新细明体)			File Name	mingliu.ttc
Typeface	MingLiU (细明体)	Family	Song	Character Set	Trad./Simp.
Sources	Comes with Windows East Asian language setup				
Samples	國這來個說国这来个说				

Font Name	SimSun (宋体)			File Name		simsun.ttc
Typeface	SimSun (宋体)	Family	Song	Character Set		Trad./Simp.
Sources	Comes with Windows East Asian language setup					
Samples	國這來個說国这来个说					

Font Name	NSimSun (新宋体)			File Name		simsun.ttc
Typeface	SimSun (宋体)	Family	Song	Character Set		Trad./Simp.
Sources	Comes with Windows East Asian language setup					
Samples	國這來個說国这来个说					

Font Name	SimHei (黑体)			File Name		simhei.ttf
Typeface	SimHei (黑体)	Family	Hei	Character Set		Trad./Simp.
Sources	Comes with Windows East Asian language setup					
Samples	國這來個說国这来个说					

Font Name	汉鼎简黑变			File Name		hdzb_35.ttf
Typeface	HanDing-CS-Fonts	Family	Hei	Character Set		Simp.
Sources	http://www.sino.uni-heidelberg.de/edv/sinopc/chinese_fonts.htm					
Samples	国这来个说					

Font Name	汉鼎简楷体			File Name		hdzb_36.ttf
Typeface	HanDing-CS-Fonts	Family	Kai	Character Set		Simp.
Sources	http://www.sino.uni-heidelberg.de/edv/sinopc/chinese_fonts.htm					
Samples	国这来个说					

Font Name	汉鼎简录变			File Name		hdzb_37.ttf
Typeface	HanDing-CS-Fonts	Family	Li	Character Set		Simp.
Sources	http://www.sino.uni-heidelberg.de/edv/sinopc/chinese_fonts.htm					
Samples	国这来个说					

Font Name	汉鼎简舒体			File Name		hdzb_39.ttf
Typeface	HanDing-CS-Fonts	Family	Su	Character Set		Simp.
Sources	http://www.sino.uni-heidelberg.de/edv/sinopc/chinese_fonts.htm					
Samples	国这来个说					

Font Name	汉鼎简特粗黑			File Name		hdzb_70.ttf
Typeface	HanDing-CS-Fonts	Family	Hei	Character Set		Simp.
Sources	http://www.sino.uni-heidelberg.de/edv/sinopc/chinese_fonts.htm					
Samples	国这来个说					

Font Name	汉鼎简中楷			File Name	hdzb_75.ttf
Typeface	HanDing-CS-Fonts	Family	Kai	Character Set	Simp.
Sources	http://www.sino.uni-heidelberg.de/edv/sinopc/chinese_fonts.htm				
Samples	国这来个说				

Font Name	AR PL New Sung			File Name	fireflysung.ttf
Typeface	文鼎ＰＬ新宋	Family	Song	Character Set	Trad./Simp.
Sources	http://www.wazu.jp/gallery/Fonts_ChineseTraditional.html				
Samples	國這來個說国这来个说				

Font Name	HanWangCC02			File Name	wtcc02.ttf
Typeface	王漢宗酷儷海報	Family	Art	Character Set	Trad.
Sources	http://www.wazu.jp/gallery/Fonts_ChineseTraditional.html				
Samples	國這來個說				

Font Name	HanWangCC15			File Name	wtcc15.ttf
Typeface	王漢宗酷正海報	Family	Art	Character Set	Trad.
Sources	http://www.wazu.jp/gallery/Fonts_ChineseTraditional.html				
Samples	國這來個說				

Font Name	HanWangFangSongMedium			File Name	wt024.ttf
Typeface	王漢宗中仿宋繁	Family	FongSong	Character Set	Trad.
Sources	http://www.wazu.jp/gallery/Fonts_ChineseTraditional.html				
Samples	國這來個說				

Font Name	HanWangGB06			File Name	wthc06.ttf
Typeface	王漢宗鋼筆行楷繁	Family	Shin	Character Set	Trad.
Sources	http://www.wazu.jp/gallery/Fonts_ChineseTraditional.html				
Samples	國這來個說				

Font Name	HanWangHeiHeavy			File Name	wt014.ttf
Typeface	王漢宗特黑體繁	Family	Hei	Character Set	Trad.
Sources	http://www.wazu.jp/gallery/Fonts_ChineseTraditional.html				
Samples	國這來個說				

Font Name	HanWangHeiLight			File Name	wt011.ttf
Typeface	王漢宗細黑體繁	Family	Hei	Character Set	Trad.
Sources	http://www.wazu.jp/gallery/Fonts_ChineseTraditional.html				
Samples	國這來個說				

Font Name	HanWangKaiMediumChuIn			File Name	wp010-08.ttf
Typeface	王漢宗中楷體注音	Family	Kai	Character Set	Trad.
Sources	http://www.wazu.jp/gallery/Fonts_ChineseTraditional.html				
Samples	國這來個說				

Font Name	HanWangKanDaYan			File Name	wt028.ttf
Typeface	王漢宗空疊圓繁	Family	Yuan	Character Set	Trad.
Sources	http://www.wazu.jp/gallery/Fonts_ChineseTraditional.html				
Samples	國這來個說				

Font Name	HanWangKanTan			File Name	wt034.ttf
Typeface	王漢宗勘亭流繁	Family	Art	Character Set	Trad.
Sources	http://www.wazu.jp/gallery/Fonts_ChineseTraditional.html				
Samples	國這來個說				

Font Name	HanWangLiSuMedium			File Name	wt021.ttf
Typeface	王漢宗中隸書繁	Family	Li	Character Set	Trad.
Sources	http://www.wazu.jp/gallery/Fonts_ChineseTraditional.html				
Samples	國這來個說				

Font Name	HanWangMingLight			File Name	wt001.ttf
Typeface	王漢宗細明體繁	Family	Song	Character Set	Trad.
Sources	ttp://www.wazu.jp/gallery/Fonts_ChineseTraditional.html				
Samples	國這來個說				

Font Name	HanWangMingMedium			File Name	wt002.ttf
Typeface	王漢宗中明體繁	Family	Song	Character Set	Trad.
Sources	http://www.wazu.jp/gallery/Fonts_ChineseTraditional.html				
Samples	國這來個說				

Font Name	HanWangMingBold			File Name	wt003.ttf
Typeface	王漢宗粗明體繁	Family	Song	Character Set	Trad.
Sources	http://www.wazu.jp/gallery/Fonts_ChineseTraditional.html				
Samples	國這來個說				

Font Name	HanWangMingHeavy			File Name	wt004.ttf
Typeface	王漢宗特明體繁	Family	Song	Character Set	Trad.
Sources	http://www.wazu.jp/gallery/Fonts_ChineseTraditional.html				
Samples	國這來個說				

Font Name	HanWangMingBlack			File Name		wt005.ttf	
Typeface	王漢宗超明體繁	Family	Song	Character Set		Trad.	
Sources	http://www.wazu.jp/gallery/Fonts_ChineseTraditional.html						
Samples	國這來個說						

Font Name	HanWangMingMediumChuIn			File Name		wp010-05.ttf	
Typeface	王漢宗中明體注音	Family	Song	Character Set		Trad.	
Sources	http://www.wazu.jp/gallery/Fonts_ChineseTraditional.html						
Samples	國這來個說						

Font Name	HanWangShinSuMedium			File Name		wt071.ttf	
Typeface	王漢宗中行書繁	Family	Shin	Character Set		Trad.	
Sources	http://www.wazu.jp/gallery/Fonts_ChineseTraditional.html						
Samples	國這來個說						

Font Name	HanWangWCL01			File Name		WCL-01.ttf	
Typeface	王漢宗新潮體一波浪	Family	Art	Character Set		Trad.	
Sources	http://www.wazu.jp/gallery/Fonts_ChineseTraditional.html						
Samples	國這來個說						

Font Name	HanWangWCL02			File Name		WCL-02.ttf	
Typeface	王漢宗特明體一標準	Family	Song	Character Set		Trad.	
Sources	http://www.wazu.jp/gallery/Fonts_ChineseTraditional.html						
Samples	國這來個說						

Font Name	HanWangWCL03			File Name		WCL-03.ttf	
Typeface	王漢宗波卡體一空陰	Family	Art	Character Set		Trad.	
Sources	http://www.wazu.jp/gallery/Fonts_ChineseTraditional.html						
Samples	國這來個說						

Font Name	HanWangWCL04			File Name		WCL-04.ttf	
Typeface	王漢宗綜藝體一雙空陰	Family	Art	Character Set		Trad.	
Sources	http://www.wazu.jp/gallery/Fonts_ChineseTraditional.html						
Samples	國這來個說						

Font Name	HanWangWCL05			File Name		WCL-05.ttf	
Typeface	王漢宗標楷體一空心	Family	Kai	Character Set		Trad.	
Sources	http://www.wazu.jp/gallery/Fonts_ChineseTraditional.html						
Samples	國這來個說						

Font Name	HanWangWCL06			File Name		WCL-06.ttf
Typeface	王漢宗仿宋體一標準	Family	FongSong	Character Set		Trad.
Sources	http://www.wazu.jp/gallery/Fonts_ChineseTraditional.html					
Samples	國這來個說					

Font Name	HanWangWCL07			File Name		WCL-07.ttf
Typeface	王漢宗粗鋼體一標準	Family	Kai	Character Set		Trad.
Sources	http://www.wazu.jp/gallery/Fonts_ChineseTraditional.html					
Samples	國這來個說					

Font Name	HanWangWCL08			File Name		WCL-08.ttf
Typeface	王漢宗粗黑體一實陰	Family	Hei	Character Set		Trad.
Sources	http://www.wazu.jp/gallery/Fonts_ChineseTraditional.html					
Samples	國這來個說					

Font Name	HanWangWCL09			File Name		WCL-09.ttf
Typeface	王漢宗粗圓體一雙空	Family	Yuan	Character Set		Trad.
Sources	http://www.wazu.jp/gallery/Fonts_ChineseTraditional.html					
Samples	國這來個說					

Font Name	HanWangWCL10			File Name		WCL-10.ttf
Typeface	王漢宗海報體一半天水	Family	Art	Character Set		Trad.
Sources	http://www.wazu.jp/gallery/Fonts_ChineseTraditional.html					
Samples	國這來個說					

Font Name	HanWangYanKai			File Name		wt064.ttf
Typeface	王漢宗顏楷體繁	Family	Kai	Character Set		Trad.
Sources	http://www.wazu.jp/gallery/Fonts_ChineseTraditional.html					
Samples	國這來個說					

Font Name	HanWangYenLight			File Name		wt006.ttf
Typeface	王漢宗細圓體繁	Family	Yuan	Character Set		Trad.
Sources	http://www.wazu.jp/gallery/Fonts_ChineseTraditional.html					
Samples	國這來個說					

Font Name	HanWangYenHeavy			File Name		wt009.ttf
Typeface	王漢宗特圓體繁	Family	Yuan	Character Set		Trad.
Sources	http://www.wazu.jp/gallery/Fonts_ChineseTraditional.html					
Samples	國這來個說					

Font Name	HanWangZonYi			File Name		wt040.ttf	
Typeface	王漢宗綜藝體繁		Family	Art		Character Set	Trad.
Sources	http://www.wazu.jp/gallery/Fonts_ChineseTraditional.html						
Samples	國這來個說						

C. Resources

Accompanying website for this book:

http://www.georgekung.com

General Chinese Language websites:

Yahoo! China
http://cn.yahoo.com

Yahoo! Taiwan
http://tw.yahoo.com

Yahoo! Hong Kong
http://hk.yahoo.com

Yahoo! Chinese (Yahoo! for global users. In traditional Chinese)
http://chinese.yahoo.com

Google China
http://www.google.cn

Google Taiwan
http://www.google.com.tw

Google Hong Kong
http://www.google.com.hk

MSN China
http://cn.msn.com

MSN Taiwan
http://tw.msn.com

MSN Hong Kong
http://hk.msn.com

Sohu (Search Engine)
http://www.sohu.com

Baidu (Search Engine)
http://www.baidu.com

Alibaba (E-commerce Search Engine)
http://china.alibaba.com

Special resources:

Xinhua news (China's official news agency)
http://www.xinhua.org

National Library of China
http://www.nlc.gov.cn

Ministry of Foreign Affairs
http://www.fmprc.gov.cn

China Statistical Information Network
http://www.stats.gov.cn

Government Information Office, Republic of China (Taiwan)
http://www.gio.gov.tw

Office of President, Republic of China (Taiwan)
http://www.president.gov.tw

The Central News Agency
http://www.cna.com.tw

National Central Library
http://www.ncl.edu.tw

Index